"In *Lead Like a Girl*, Dalia Feldheim shares her wit, wisdom, and worldliness. By combining storytelling and scientific research, she provides clear and accessible advice for women (and men) who strive for a meaningful, purposeful, and successful life."
—**Tal Ben-Shahar**, PhD, *New York Times*–bestselling author of *Happier*

"Until 'you're leading like a girl' is a compliment the world over, we will need books like this. Fortunately, Dalia has written one that is inspiring, actionable, and fun to read!"
—**Hanneke Faber**, chief executive officer, Logitech

"Dalia Feldheim is and has always been an exceptional leader. This is evident throughout her book, *Lead Like a Girl*. It is filled with leadership lessons and practical advice backed by thoughtful research, as well as wonderful stories about what it means to lead with courage and authenticity. A must and easy read for every leader out there."
—**Melanie Healey**, board director, Verizon, Target, PPG, and Hilton; former group president and CEO, Procter & Gamble North America

"Dalia Feldheim captures in concrete, easily understood, yet fresh terms the qualities of outstanding leadership. She shows how to take advantage of natural attributes particularly possessed by women—empathy, nurturing, intuition—and encourages women to take advantage of their natural strengths, to recognize their purpose, and take strength from their passion. She has, I think, very effectively encouraged men like me to do the same."
—**John Pepper**, retired CEO/chairman, Procter & Gamble

"I've always believed that instead of trying to 'fix' women, we should learn from them. I had the pleasure of awarding Dalia the P&G Europe diversity award in 2003 for her internal maternity guide 'Mom' and am excited she is bringing all her knowledge to a broader audience. Dalia's book *Lead Like a Girl* is brilliantly crafted, combining her personal experience as a senior leader, her vast academic knowledge, and practical advice for what leaders can do to allow women and men to lead from their heart—a must-read for all managers aspiring to become inspirational leaders—women and especially men!"

—**Paul Polman**, coauthor of *Net Positive*; former CEO, Unilever; former president, Procter & Gamble Europe

"Dalia brings two decades of corporate wisdom, coaching, and academic teaching to this book written with love. Each chapter captivates you with stories, research, and practical tools to encourage us all to lead from the heart. A true gem and a must-read for any leader who has the courage to lead from the heart!"

—**Claude Silver**, chief heart officer, Vayner Media

"*Lead Like a Girl* is a motivating read that will help you recognize that figuring out your passion is what gives you creativity and strength—a terrific read for those searching for inspiration and ideas to help you find your path."

—**Kara Goldin**, founder and former CEO of Hint, Inc., and author of *WSJ* bestseller *Undaunted*

"In 2018 (the year I turned 60), I was given a priceless gift by my coach, Suzanne. After listening to my life story, she said, 'Do you realize that you spent the first 45 years of your life trying to impress your father, and the last 15 years honoring your mother with your work?' That insight struck me with the force and clarity of a thunderbolt. I realized that my work in Conscious Capitalism had really been about bringing my mother's essence—her unconditional love, empathy, and compassion—to the world of business and leadership. This is what the world needs and this is what the world has been missing. It is what Dalia Feldheim's wonderful book brings to the fore: the power and beauty of the empowered feminine in every sector of society. This important book will help awaken humanity to the fact that the answer to most of our problems—planetary, societal, business—are right in front of us: the long-overdue elevation and celebration of the feminine energy that is our most distinguishing quality as humans. That energy is available to men and women alike. We must recognize it, cherish it, and harness it."

—**Raj Sisodia**, cofounder, Conscious Capitalism Inc.

LEAD LIKE A GIRL

The New Leadership Playbook for Women and Men

Dalia Feldheim

ROWMAN & LITTLEFIELD

Lanham • Boulder • New York • London

Published by Rowman & Littlefield
An imprint of The Rowman & Littlefield Publishing Group, Inc.
4501 Forbes Boulevard, Suite 200, Lanham, Maryland 20706
www.rowman.com

86-90 Paul Street, London EC2A 4NE, United Kingdom

British Library Cataloguing in Publication Information Available

Library of Congress Cataloging-in-Publication Data available

ISBN 9781538194119 (paperback)
ISBN 9781538194126 (electronic)

♾™ The paper used in this publication meets the minimum requirements of
American National Standard for Information Sciences—Permanence of Paper
for Printed Library Materials, ANSI/NISO Z39.48-1992.

CONTENTS

DEDICATION

I would like to dedicate this book to the wind beneath my wings—my husband, Dror, and my parents, Irene and Ron. To my inspiration, my kids—Mia, Liam, and Anna. And to all the incredible women and men, my managers, mentors, and mentees who have inspired me with their passion to become more compassionate leaders.

I would also like to dedicate this book to my dear friend and women's empowerment advocate, Vanessa Steenkamp, who helped me write the chapter on women's advancement. She unexpectedly passed away in July of 2021 at the young age of thirty-nine—she loved, laughed, and shone her light so brightly! I hope her son, Oliver, and her prematurely born daughters, Mila and Vivian, who never met their incredible mother, will read this book and carry forward her legacy.

Committed to Make a Difference
A percentage of all profits will be dedicated toward "Lead Like A Girl" schools for underprivileged girls.

In addition, if you know of a bully boss who will benefit from reading this book, you can anonymously send them a copy. Sign up online for our free "reformed boss" program at https://daliafeld heim.com.

ACKNOWLEDGMENTS

To My Family

My hubby, Dror—for teaching me to be a present and playful parent, the best career decision I have ever made. My *Ezer Kenegda*—help against—my help and my challenger and my biggest supporter.

My eldest, Mia—the one I fell in love with first, who makes me so proud of the heights she can get to since she started to believe she can and turned from a worrier to a warrior!

My sausage in my sandwich, Liam—for teaching me that hugs can go deeper than words and that when there is a will, nothing is impossible.

My tough-cookie baby-girl, Anna—for showing me that everyone has emotions, but some are more prone to keep them to themselves; it is up to us to stay present and uncover them.

My mum—for giving me the desire to achieve and the security to focus on enjoying the game regardless of the outcome.

My dad—for giving me the optimistic gene and the love of people and teaching.

My brother, Ilan—for teaching me that happiness isn't getting what you want but being happy and content with what you already have.

My sister-in-law, Mayan—the little sister I always dreamt to have—who has so much to offer to further enlighten this world. The best is yet to come!

My Booby, who died six weeks before her 105th birthday as sharp and content as always—for teaching me the value of optimism and never going to sleep angry.

My grandmother, Nana—for teaching me about the importance of financial independence and to always stand on your own feet.

To My Friends

My BFF, Tzurit—who as my platoon commander stayed up with me all night so we got the pinpointed feedback right—for her unconditional friendship for over 20 years.

Batsheva—for restoring my belief in non-transactional sisterhood.

My very special mentee-friend, Roi—who is showing me what courage is every day.

My best friends at work—my first HPO at P&G and to Kathy (coffee shop!), Dor and Jutta, my P&G soul mates.

My tribe—BFMABS—Nira & Eli, Neta & Yoli, Yael & Yair, Anat & Kobi, Effie & Adi, Merav & Arik, Smady & Shlomi, Wellness tribe—Dana & Keidar, Karin & Yoad, the bold and the beautiful— Ayelet & Roy, Mirit, Limor & Gadi, Shirley & Guy, Yael & Yaniv, Noa, Yifat, Tal, Vivi, Roni, Yodfat, Michal, Laurence, and our dear Kadosh Daniel (RIP)—life wouldn't be the same without you and your love and support to me and my family!

All of my mentees, coaching clients, direct reports, students— from my soldiers to my first high performing organization in Russia to my team of 100 in my last job to my students—I always said I learn more from my people than from my bosses.

To My Amazing Bossess and Mentors

Jim—my first boss, friend and mentor—for giving me the permission to be human and setting the bar so high on what great people leadership looks like.

Alex—for the power of a sharp strategy, hard work, hard play (aka night swimming with the agency), and the value of undivided attention.

Regi—for teaching me the value of "lift as you rise" and "self-fullness."

Stassi—for the epic support with pregnancy and teaching me never to give up.

Tammy—for giving me the first glimpse at being politically savvy and enjoying the ride, aka being late to an agency meeting in London as we had to buy shoes . . . ;-)

Nada Dugas—for teaching me and role modeling—no regret—live life to the fullest—when you're home, be a hundred percent there, and when at work, make it count!

Elena—the Russian ice queen—what doesn't kill you makes you stronger and pressure makes diamonds.

Daniella—for teaching me that women don't need to behave like men in order to succeed.

Edgar—for role modeling compassion.

Melanie Healey—one of my most amazing senior leaders—demanding yet so caring.

Patricia Lopez—for role modeling vulnerability and strength.

Christina Angco—for your tough love feedback.

Paul Polman—for role modeling to the world purpose-led leadership and awarding me diversity initiative of the year 2002 for my company-internal booklet on managing maternity—setting the stage for this book.

John Pepper—the most approachable humble CEO I have ever met.

Jim Stengel—P&G ex-CMO—for role modeling and advocating passion and purpose at the workplace.

Marc Prichard—P&G CMO—thank you for recognizing mums as having the best job in the world and being a role model for leading from the heart—with vulnerability and humility. You made me cry twice—when showing me the Mum Olympic ad for the first time, and when you wished me luck for the TED Talk years later.

Dennis Andrews—for establishing women supporting women and creating a legacy of sisterhood power.

Hanneke Faber—my first P&G women network sponsor who inspired me to be a gender warrior and continues to inspire as a Lead Like a Girl role model.

Mary Kay and the global team—in a sea of darkness, you were the light.

The whole marketing team at Elux as well as my peers—Jessie, Simon, Enrique, and Joanna—in a pool of sharks, you were my life buoy.

And my most recent "tissue box" boss—through presenting the dark side, I am grateful to you for helping me remember what really matters and defining how I want to show up as a leader. In the weirdest way, you pushed me to write this book.

To My Newly Found Writing and Speaking Tribe

Margie, Tanvi, Fredrik, Ritu, Dee, Meital, Avi, Joanna, Tim— thanks for your generosity of sharing.

The EVE legends who started the journey—Anne, Christine, and my luck-charm Marie-liesse.

The Keynote women directory and the Equity in action 2020 family—especially Mette, Binu, Abam, KG, Aurelie, Christine, and Uma—for believing this is an idea worth sharing.

My special TED tribe—Adam, Barry, Galia, Lybi, Adi, Ayat— for the inspiration and support and for reminding me what working with passion looks like.

HumansFirst tribe and such incredible soul brothers and sisters— Mike, Paul, Brian, Shelley, Claude, Andrea, Samantha, Alexandra, Garry, Ozlem, Teresa, Mark, Josia, Linda, Terry, Quinn, and Stephynie.

My Uppiness at work uppy family—Oren and Ofra, Cassandre, and 500 Uppiness coaches to come.

Tal Ben-Shahar—my humble, generous prof. at the Happiness Studies Academy, now mentor and friend—I am a happier whole person, thanks to you.

My committed agent, editors, and expert readers who taught me editing is just as important for the book as the writing to get the message across, if not more ;-)

Peppur Chambers, Maryann Karinch, Suzanne Staszak-Silva, Hannah Fisher, Eran Zmora, Maya Lahat, Yoram Ros, Kimberly Peticolas, Liat Behr, Michal Harel, Leasanne Brook, Nitin Goil, Tal Ben-Shahar, Jim Lafferty, Michèle Telio, Nathalie Bariman, Samantha Suppiah, Neta Bar-El, Kathy Litalien, Sowmya Kolluri, Dee Allan, Ocean Reeve Publishing, and my dad, the English professor and master editor.

All the amazing women and men I have mentored, coached, touched—be it through university work or speaking convention—you are the reason and inspiration for my writing, and I hope my stories and learning from my journey may help you on yours!

Thanks for making me a better person every day and for enabling me to dare—#DaretoLeadLikeaGirl.

I would like to finish off with my advice in the area of happiness:

Remember happiness is contagious—share positivity!

Choose to be generous—NATAN—giving is a two-way street—when you give you get.

DON'T LET ANYONE ELSE OWN YOUR HAPPINESS BUT YOU! Happiness cannot be given TO you or taken FROM you, it must come FROM WITHIN you.

I am forever grateful,
Namaste, Dalia

FOREWORD

Sheryl Sandberg

Over the last decade, I've traveled around the world asking hundreds of women and men to raise their hands if they've ever been called bossy as a child. Time after time, most women's hands go up while few men raise theirs. When I follow up by saying that girls should be described as having "executive leadership skills" instead of bossy, people chuckle. But why is celebrating confident, bold girls who aren't afraid to step up seen as funny? Those girls become the women leaders of tomorrow, and there are still too few of us. Changing and expanding perceptions of what it means to lead and who's up for the task not only paves the way for more equal representation, but also creates better, well-rounded leaders in everyone.

For too long, narrow definitions of leadership have left out girls and women. In childhood, girls are discouraged from leading. They are called on less and interrupted more in the classroom, and by middle school, have less interest in leadership than boys. Those trends continue into adulthood, creating a gender gap in power. For example, men are evaluated on their potential, while women have to prove their worth—over and over again. Men are hired and promoted into manager roles at higher rates than women despite having a similar amount of experience. Assertiveness in men is seen as strength but makes women less likeable in the eyes of others. And traits often associated with women—such as vulnerability and empathy—are categorized as "soft skills," and separate from other skills needed to be professionally successful.

People's views on gender and leadership are shaped by the hundreds of messages that they're exposed to every day. Unfortunately, many of these messages—from media to advertisements to casual conversations—are rooted in gender stereotypes. But women are pushing back and defying expectations every day. We are leaning into being our authentic selves at work and beyond. We are fighting for representation in spaces that have historically shut us out. Most important, we are challenging bias in all its forms.

In 2015, my foundation, LeanIn.Org, created the Glass Lion Award for the Cannes Lions International Festival of Creativity. The goal was to celebrate marketers who were using their platforms to promote messages of gender equality. Dalia was part of the amazing team that received the award for the very first time. Her team created an important campaign that destigmatized menstruation and sparked a larger cultural conversation with an empowering call to action. Dalia has helped produce other game-changing commercials and continues to expand the narrative about women beyond the world of marketing.

Dalia and women like her give me hope. They represent courageous, expansive leadership, but also lift up others with them by sharing their journeys and the lessons they've learned along the way. Everyone—regardless of their age, gender, background, or the industry they work in—can be inspired by this book and the example girls and women set every day to redefine leadership and change their communities and workplaces for the better.

—Sheryl Sandberg

PREFACE

The Story Behind This Story—
What It Means to Lead Like a Girl

In 2014, I was the marketing director for FemCare (Always, Tampax brands) at Procter & Gamble (P&G) and I was working with my global marketing team to rework the equity of the brand. We were redesigning our feminine pad and wanted to create a marketing campaign that was more purpose driven. After deep consumer-insight work and realizing the impact an effective pad has on a girl's self-esteem, we aligned to shift our focus from the functional benefit of protection to that of a higher-order life benefit—empowering women to be the best that they could be.

This equity reinvention led to a global brief that directed our advertising agency, Leo Burnett, to present to us a new campaign called "Always #LikeAGirl."

We opened the commercial with a provocative question: What does it mean to run like a girl?

Results showed that while young girls understand the phrase "run like a girl" to mean "run as fast as you can," something starts to change at puberty. Doing things "like a girl" becomes an insult. Our goal was to change the meaning of those words and challenge men and women to reclaim the phrase "like a girl" to mean being proud of who you are. We closed by challenging consumers and society with: *Why can't "run like a girl" also mean "win the race"?*

I remember seeing the completed advertisement for the first time and my heart jumped; we were empowering women, making change. This was exactly what had made me get out of bed every day for the past seventeen years and was the type of impact I wanted to make in the world. I showed it to my eldest daughter, Mia, then eleven years old, and she cried and shared it with all her friends. But what is even more meaningful—five years later—my youngest Anna, who was then eleven, called me from school all excited: "Mum, you will not believe it, but they are showing your ad in social studies!" This campaign went on to become the most viral advertisement of 2014. It won fourteen Cannes advertising awards and was the first FemCare advertisement to ever be shown during the Super Bowl, an American football prime-time television sporting event, and it was chosen by *Forbes* as one of the top ten most influential campaigns of the decade.[1] More than a commercial, Always #LikeAGirl had become an icon for women's empowerment.

Now what if I asked you, "What does it mean to LEAD like a girl?"

After having spent more than two decades as a marketing executive and most recently as one of the only female executives on an mostly-male team, I believe it's time to reclaim the phrase "like a girl" once again—this time, in the world of leadership.

While this book is aimed at both women and men, I have decided to call this book *Lead Like a Girl* as a provocation against current leadership bias and to pay homage to this game-changing and poignant campaign.

What does it mean to lead "like a girl" and why is it critical, today, more than ever?

Leading like a girl is leading from the head *and* the heart—leading with compassion.

From an evolutionary point of view, men were hunters (strong and bold) and women were gatherers (warm and nurturing). Our models of leadership today reflect much of this archaic view. Leaders are expected to be strong, bold, decisive, assertive, and somewhat impersonal, all of which has been associated with male behavior in the past. On the flip side, being a leader who is warm and nurturing is seen as being weak. This is a socially constructed, yet, I argue, old-fashioned stereotype, and it's becoming imperative that we change this; in today's world, feminine qualities are exactly what we need in our leaders. We are in the midst of a leadership crisis. Our previous hunter/warrior/industrial efficiency models of leadership just don't cut it anymore. The poor condition of our employee engagement status exemplifies this.

A Gallup global engagement research poll conducted in 2016 found that 87 percent of employees are unhappy in the workplace and feel they work for companies that don't care for them as human beings. Even worse, 20 percent of employees are actively hostile.[2]

"Harassment and bullying at work are commonly reported problems, and can have a substantial adverse impact on mental health."[3] In fact recent research has found that the number-one driver of the great resignation is a toxic work environment (10x more than poor pay). An employee who experiences a toxic environment is up to 55% more likely to fall chronically sick.[4] This drops straight to the bottom line—in fact, work-related "depression and anxiety have a significant economic impact; the estimated cost to the global economy is US$ 7 trillion per year in lost productivity."[5] The good news is there are many proven interventions organizations can do to build a healthy culture and limit this mental health challenge. Research has shown an estimated ROI (return on investment) of 1 to 4—"for every US$ 1 put into scaled up treatment for common mental disorders, there is a return of US$ 4 in improved health and productivity."[6] Current leadership methods are hindering engagement and performance.

In the midst of such a leadership crisis, we need the emotional traits traditionally associated with women—like resilience, value-based decision making, and empathy—more than ever before. COVID-19 deepened this mental health crisis and hence these needs even further.

Let's start with the "softest" of skills—emotions. Displaying emotion is considered a feminine trait and many still argue that bringing emotions to work makes you seem weaker.

Research has shown that emotions, especially empathy, are critical to creating an environment of psychological safety, which is the number one driver of high-performing teams as found by Google research.[7] *Psychological safety* is a term coined by psychologist William Kahn in 1990 to describe a working environment where an employee "is able to show oneself without fear of negative consequences to self-image, status or career."[8] In cultivating such an environment, becoming a compassionate leader is not just nice, it is a necessity. In psychologically safe teams, employee potential and team effectiveness are maximized as a learning environment is created.[9]

In addition to being vital for engagement and learning, emotions—and particularly empathy—are also critical to understanding employees' and stakeholders' resistance to change. Even more fundamentally, empathy is needed for innovation and the ability to understand unexpressed consumer needs.

Yet empathy is considered a feminine trait, and that is supported scientifically, as women tend to score higher on most measurements of emotional intelligence, especially empathy. This is also proven in neuroscientific research showing that when an emotion is expressed by another person, women on average tend to connect and stay with the emotion. Men tend to sense empathy in others for a brief moment, but then tune out and activate the parts of the brain associated with problem solving. That is why so many women feel that their man doesn't listen and instead jumps to fix a problem when all they want is empathy and to feel "felt."

While empathy is so critical to dealing with the challenges of the future, we are currently experiencing an "empathy crisis." Research has found a 40 percent drop in empathy among Generation Y—the twenty-five- to thirty-year-olds—and millennials in the workforce compared to thirty years ago.[10] With digital transformation and kids having fewer face-to-face emotional interactions, this is not surprising. Workplaces are also struggling with short-term financial focus and a decrease in job security, all leading to a reduction in empathy, as workers are less able to attach emotionally to their jobs and work environments.

This combination of the workplace becoming less empathetic and the world demanding more empathetic strategies to drive engagement, creativity, and innovation indicates that this "female" trait of empathy is an important leadership skill we need now and in the future.

Needless to say, COVID, its mental health challenges, and the remote work environment we should expect to see more of, have further deepened the need for empathy and more traditionally feminine leadership traits.

So what are these feminine traits and what is more effective in today's world?

A recent *Harvard Business Review*[11] article found that not only are women just as effective as men, women actually score higher than men in seventeen out of nineteen leadership traits. I have based much of my 5P model—the foundation for this book—on this

Figure 0.1.   Women Score Higher Than Men In Most Leadership Skills.
Source: Jack Zenger and Joseph Folkman, "Women Score Higher Than Men in Most Leadership Skills," *Harvard Business Review,* June 25, 2019.

research. These traits include: bold leadership (courage), integrity and honesty, establishing stretch (yet achievable) goals, resilience, empathy and emotional intelligence, and a variety of people skills like inspiring, motivating, and developing others (figure 0.1).

So why is "lead like a girl" still seen as an insult?

In this book, I argue that these skills are often underrated, that women need to be proud of, and men need to embrace, these critical "feminine" traits.

Sometimes referred to as the tension between left and right brain—where the left brain represents the logical brain while the right brain represents the more emotional and creative brain—the reality is that we need leaders to be holistic and flexible and to embrace both sides of their brains.

This concept referred to as the genius of the "and" versus the tyranny of the "or,"[12] developed by J. C. Collins in the book *Built to Last*:

> Builders of greatness reject the "Tyranny of the OR" and embrace the "Genius of the AND." They embrace both extremes across a number of dimensions *at the same time*—purpose AND profit, continuity AND change, freedom AND responsibility, discipline AND creativity, humility AND will, empirical analysis AND decisive action.

In the same way, I argue that a leader needs to embrace both masculine left-brain traits (like logic and data) as well as traditionally feminine right-brain traits (like emotions) in order to deliver both the short-term objective and the long-term impact that comes from developing people.

This book is not about women versus men. We all have within us both masculine and feminine traits. And a leader needs to connect to these positive masculine and positive feminine traits.

The issue, as my friends Nilima Bhat and Raj Sisodia share in their book *Shakti Leadership*,[13] is that the business world has sunk into something they call "the wounded masculine"—a world of competition over collaboration, scarcity over abundance, and power *over* people versus power *with* people. In the same way, many women—when confronted with a wounded masculine business world—will either choose to "hide" their feminine traits and act like men to succeed, or they sink into their "wounded feminine," becoming overly dependent on external validation or too empathetic and over-pleasing without boundaries until they reach a state of burnout. Interestingly, young girls feel strong and confident yet are socialized when reaching the workplace to behave like men to succeed. "Lead like a girl" is not only a cry to men to adopt feminine traits but also for women to remain true to how they were as girls.

This book is hence an urgent invitation to ALL leaders to adopt this genius of the AND—to adopt the positive masculine, that of direction and logic, AND to adopt the positive feminine, that of empathy and nurturing teamwork. In other words, we need to shift the current skew in the business world and encourage all leaders to connect to their more feminine side and **lead (more) like a girl!**

When we talk about daring, former Unilever CEO Paul Polman states:

> The word *courage* has been misinterpreted as brave, or making decisions that others are not willing to make. Courage comes from the French word *coeur*—which means heart. Courageous leaders lead from their heart.

In that same interview Paul Polman also mentioned that instead of trying to fix women or force them to behave more like men, maybe it is time we learn from them!

What's in it for you?

Lead Like a Girl is for all women and men striving to be inspirational leaders and struggling to keep it all in balance. After writing my first blog under this title, I was grateful to find that more than 60 percent of comments came from men who were inspired by the blog to be a better husband and/or father, and to evolve from the role of a manager to that of an inspirational leader. This was further proof that we *all* struggle with how to be happier in our lives, how to leverage our strengths and manage our weaknesses, and how to balance our different life roles and add value in a way that is in line with our values and our hearts.

Some of my stories may seem privileged or optimistic to some. They probably are. I am very grateful for my hard-earned privilege—earning my own dime since I was 14 as a gymnastics coach, and working 16- to 18-hour days most of my career. I hope you can still draw the key strategies and insights that are helpful for you. I guess leading like a girl is never apologizing. And remembering that "the difference between privilege and entitlement is kindness." So I am sharing myself and my journey as openly and authentically as I can, in hope that it may help you on yours.

After the first draft of this book was written, I was invited to give a TED Talk on this topic.[14] I was again blown away by the impact this would have. I was contacted by many—from young students and working mums who were challenged to "man up," to men who were denigrated by being told that they "lead like women." But probably the most surprising comment was from a guy who admitted he was a "reformed asshole" and was inspired to woman up and try a softer path. I am grateful to be able to further this important conversation on equality and the much-needed leadership paradigm shift.

As I state in my TEDx Talk: Courage is not the absence of fear, so face your fears, go back to the heart, dig into your superpowers, and lead like a girl. This book is an attempt at exactly this: How can we better understand these softer, more feminine leadership traits and embrace them?

When my friend and mentor, Tal Ben-Shahar, first heard me speak and told me I needed to write a book, my first reaction was— "Me? My stories are like any girl next door."

"But that is why they are so relevant," he said. Many of the experiences in this book could happen or have happened to many young women. By sharing my personal learning and the scientific underpinnings I have picked up along the way, combined with actionable tips you can start implementing immediately, it is my hope that you will be inspired to **lead more like a girl!**

Become a compassionate leader—leading from your head and your heart.

Be strong enough to seem weak.

Recognize and be connected with your superpowers.

Be the leader you aspire to be.

With deepest gratitude.
Namaste,
Dalia Feldheim
Singapore, June 2020

INTRODUCTION

Are You a Compassionate Leader?
The 5P Model—Self Assessment

Like a roadmap that helps us get to where we are going, we must make sure that we are prepared to travel. For most of us who have been broken apart bit by bit by life and work, this means putting all of the pieces together.

> The only definition for happiness is wholeness.
>
> —Helen Keller

The word *health* in Latin, "salus," is derived from "sarvas," which means "whole." You cannot be mentally healthy if you are not whole. Said differently, while we don't need to be scoring 10/10 in each of the dimensions in the model, we do need to be growing and making progress in each of them. You may be very spiritual, positive, and adamant about your physical wellness, but one challenging relationship that you ignore robs you of being truly happy.

Based on these drivers of whole-person well-being, as Tal Ben-Shahar calls them, and the critical traits of effective leadership—especially those where women tend to outperform men—I have created this model of what it really means to "Lead Like a Girl." Inspired by my marketing experience, I call this model the 5Ps of resilience and compassionate leadership—**the 5Ps of leading like a girl.**

The 5Ps are focuses on purpose and integrity, power up, physical wellness, perspective and mental perseverance, people and social skills, and positivity and emotional bravery. Let me briefly expand on each:

1. Leading with **purpose** is about understanding your strengths, passions, and values and bringing your best self to work and life every day. It's about having integrity and making value-based decisions, and about setting stretch goals.
2. **Powering up** is about physical wellness, managing your energy, and finding more balance in your life.
3. **Perspective** and mental **perseverance** means understanding our limiting beliefs and embracing these as an opportunity for growth by cultivating the mental resilience to be able to bounce back and grow from hardship.
4. **People** is about investing in relationships and redefining ROI to mean Return On Interaction instead of Return On Investment. It's about bringing out our typical female gathering skills in a holistic view as partners, parents, and leaders fostering teamwork, inclusiveness, and personal growth for all.
5. **Positivity** is about emotional bravery—recognizing our own emotions and those of others as a sign of passion not a weakness.

Because with **Purpose, Power, Perspective, People**, and **Positivity**, who says that leading like a girl can't mean winning the game?

Before we start the journey of self-growth to lead (more) like a girl, I invite you to do an assessment of where you are today. On the list below, give yourself a mark from 0–10, with zero (0) being *I am not at all good at this* and ten (10) being *I am great at this*.

PURPOSE

1. Purpose:

   a. I clearly understand my purpose and what I do
   b. I set clear goals
   c. I make decisions based on values and personal integrity

2. Strengths:

   a. I am aware of my strengths
   b. I bring them to life every day

POWER UP

3. Physical Wellness:

   a. I am successful with managing my energy
   b. I am mindful about what happens in my life
   c. I meditate regularly
   d. I am conscious about what I eat
   e. I sleep 7 to 8 hours each night
   f. I take real vacations
   g. I work out regularly

4. Physical Environment:

   a. I am happy about my physical environment
   b. I am happy with where I live
   c. I am happy with where I work

PERSPECTIVE AND MENTAL PERSEVERANCE

5. Learning and Growth:

   a. I am happy with my self-learning/education
   b. I am happy with how I am doing in my career

c. I am happy with how I am managing my finances

d. I am constantly asking questions, listening, being curious

6. Perspective and Mental Perseverance:

a. I am happy with how I manage stress and adversity

b. I can step back and reflect on my perspective recognizing what could be my interpretation of the event versus what really happened

c. I think I have no beliefs that hold me back

d. I am good with dealing with failures and drawbacks

PEOPLE

7. People:

a. I am mindful about my relationships

b. I am happy with my relationship with my partner

c. I am happy with my relationship with my family

d. I am happy with my relationships with my friends

e. I am happy with my relationships with my colleagues

f. I feel I leave others happier after meeting with them

8. Relationship with Self:

a. I am satisfied with my relationship with myself

b. I am satisfied with my self-care

c. I am satisfied with my self-esteem

d. Positivity and Emotional Growth

POSITIVITY

9. Positivity and Emotional Growth:

a. I believe I am emotionally brave about accepting the full range of emotions

   b. I am able to express my own emotions in a manner that is helpful for others versus destructive

   c. I am empathetic and emotionally brave about understanding and accepting others' emotions

   d. I live with an attitude of gratitude

   e. I am overall positive and optimistic about the future

10. Play and Creativity:

   a. I am content with the level of play in my life

   b. I am content with the level of creativity in my life

   c. I am content with the overall level of happiness in my life

I invite you to explore how to grow in each of these areas and lead from your heart, with authenticity, courage, and conviction to become an inspirational and compassionate leader.

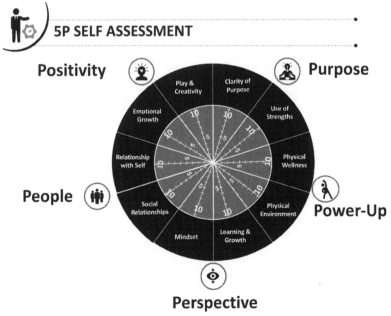

Figure 0.2. 5P Self-Assessment.

I

PURPOSE

Leading with *purpose* is about understanding your strengths, passions, and values and bringing your best self to work every day. It's about having integrity and making value-based decisions, and about setting stretch goals.

I

LEAD WITH PURPOSE, LIVE IN FLOW

It was 1998 and I was twenty-five, a young associate brand manager (ABM) at Procter & Gamble in Geneva, Switzerland, leading the FemCare brands for Israel. That meant I handled brands like Always, Alldays, and Tampax and my job was to promote sales of the products for Israel and the West Bank markets.

This was important business as these brands were market leaders and a key profit driver for the Near East group at the time. Our key competitor, Kotex, announced they were going to enter the Israeli market. Their top brands were hard on our tails for market share, and we didn't want to lose our leadership position. In brand marketing, you learn early on that in a situation like this, your best defense is fortressing your strengths. I learned to apply this tactic to my life as well. But more about that later.

I decided to fortress my business not by pushing the product but by better serving the needs of women at each life stage. We came up with a campaign that ran much deeper than a great product; it spoke to the sense of self-confidence women should feel any day of the month.

We narrowed our focus on Point of Market Entry (POME) and together with my fearless PR manager, Nada Dugas, we partnered

with the Ministry of Education on a mission to educate young
girls on hygiene at schools and started a nationwide program in all
schools for the twelve- to fifteen-year-olds.

However, we found our weak spot was Point of Market Change
(POMC) with female consumers between the ages of eighteen and
twenty-two. This was because at this age, Israeli women enter
the Israel Defense Forces, as military service is compulsory for
both men and women in Israel. With their tightly budgeted army
pocket-money, many start buying cheaper products. We needed to
increase relevancy and value for this age group and create trials for
our new products. We decided to approach the army and offered
product samples to the women, providing them with a wash kit that
had special sealed-off compartments for their pads and tampons.
As an ex-platoon commander for women just five years before, I
remembered the embarrassment of having to carry these supplies
to the outside showers, and the pain, as they would often get soggy
and ruined in the standard wash kits. The army loved the idea and
gave us permission to provide a sample to every eighteen-year-old
recruited.

But I wanted to add a more personalized note of encouragement.
And so, I sat down and started to write a note to these women as an
inspirational starting point for my advertising agency. I distinctly
remembered my first day in the army, having gotten on the bus after
saying goodbye to my parents and friends and not knowing anyone
yet. I recalled looking at my new uniform and through some of the
gifts I'd received from friends and family and thinking, "How will I
manage? Who will take care of me now?"

This was all fresh in my mind as I wrote this personal note. I believe being a platoon commander shaped a lot of my understanding
of how to lead like a girl. I wrote about the importance of hygiene
in the army, but also about the pride they should feel as women
stepping up and serving their country as equals to their male counterparts and the huge impact this experience would make on building
their resilience.

I lost track of time and worked into the wee hours of the morning.
When my boss Jim came in the next morning, I showed him the note.

He had a tear in his eye and asked me not to have the agency rewrite it but to print this letter of encouragement "as is." He insisted I sign my real name and former title, so the soldiers would know it was authentically written by an ex-platoon commander. He didn't allow this letter to be touched for the five years we were running the army sampling program. Jim saw my ability to empathize with the target audience and use it to better connect. He was one of my first role models for what it means to lead from the heart.

What happened next shocked me. Two days after this delivery, our service line was overwhelmed with calls and notes from the young women and their mums thanking us for the insightful gift and note, and for being there and supporting them on such a critical day.

That was my first encounter with **purpose**. It was then and there that I realized *I was not in the business of selling pads but promoting self-esteem and women's empowerment.*

As an anecdote—the other week I went to say goodbye to my own eighteen-year-old who decided to join a yearlong premilitary program in Israel. She invited me to her dorm and when I went into the toilet, my heart jumped—hanging there was the wash bag I designed that was given to my daughter's friend by her mother, who got it from me some twenty-five years ago.

Our P&G next point of weakness was a special sector of the population: ultra-Orthodox Jewish women. We needed to find a creative way to market to them since they do not consume public media or advertisements about period products, even in their own media outlets, as it is considered extremely inappropriate. We knew we needed a forum where women were alone. A husband or son bringing a sample of the pads to the house was a big no-no among this community.

As I was preparing for my own Jewish wedding (which had to be an Orthodox ceremony in order for the marriage to be recognized in Israel), I learned that all Orthodox women meet at the *Mikveh,* a community bath that offers the gift of purity and holiness after their menstruation and is also a requirement for every woman before her wedding. This sparked an idea. We aligned with the managing authority of the *Mikveh* association to offer samples to these ladies.

But again, we didn't just sample the product, we shared a note on women's equality.

In order to determine the effectiveness of the program, we visited the baths. On a visit to one of the biggest purifying baths, the women there asked me to talk a little bit about myself and my journey. A year later, I went back to tour the *Mikveh* program to assess how it was going. A young Orthodox woman walked up to me and said, "*Mazel Tov* [congratulations], Dalia. I see you got married." I was shocked. She not only remembered me from the previous year but also noticed that I now had a wedding ring on my finger. She told me my talk inspired her to delay her arranged marriage and finish her studies. She shared that she had opened her own business and was doing very well and was going to marry the following year, but now as an equal as she had now established a path for financial independence.

I was amazed by the impact my little talk had . . . I realized then my purpose was *to inspire and enable people to be the best they can be.*

By the end of a twelve-month period, we had a strong marketing defense plan and our shares soared. Even better, Kotex delayed their entry into the market by three years and P&G's strong market leadership in Israel was established.

That year I didn't sleep much. I was so passionate and happy about what I was doing. I felt a huge sense of purpose. I was bursting with ideas. I was glowing. *I was in flow.*

The term *flow* was introduced by professor Mihaly Csikszentmih-alyi,[1] one of the fathers of Positive Psychology (who recently passed in October of 2021), to describe a state of complete absorption in an experience that is both challenging and rewarding. Sometimes, it is also referred to as meditation in action, being in the "zone," losing yourself in what you are doing, and being in a state in which action and awareness are merged.

Having purpose means being useful and contributing to others and yourself and it affects all the other Ps because it drives *mood and motivation.* From a neurological perspective, the reward of contributing to something outside of yourself comes in the form of a rush of oxytocin, dopamine, and serotonin—what neuroscientists call the "Happiness Trifecta."[2] Oxytocin supports empathy and social bonding. Dopamine plays a major role in motivation and movement. Serotonin regulates mood and creates a feel-good phenomenon.

Not only does being pulled by something bigger than ourselves affect mood and motivation, it has also been scientifically proven to make us *more resilient*. Or as Nietzsche said, "He who has a why to live, can bear almost any how." This is examined in *Man's Search for Meaning* by Viktor Frankl,[3] Austrian psychiatrist and Holocaust survivor. When he went into the camps, not only was he stripped of his clothes but his lifelong research was taken away from him, too. He shares how it was his *purpose*, to reunite with his family and mentally reconstruct his studies to continue teaching, which gave him extraordinary strength to survive.

At a corporate level, having a brand or company purpose has proven to drive company performance. My former P&G CMO (chief marketing officer) Jim Stengel dedicated his second career to the importance of corporate purpose and, together with Millward Brown, created a list of the world's fifty fastest-growing brands based on ten years of empirical research involving 50,000 companies. Known as the Stengel 50, they found that these purpose-driven companies saw 400 percent more returns on the stock market than the S&P 500. This is due to proven impact on employee engagement, especially the younger purpose-driven Gen Y, as well as customer satisfaction.[4] As Paul Polman, my ex-P&G president who later led Unilever to purpose and sustainability, advocates, "We cannot choose between growth and sustainability, we must have both." This focus on purpose further inspired the movement of Conscious Capitalism.[5] B Lab has taken this mission further by certifying companies that balance profit with purpose and use their business as a force for good. When I went to do my master's at INSEAD business school, I was happy to learn their selling line and mission is to be a "force for good."

Finding your purpose is not about leaving your day job to be a monk in Tibet; rather, it's looking at your current job and identifying what you are *good* at—your strengths, what you are *passionate* about—your values and motivations, and how you can use this to drive value to consumers and the world. It is about looking at what you are currently doing and aligning it with your strengths and passions. It is about turning your job into a calling. When I recently started coaching individuals and companies to find purpose and joy at work, I created a workshop which quickly became my most popular. I help employees find their personal purpose and reignite their spark at work by linking it to the company purpose. Paying homage to Simon Sinek's golden circle concept highlighted in his TED Talk "Start With 'Why,'"[6] I have called this process discovering the "golden link," which is being able to align one's personal purpose to that of the brand and of the company and, as a leader, being able to help your employees fulfill their purpose by designing roles that focus on their strengths and passions, while driving the company's goals. I will describe this process using my own journey to discover my golden link.

P&G is a purpose-led company. Its purpose is "Touching Lives, Improving Life." I kept being drawn back to work on FemCare as I was personally aligned with its brand purpose—"No girl left behind." And so, from an early stage, I was able to focus 100 percent of my time on my purpose: people empowerment. From the teams I built, the training I led, the women's networks I participated in and later founded, to the consumers I served, my career wasn't a job, it was a calling. This was because I was living and working toward my purpose, which was linked to the company purpose, grounded in brand benefits and deep consumer understanding, and as a result drove business success.

I have shared with you how I discovered my golden link. Let me now share two examples which bring this golden link between personal and company purpose to life.

I was over the moon when, in 2010, I landed the role of FemCare marketing director for Asia and we moved to Singapore. One of my biggest markets was India and I fell in love with the women of India. I was in awe of their passion for and commitment to self-development. During one of my first trips to India, I encountered a young girl, eleven or twelve years old, sitting on a stool trying to read a book. There was no light in her house, and so she was reading the book by the light of the passing cars. I was astonished with her commitment to growth. I later heard so many stories about the challenges young girls deal with just to keep up and yet they remain brave and determined. As a foreigner, I also was in awe of their cultural beliefs.

To learn about how our products might improve people's lives, P&G goes into consumers' homes to better understand how they live, their unmet needs, and how its products are used. I vividly remember the day we walked into a middle-class home and I noticed a girl sitting on the floor. I remember looking at the blue wall behind her and noticed the paint was peeling and worn out just in that spot, as if she sat there often. When her mum came in with drinks, she served the young girl a drink where she was on the floor! I was puzzled. Uncles and aunties came in and greeted the family and then greeted her on the floor. As she greeted them back, I noticed a sad, embarrassed look on her face. *What was going on here?* I thought.

When we left the house, I asked my local agency representative, "What was that all about?" And they told me, "She has her period." I asked, "So what?" They told me, "Well, we believe women should stay isolated during their period."

I was stunned. I now understood the sad look on the girl's face. My agency partner went on, "The basis of this was originally positive. Women were overburdened with house and childcare, so they got a week off and were not allowed into the kitchen to avoid them being sucked into work. Also, with no sanitary protection, areas which are religious should be avoided as bodily waste is considered impure." She smiled and said, "We even believe women on their periods are not allowed to touch pickles as we believe the bacteria in the menses will make them go bad." She added, "Yes, despite modern sanitary progress, the nation is still struck by regressive myths, casting girls away for a week every month."

While this cultural behavior may have had solid reasons in the olden days, we were both saddened by the repressive, negative connotations that periods still have today and the impact such perceptions must have on young girls.

That night, I couldn't stop thinking about that young girl's sad, embarrassed look. Together with my local team and agency, we decided to try to tackle this cultural norm in the most respectful way. For the next year we were deep in research and developing our campaign to change the stigma behind periods. Finally, in the summer of 2014, we launched our campaign: Whisper "Touch the Pickle."[7] We used humor to tackle the myth and it worked!

This advertisement ended up becoming the most virally watched ad in India in 2014. It also was the winner of the first-ever Cannes Sheryl Sandberg Glass Lion Grand Prix Award,[8] which is awarded to an ad that "implicitly or explicitly addresses issues of gender inequality or prejudice," and, more importantly, drove the conversation that's still going about women's equality in India.

That same year, the global team for Always was looking to redesign the global equity for the brand. We knew we wanted to evolve from selling pads to promoting self-esteem and we wanted to find a way to do this on a global scale. My general manager, Edgar Sandoval, a huge purpose advocate and now president of World Vision, and my president, Melanie Healey, loved this new direction. We challenged our advertising agency, Leo Burnett, to come up with a breakthrough that would, for the first time, focus on the purpose of the brand instead of hard selling the new product we were launching. That's when the iconic Always #LikeAGirl campaign was launched.[9]

Melanie Healey is another amazing role model of mine for leading like a girl—her ability to empathize both with her employees and customers is key to her success and to the sound business decisions she made as FemCare global president. Melanie is credited with inspiring this campaign idea. Her daughter, then twelve, was about to play in a crucial sports game and got her period. Melanie just told her, "It's okay. Periods should not stop you, now go on and play like a girl and win the game." She shared this with the agency and the idea was born.

When we saw the first video cut of the idea, our entire team teared up. The agency had nailed it. This was exactly what we were looking for. I personally felt my years of focusing on purpose in our communication had reached a new high. Within two weeks we were able to persuade twenty-six markets across North America, Europe, and Asia to invest, even though it was the last day of the fiscal year. The campaign went on the air on June 26, 2014, and was the most viral ad of the year with almost 70 million views, fourteen Cannes advertising awards, and recognition as one of the most influential campaigns of the decade by *Forbes* magazine.[10] But more importantly, the commercial had become an icon for women's empowerment, inspiring a reframing of the phrase "Like a Girl" to mean be the best that you can be.

I am proud of many things about my career at P&G, but I am most proud of being able to use my passion and empathy (two characteristics of feminine leadership) for good—to drive purpose and profit. From creating the unique army and Orthodox markets sampling products, to establishing women networks within P&G, to starting the women's empowerment conversation in India and later the world, I was in a state of flow as I was able to create the golden link. My personal passion for women's empowerment was linked to my brand and company purpose and it drove me, with renewed energy, to deliver better business results.

Leading like a girl is leading from the heart—with empathy, connecting your work to your core values and having high integrity to make business decisions in line with those values. The *Harvard Business Review* research I referred to in the preface[11] shows women tend to score higher than men on these elements—high integrity and honesty. Men and women both can become better leaders by finding their purpose, which will boost their passion for their work and help them make honest, value-based decisions.

PERSONAL ACTIVITY

Activity: How can you find your purpose and create the golden link?

You can sign up to do the exercises online,[12] or find yourself a coach or even a good friend to complete the exercises with, as they are particularly challenging to do alone.

One of my favorite parts of my "Wellness at Work" corporate programs is finding your *why* module. It helps employees find their strengths, align their core values and motivations, and reignite their passion for their work, resulting in increased engagement and increased performance. I have brought into this workshop the great work by Simon Sinek, further enhanced by the INSEAD leadership program, and included the power of illustration in experience to reveal the subconscious. It relies on three exercises.

Before you begin, find a quiet place and put on your favorite music. Allocate an hour-and-a-half to two hours for Exercise 1; one hour for Exercise 2; and ten minutes for Exercise 3. Take fifteen to thirty minutes at the end to bring your responses to the exercises together. Get yourself the following—tabloid-sized paper (or stick two pieces of letter-sized paper together) and colored markers.

EXERCISE I

What can your history tell you about your purpose?

Your purpose is driven by your heritage and the roles you carry throughout your life. Looking at your life map through a reflective lens allows you to find themes that help you assess your current purpose.

Step 1 (10 minutes): Your story.

Draw your life map. Drawing will help you dig into your subconscious.

- Draw five to seven events that had the biggest impact on who you are today. Make sure no words are used at this stage, only drawings.
- Try to include stories from different stages of life (0–5 years old, 5–10 years old, etc.).

To help you in this task, I invite you to think about the following:[13]

1. What is your earliest defining moment—the happiest or saddest moment that made a big impact?

2. Who was a person who had a big impact on you?

- What did this person say or do to you?

3. What was a pivotal moment in your life, a time when you realized life would never be the same?

4. What have you accomplished that you are very proud of?

- Who supported you?

5. Think of a time you were in the zone—what happened that made you feel that way?

Step 2 (30 minutes for each storyboard point): Finding meaning in your stories.

- Ask your friend/mentor to make a line down the middle of a page. On the left, they write down your story, and on the right, they write down its meaning, emotions, the contribution others had on you, the impact it made. Share the stories drawn in Exercise 1 and dig into the meanings of these stories.

- Tell the stories with as much detail as possible.
- Your friend/mentor probes you on the meaning by using the following questions:

  a. How did the story impact you?
  b. When this happened, how did it make you feel?
  c. Who else was involved and how did they make a difference?
  d. What is it about this story that was so impactful?
  e. How did this experience affect you?
  f. What was its contribution to who you have become?
  g. What is the lesson you learned from the experience that you carry with you today?

Step 3 (10 minutes): Find themes.

This is the part where you realize that unrelated stories create a theme.

- Circle any word on the meaning side of the page that repeats itself.
- Write down what repeating threads come up, for example: protecting others, empathy, bringing people together, etc. Choose the theme that best resonates with you and your purpose.

Step 4 (15 minutes): Write your purpose statement.

This last stage is not easy but be sure to write something down. It takes years to refine and finalize your purpose statement, but it is important that you write down your first draft, which we will further refine.

Use the themes that come from your heritage life story to create a draft purpose statement. Simon Sinek uses the following format:

My purpose in life is to_____ (verb to describe your contribution) so that_____ (impact on others).

For example: My purpose in life is to empower and enable people to find purpose and joy so that together we can light up our world.

EXERCISE 2

What can your strengths and passions tell you about your purpose?

This exercise is based in *Ikigai*, a Japanese term meaning *the reason for being*. The term is used to indicate that sweet spot or balance where the three elements of your strengths, your passions, and your contribution to the world converge. Look at the diagram in figure 1.1 and think about what is your *Ikigai*. Where do these concepts intertwine for you?

What are you good at?

Write down your strengths. Previous job assessments and/or 360 feedback should be able to help you recognize these strengths; or feel free to use the strength-finder assessment found in this link: http://www.viacharacter.org/www/Character-Strengths-Survey.

What are you passionate about?

Sometimes you can be great at things you're less passionate about. Now think about the things you *love* doing—things you would do

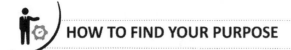

HOW TO FIND YOUR PURPOSE

Figure 1.1. How to Find Your Purpose. *Source:* **García Héctor and Francesc Miralles,** *Ikigai: The Japanese Secret to a Long and Happy Life* **(New York: Penguin, 2018).**

without pay or that you easily get sucked into. Another way to come up with what you are passionate about is to look at your values. What are your five most important values?

What does the world need?

This is about mining the external environment to understand what unmet need exists in the lives of the people you want to serve.

Where can you add the most value?

Now spend some time reflecting on the three elements above; what can you offer the world that is uniquely yours, about which you are strong and passionate, and for which you know there is a need?

Now go back to your written statement and see if there are any adjustments you want to make.

My purpose in life is to_____ (verb to describe your contribution) so that_____ (impact on others).

For example: My purpose in life is to empower and enable people to find purpose and joy so that together we can light up our world.

EXERCISE 3

What can your friends tell you about your purpose?

This is a beautiful exercise I have also adapted from Simon Sinek and which my coaching clients and mentees find both the most challenging and the most rewarding.

Choose five to ten of your closest friends as well as your partner and send them the following email:

> I am doing a leadership development program and I am asked to collect feedback from my closest friends. Can you help me answer the following questions?
>
> Why are you my friend?
> What is it about me that makes you want to be my friend?
> What value do I add to your life?"

Once you receive an answer, you will add this to your work.

Now you have three pieces of feedback—your past heritage, your current role, and themes of how you are contributing to your best friends. With this you should be in a better place to write down your initial purpose statement.

This process was refined with over five thousand clients and mentees. I have done this individually as well as within group coaching sessions and even online.

Let me give you an example based on the very first workshop I completed with my coaching client and friend, Dana.

Dana is a lawyer and a mediator. She came to me because she was in the midst of identifying her purpose and aligning her actions.

After drawing her life map stories and talking about them, she was amazed to discover there was a red thread in her life map stories and that was around "protection" and "empathy." Without going into too much personal detail, she realized all her stories included these two ideas:

1. Not being protected in the past, and
2. Being able to protect her own children and other helpless children.

We then looked at her magic interception between her strengths, her passions, and what the world needs.

Her strengths are her ability to resolve conflict through healthy communication and mediation, using humor and simplicity.

She is passionate about the world's empathy crisis, especially between parents and teens.

She believes there is a need in the world to help others resolve conflict through empathy.

Together, we constructed her purpose as: "Awaken empathy for people to be their best selves and inspire others. Like raindrops on a lake, the ripples of goodness expand, and together we impact more and more human beings around us to brighten our world."

She went on to move away from business mediation to focus on her passion: education—inspiring and enabling happy parenting.

Dana now leads workshops for parents of teens and has written a best-selling book *Flight or Fight* on limiting conflict when traveling with children. Dana even decided to use her sense of humor to run an annual stand-up comedy event about conflict resolution between parents and kids to raise money for kids in Nepal. She is now clear about where she is headed, and she is on fire and energized.

I have run this refined process with hundreds of women and men, and a handful of brands, and I am always so thrilled to see the shift people take when they are clearer on why they are here on this earth.

What is the higher purpose you are here to serve?

What is within the current work you are doing that is most aligned with your purpose and should be expanded for more job satisfaction, flow, and for a boost of your energy that will reignite your spark and step-change performance?

With more clarity on your purpose, you are now equipped to create a vision and set goals in line with your purpose, which we will further explore in the next chapter. Finding your purpose and setting goals will boost your leadership potential at work and in life.

> Love the work you do, and you will never work another day in your life.
>
> —Anonymous

2

THE SCIENCE OF GOAL SETTING

Shoot for the moon. Even if you miss, you'll land among the stars.

—Norman Vincent Peale

In 2001, I was a young associate brand manager at Procter & Gamble, newly married, living on one salary as my husband was still studying at university. I attended an inspiring lecture at P&G. The keynote speaker spoke of her father, an encyclopedia salesman. Every year her dad would write how much he wanted to make that year and place that note in his wallet. Once he reached that goal, he would take out a pen and write a new goal and put the paper back in his wallet. Slowly, he moved up to head salesman, took out a small loan, opened the first stamp loyalty business, and later became owner of one of the biggest global travel agencies. This man was Curt Carlson, founder of Carlson Wagonlit Travel, and the speaker was his daughter, Marilyn Carlson Nelson, who was later promoted to CEO of the company.

At the end of her talk, she gave each of us a little card. On one side there was the company credo and her personal moto which I still remember today—

*They drew a circle in the sand and left me out, I drew a bigger circle
and included me in.*

On the other side of the card there was a blank space where she
urged us to write down five goals we wanted to have achieved in
five years. I remember she encouraged us to dream big, so I wrote a
few ambitious things:

1. I want to be a mum of two (I was newly married).
2. I want to be promoted twice to Associate Director (this would
   normally take eight years).
3. I want my husband to be a successful businessman making
   one million dollars in his own right.
4. I want to have an international experience.

And then I added a total wild card:

5. I want to own a house in Geneva by the lake.

She did say to dream big!

I put that card in my purse and totally forgot about it. Life was
a whirlwind over the next five years. I got pregnant fast with my
daughter and had my son three months after going back to work, so
that meant I had them only fourteen months apart.

My husband got a job offer in Moscow and we decided to take
it. Moving as expats with rent and our schooling fully paid enabled
us to save some money for the first time in our lives. This move was
not only good for us financially but my husband also did well in his
job, and so did I.

I had amazing bosses rooting for me and got promoted twice
within five years (instead of eight years). And bizarrely enough,
when we returned to Geneva in 2006, we took the money we'd
managed to save and bought a house within walking distance of
Lake Geneva in Switzerland. This house was significantly under-
valued due to a tenant who refused to leave and hadn't made any
improvements in years. With a stroke of luck and good people skills,

we managed to get the tenant out and my husband proved to be an excellent creative project manager—he would take me to choose the materials I liked and then find a way to get the same for half the cost. For example, we built our pool based on the number of tiles he found on eBay from a lady who had bought too many!

One day, as I was unpacking in our new home, I found that card I had written back in 2001 in an old purse, that absurd "dream big" note I had written five years ago. I looked at it and couldn't believe my eyes, *everything on my dream list had come true!* I had no idea back then that we would get the offer to move to Russia that would make a lot of my dreams possible. I looked at the card again in total disbelief, but indeed everything I'd dreamt back in 2001 had come true in five years. I sat there looking at the card, looking up at my kids playing in this beautiful house we'd built with our own hands and started crying with gratitude.

Ever since then, I have been a big believer in goal setting.

Neuroscience, the study of the nervous system and the brain, has proven that setting goals is key for a successful life and that people who set goals are more likely to achieve better results and obtain overall well-being versus those who do not set goals.

The science behind it is simple. When you set goals and imagine yourself achieving these goals, your brain releases dopamine and other feel-good hormones. It also decreases cortisol and inhibits other stress-related hormones, enabling you to release more energy toward creativity and problem solving, which then gives you the focus and resources needed to achieve these goals.

Pretty amazing right? By setting goals, you'll know where you are heading; you will start noticing elements and opportunities re-lated to your goals and even subconsciously take risks getting you closer to your goals, like our somewhat zany decision to move to Russia.

It's long been proven that good leaders set stretch goals for themselves and others and help their people attain these goals. The *Harvard Business Review* research mentioned in the preface shows that women tend to perform better than men in establishing stretch goals. While there is not much statistical evidence as to why this is true, there are a few hypotheses to consider. First, stretch goals involve investing in personal learning, an area women tend to score higher on. Second, setting stretch goals may mean there is a risk of losing power and authority if the goals are not met. The same study demonstrates that women are less power driven. Third, women are generally more emotionally expressive and tend to attach more emotional value to their goals, proving to aid goal attainment. Finally, women are more inclined to see goals as a team effort and ask for support to achieve challenging goals. Additional research will be needed to support these hypotheses, but, clearly, stretch goal setting while seeking the support system to achieve these goals is a "must" component of leading like a girl for both men and women.

Knowing that you need to set goals is one thing; knowing how to do that is another. First you must look at the type of goals you are setting.

Happiness expert Tal Ben-Shahar, a great man and now a close friend of mine, created Harvard's most popular course in positive psychology. Much of the science in this book is based on his excellent online course.[1]

To be at your happiest self, he suggests that your goals fall into the "want to" category versus the "have to" category. To ensure you are going after these types of goals, he suggests your goals have the following components. These components are called the 3As:

1. **Affection**—These are goals you are passionate about. Ask yourself: *What do I really, really want to do?* versus *What should I do?*
2. **Authenticity**—These goals are in line with your values and strengths.
3. **Autonomy**—These are goals that you have selected on your own versus those set for you by your parents or others.

READY TO GET STARTED?

You can go to a coach to help you set goals, which is a great experience, or, with a bit of time spent self-reflecting, you can set goals yourself.

Many people avoid setting goals as they don't know how they are going to achieve them. The advice here is, don't worry about the *how* yet. Focus on the *why* and the *what*, and when you are clear about the destination, the road map will present itself to you. I couldn't have imagined moving to Moscow, but the opportunity came and we jumped at it, and that willingness to leap made all the difference. In this case, we were more focused on the why; we knew we wanted to have an adventure and to do what was good for our family and our careers.

Leadership expert Simon Sinek advises to start with the why.[2] I covered this indepth in the previous chapter, but here are the key questions to get you started.

1. What are you good at?
2. What are you passionate about?
3. What does the world need and in what areas can you contribute?

With that in mind, spend some time envisioning your brightest future.

1. What will people say to you on your eightieth birthday?
2. What do you want to *be* as a human being?
3. What do you want to *have*?
4. What do you want to *do*?

Sit down in a quiet place, put on some relaxing music, and write it all down. Dream big!

Another more creative way to envision your best life is to create a vision board. Again, I recommend finding a quiet place so you can better create the vision of your best life!

1. Take the wheel of balance I shared in the introduction.
2. Now find a picture or two that best represent what "best" looks like to you. You can set this in the future. I recommend ten years; in ten years, if this area of your life was the best that it could be, if you were performing at peak in this area—what would it look like? You can pull pictures off the Internet, cut pictures from magazines, or download the Pinterest app and pin the pictures you like onto your virtual board.
3. Create a collage using two pictures of each of the areas of your life. Add quotes if you wish, but make your board visually appealing
4. Now give your board a name—it could be your purpose statement or a summary phrase to bring to life who you need to be to live your vision board. Your vision board should represent BE, HAVE, DO. You can add a personal manifestation—I am gratitude, I am wisdom, etc.
5. Hang that board somewhere visible. Achieving goals is not easy; it requires habit change. Your vision board will act as the pull to get through the grind of daily habit change, as you know the bigger picture—you are creating your best life!

If your dreams do not scare you, they are not big enough.

—Ellen Johnson Sirleaf

With clarity of your why and where you are heading you can start asking yourself—what is preventing me from getting there? Often there are limiting beliefs you need to address (see chapter 5), but it all comes down to a better understanding of the areas that need most work. Goal setting usually comes up for people because they want to change something in their lives.

What areas of your life need work?

Go back to your self assessment in the introduction section to see which areas you want to focus on. For example:

Do you feel good about your eating habits?
Do you make it to the gym five times a week?

If that's what you want in life and you scored lower on this area, this is an indication that health needs to be high on your priority list.

Are you so busy at work that you barely make it home in time to feed your cat, change into your pajamas, and roll into bed, with no time for friends or weekend brunch?

If this is the case and you scored low on this area, and if it is important, then maybe the social life pie piece should be high up there as well.

This is a great way to see how you are doing on each of these critical dimensions. The results may surprise you. The great thing is, once you have your numbers, you can see which areas to focus on to help you set goals that will help you achieve a balanced and fulfilled life.

Setting goals isn't enough. You must make sure your goals are SMART.[3] That is: Specific, Measurable, Actionable, Realistic, and Time-bound. Doing this ensures that your goals are stretched enough to keep you pumped and inspired but not so totally out of whack that you don't even know how to take the first step. Also make sure they are clearly defined and measurable over a specific period. Coaches usually recommend setting three to five goals for six months. In six months, what tangible results would you like to have achieved?

For example: Don't just say, "I want to be healthier." Make it measurable. "I want to lose fifteen pounds and lower my blood sugar from 96 (prediabetic) to 85 (healthy range)." Once you have defined it, I encourage you to "shine" this goal by creating a picture of success—it could be a real picture or a sentence—anything to inspire and set your brain toward what you want to achieve.

Now that you have three goals SMARTly expressed, it's time to sit down and create the strategies and actions to get there. I have adapted this spreadsheet from Tony Robbins's Rapid Planning

Methodology: Results-focused, Purpose-driven, Massive action plan (RPM).[4]

I create an Excel sheet which I update once a week:

Results: On the left I write the SMART results I want to achieve in six months.

Purpose: In the next column, I write how each result helps me achieve my purpose.

MAP (Massive Action Plan): In the final columns I write how to get there. These are tangible actions I will do this week toward that goal.

Do the same for each of your three goals. Schedule time once a week to review your progress against your MAP and set new actions toward your goal for the following week. Breaking the lofty goal into tangible actions helps you make them actionable. Keep your eye on the end goal, but your focus should always be, "What is my next step?" Make your goals stick.

SHOUT IT FROM THE ROOFTOPS!

Find someone to share your goals with. A coach is great; a friend or partner will do. Write your goals down and maybe keep a notebook by your bed and get back to them weekly.

Define and schedule.

Each week, look at your three to five goals and define one action you are going to do immediately that coming week in each of your focus areas. Take out your calendar and schedule it in now.

Turn intention into rituals.

Neuroscience proves that habits are deeply wired into our brains. To create a new habit, we need to wire a new pathway and do the new habit repetitively. Repetition creates ritual, and this requires a signal, a trigger to drive action.

Want to work out more? Make it a ritual at least three times a week first thing in the morning. Leave your running shoes by the door as a trigger.

Want to become more mindful? Wear a red bracelet to remind you to start every morning with five minutes of mindfulness.

Want to remember to tell your spouse you love them? I heard about a husband who became conditioned to tell his wife he loved her by touching his wedding ring as a reminder to do so.

Every voyage starts with a single step. Don't try to do all your goals at once, as you will just get discouraged and ditch your plans.

Define your first baby step.

Once you have successfully achieved this, you can go on to the next one. Define these steps weekly; at the end of the week, set a new action plan for the following week. When I attended Tony Robbins's Life Mastery adventure retreat, we had to jump off a telephone pole. As we climbed up, we were asked to focus on one thing only: "What's your next step?" While the goal was to jump, we had to take one step at a time to reach that goal.

Let me share with you another personal example, which will hopefully help turn the theory into action and maybe inspire you to get started.

After twenty years in a lucrative corporate career, I decided to leave my job as CMO Asia with a big company and took a leap of faith to dedicate more time to my purpose: inspiring and helping people grow.

I knew I wanted to create a life that would be grounded in growth, contribution, and love—this was my *why*. I wanted to continue self-learning, to help others achieve greatness, and to strengthen important relationships in my life.

And so, in April 2018, I sat down to write my five key goals for the next six months in line with my why and my vision of an ideal future.

1. **Purpose**—Create a business plan against my newfound purpose to inspire others to be the best they can be. Lead women's empowerment retreats. Give one talk a month.
2. **Physical Growth**—Lose seven kilograms and reduce my sugar from prediabetic to normal. Exercise three to four times a week.
3. **Perspective and Mental Growth**—Go back to school. Develop a portfolio career by working multiple part-time and freelance jobs.
4. **People and Relationship Growth**—Move from a score of five to eight on my relationship self-assessment. Spend quality time with my parents, kids, husband, and friends.
5. **Positivity and Emotional Growth**—Bring to zero anger outbursts and start a five-minute gratitude practice.

By September 2018 (six months later), this is what happened:

Purpose—I resisted the temptation and three offers to go back to the lucrative and safe corporate world and created my own ideal portfolio career combining time to study, speaking, teaching, training, and coaching. I signed up to APSS (Asia Professional Speakers Singapore) and gave monthly keynotes on my areas of passion—purpose-led leadership and happiness at work. I spoke at the amazing EVE women's empowerment event in Singapore and met great role models like professor Tal Ben-Shahar while there. Lastly, I started monthly women's empowerment yacht retreats which not only help inspire growth in those participating but also contribute to an NGO helping women in Sri Lanka to open their own micro-businesses. I took on another major volunteering project by joining TOM (Tikkun Olam Makers) and connecting people with disabilities with the local technology community. Every evening I evaluated whether I spent my time 100 percent toward my purpose. I was at a high 80 percent.

Physical Growth—I went to a nutritionist, managed to hit the gym four times a week, and lost the desired fifteen pounds. I obtained a SUP yoga teacher diploma. I practiced and taught weekly, started a supplement program, and got my sugar in balance (see chapter 3).

Perspective and Mental Growth—I decided to go back to school to obtain my INSEAD Executive Masters in Change (EMC). I took on an extra stretch goal, a yearlong online diploma in Happiness Studies (HSA by Tal Ben-Shahar), which opened the door to a whole shift in my career and a role as an adjunct professor at Singapore Management University.

People and Relationship Growth—I pampered my parents with a trip to Japan. I spent the longest summer holiday with the kids by inviting fifteen of their best friends to a surfing camp at a beach house we rented. We went on family trips to Italy and the Japanese Alps. For the first time, I joined my husband as trailing spouse on his two-week business travel to the United States. I spent time at home with my daughter preparing for her Cambridge IGC-SEs, and I also managed to spend one hour per week alone time with each of my three kids and get back to a weekly date night with my hubby.

Positivity—I created a Post-it note which says "Gratitude" and placed it on my mirror. Every morning while brushing my teeth I would state out loud what I was grateful about the previous day as well as prime myself for the coming days. Doing this while brushing my teeth proved very helpful, not only to my general well-being but also to my dental health ;-)

That's quite a lot for six months, but it all started from being clear on where I was heading and taking risks on opportunities the universe presented in front of me, as I truly believe that—the universe aligns with a made-up mind!

One final thought to leave you with: research shows that it is not the attainment of your goals which is important, as this leads only to a temporary high; it is the journey toward purposeful goals grounded in your strengths that leads both to prolonged success and happiness.

Leading like a girl is about prioritizing growth toward your goals and putting in place the support systems to help you and your team achieve these goals.

Happiness is not about making it to the peak of the mountain nor is it about climbing aimlessly around the mountain; happiness is *the experience* of climbing toward the peak.

—Tal Ben-Shahar

II

POWER UP

Power up is about using self-care to manage your energy. It is about role modeling work-life balance, thus encouraging and enabling employees' holistic well-being.

3

MASTER ENERGY, NOT TIME

In September 2018 I fell sick. I was supposed to get on a plane to a leadership meeting in Indonesia and I couldn't get out of bed. My whole body ached, and I was lethargic. I ended up taking the two-day meeting over Zoom (which wasn't very common prior to COVID-19).

I don't get sick often. I admit, I was pretty scared. *What was wrong with me?*

I thought it might have been Mycoplasma (a tropical bug I had caught in the past), so I decided it was time for an all-inclusive body checkup. I went in and they didn't find any tropical bug; what they found was abnormalities in my breast.

The fear of breast cancer crept in. That year, a brave friend of mine was battling cancer. She survived but another friend, Mark Walden (RIP), died very unexpectedly after a long battle with cancer. I prayed for the best. Thankfully, the lump in my breast was normal and the only red mark I received on my health report card was simply that I was fat. Yes, according to Asian BMI charts, I was twenty pounds overweight and defined as pre-obese. Not fun.

I was still feeling sick, so I engaged in more robust checks and found my sugar was too high (prediabetic) and my hormones were out of balance. My levels of both testosterone and estrogen had sky-rocketed. My poor family—I was both aggressive and emotional. I felt out of control and I am embarrassed to admit this, but after a long flight with little sleep, I even slapped my eldest daughter for the silliest reason. This was simply not acceptable and was a huge wake-up call. I was unbalanced. The root cause was my job. I was going through the toughest time in my life then, and three years of suppressed anger and stress had taken its toll on me both profession-ally and personally. It was time for a change.

Being healthy is crucial to your leadership ability. Think about it. How can you be compassionate when you're cranky? How can you deal with adversity when you are not getting enough sleep? How can you inspire your team to greatness when you can't motivate yourself to get out of bed? You can't.

I knew a little about the healthy mind/healthy body connection, so I started reading and investigating everything there was to know about managing your health. I studied the gurus: Dr. Robynne Chut-kan, creator of the "Live Dirty, Eat Clean" plan;[1] Dr. Mark Hyman, author of *The UltraMind Solution: Fix Your Broken Brain by Heal-ing Your Body First*;[2] and Dan Buettner, author of *The Blue Zones*;[3] among others. I also decided to join Tony Robbins's Life Mastery experience in Fiji and engaged my nutritionist friend Karin Reiter on my journey. I am not a health expert, but I got started and got healthy. And in this chapter, I will summarize some of these experts' findings that worked for me. If getting healthier and more balanced is on your goals list, I hope you will find a few strategies that will work for you too.

Finding work-life balance (WLB) is a struggle for any leader, but as women who still bear the majority of the housework and parent-ing, leading a balanced life becomes a survival skill. Sadly, men bosses who do not take an active part in child and home care are also less tolerant of women's desire for WLB, making any attempt to maintain WLB even more challenging, creating a downward spiral where leaving early and prioritizing health is frowned upon.

It all starts with raising awareness and setting holistic expecta-tions. In one of our most effective WLB initiatives for the P&G network, a colleague of mine wrote a funny short story about the life of a working mum—it was an eye-opener for many leaders, especially the men leaders who had no clue what a hectic morning of a working mom looks like. So, if you want your boss to better understand what you are going through—feel free to invite them home at 7:00–8:00 a.m. Hopefully COVID-19 helped many working men understand and get more involved in sharing the load, but most of the challenge still falls on working moms.

Sadly, many don't realize they have a WLB issue until it's too late and they hit a crisis—sickness, burnout, or even death. While the WLB initiatives created by our women's network were aimed at solving this challenge for working women, men benefited just as much and even more, with many men claiming, "Suddenly I felt comfortable saying I need to leave earlier to pick up my kids from school."

Luckily for me, most of my bosses (predominantly men) placed a huge value on being good parents themselves and encouraged WLB with their people—recognizing this balance is key for overall well-being, motivation, and, ultimately, long-term performance.

Leading like a girl is hence about powering up—prioritizing self-care (before it is too late) as well as role modeling this balance, thus encouraging and enabling employees' holistic well-being. As burnout is one of the biggest pandemics of the twenty-first century affecting men as well as women, this chapter addresses core skills needed by any leader.

LET'S GET STARTED

This chapter will focus on your physical health, while the next will focus on taking time for rest and recovery. There is a reason this chapter follows my chapter on goal setting. You can do this. Getting healthy can be overwhelming, but it doesn't have to be. You have to take one step at a time.

If you manage how and where you direct your energy, you'll lead a healthy life. This means that you want to focus your energy on a lifestyle that promotes longevity and happiness. It can be done.

Through investigative studies, longevity expert Dan Buettner discovered what he calls the Blue Zones. These are locations where people are living longer and managing their energy exponentially. These are: Okinawa, Japan; Sardinia, Italy; Nicoya, Costa Rica; Ikaria, Greece; and Loma Linda, California. Key areas to prioritize include:

1. **Purpose**—knowing why you wake up in the morning makes you healthier, happier, and increases life expectancy.[4]
2. **People and social engagement**—a strong sense of belonging and social connections add up to another fourteen years of life, according to Dan Buettner's research.
3. **Breathe**—taking the time to meditate.
4. **Eat**—you are what you eat.
5. **Touch**—proven to reduce pain and enhance well-being.
6. **Recovery down time and sleep**—critical for physical, psychological, and cognitive health.
7. **Movement and light physical activity**—which has proven to affect not only the body but also the mind.

The first two are covered in other chapters, but when focusing on the physical magic pill, my students presenting their year-end project came up with this acronym—BETR Me (see figure 3.1).

Breathe and Meditate

When my daughter Mia was twelve, I decided to take her to the school psychologist. She had never managed to sleep outside of the house and most field trips ended in me coming to pick her up. The two-week trip to Chiang Mai was coming up and she really wanted to go. The psychologist did a simple biofeedback session with her, teaching her how to take deep breaths every time she was struck with anxiety about the trip and she saw how her heart rate and anxiety would diminish. I also gave her Rescue drops and hoped for the best.

BETR Me - **MANAGE YOUR ENERGY!**

Breathe	Eat	Touch	Recovery	Movement
• Activate the parasympathetic system	• Plant based / rainbow • Protein as condiments • Quality over quantity • Water	• Releases opioids • Reduces pain / calms • Hug more • Weekly touch therapy (massage)	• Sleep 8H (physical psychological and cognitive impact) • Take real breaks to sharpen the "saw"	• Like taking an antidepressant • Immune system • Memory

Figure 3.1. BETR Me.

Whether it was the drops or the breathing, she felt she was in control and while she called me crying the first night, she decided to stay the full two weeks! She ended up crying more the last night but this time it was because she was sad it was over! Breathing gave her a sense of control. She could conquer her fears.

The Breath

Research has proven the benefits of breathing or pranayama—a Sanskrit term that describes the regulation of breathing—inhalation, retention, and exhalation.[5] Research shows it helps reduce stress by activating the parasympathetic system, which acts as a seesaw with the sympathetic system—our fight-or-flight response. It has proven to calm emotions, improve cognition, and even boost the immune system. I will talk about breath and meditation in the next chapter. But I invite you to close your eyes and try this simple exercise of 4x4, sometimes referred to as box breathing—four-second inhalation, four-second hold, four-second exhalation, four-second hold. Repeat this four times and noticed how things feel calmer already. You are ready to tackle the next step.

Eat[6]

This is what worked for me to lose the desired fifteen pounds. (Please note this is my personal experience—please see a medical professional for a more robust, personalized approach.)

Detox

How "tox-sick" are you? How are you doing against the 3Ps of detoxification—Poo, Pee, Perspire? You should be pooing at least once every day. If you are not, you are considered constipated and should increase the dietary fiber in your body to get to this desired state. Peeing is also a great way to remove toxins, and your urine should be almost clear. Finally, you should break a sweat every day doing some kind of exercise.

A personal experience here: I decided to try colon therapy during the Tony Robbins's Life Mastery retreat. The idea is simple—our health isn't determined only by what we are eating now but also by what we ate in the past. If you're putting healthy stuff into a toxic waste environment, this isn't helpful. Colon therapy is about removing that waste. It is an intense procedure, but not as traumatic as it sounds. The minute the process started at the retreat, my hilarious friend Dana texted me, "Hallelujah! I LOVE seeing this shit coming out of my body!" A poo party might not be your thing, but it's something to consider.

Eat

I have never successfully dieted in the past. I tried, *once*. My husband laughingly called the system "Whale Watchers" because I didn't lose weight, I gained it. It's an amazing program, but I wasn't disciplined enough, and I didn't have a strong enough *why*. I also tried going vegan, but really struggled. I found I was low in vitamin B12 (cobalamin), so I went back to meat, but only high-quality, grass-fed with no antibiotics. It costs more, but the alternative is quite horrific when you consider the health of mass-produced meat and chicken. If you limit your diet to only 30 percent meat, you may be able to afford the healthier variety. If you're eating fish, the smaller the better. Focus on SMASH,[7] an acronym used to denote salmon, mackerel, anchovies, sardines, and herring. These fish are higher in omega-3 fatty acids, which are essential to overall health. But when buying fish, again, quality makes a huge difference, especially given the mercury levels in most fish today—prioritize high quality protein.

The first intervention that really worked for me was when I followed my nutritionist's advice to do a simple blood test to find out what foods I was sensitive to. I discovered I was lactose sensitive and by replacing cow's milk with alternatives such as almond milk, sheep feta, and coconut-based yogurt, I lost my first six pounds easily.

The second, and probably the most talked about weight loss technique currently in food health intervention, was intermittent fasting. Intermittent fasting is an eating pattern where you cycle between periods of eating and fasting.[8] There are many variations but the three most popular ones are:

- The 16/8 Method: Fast for sixteen hours each day. For example, only eat between noon and 8:00 p.m.[9]
- Eat–Stop–Eat: Once or twice a week, don't eat anything from dinner one day until dinner the next day (a twenty-hour fast).
- The 5:2 Diet: Two days of every week, eat only about 500–600 calories.

I used to think that I could never fast. Maybe it's the Jewish Holocaust subconscious, but even before a three-hour drive, I would stock up as I hate feeling hungry. But the data behind intermittent fasting is quite compelling, so I tried.[10] I have a black coffee when I wake up and then my green juice at 11:00 a.m. and lunch at 1:00 p.m.—as black coffee is not counted, from dinner at 7:00 p.m. to my first green juice at 11:00 a.m. gives me a fifteen to sixteen hour gap and was another relatively easy eight-pound loss. Both are now a habit. I don't feel like I am dieting.

The third easy step for me was to increase my healthy fats. Udo Erasmus in his book *Fats That Heal, Fats That Kill* talks about the criticality of fats.[11] Good fats increase energy and metabolism, improve skin condition, prevent leaky gut, lower blood pressure, stabilize heartbeat, and elevate mood and brain functioning. Good fats include: MCT oil (medium-chain triglyceride), coconut, flax, avocado, oily fish, nuts, and seaweed. So I added a teaspoon of MCT oil to my smoothies and a quarter cup of nuts at 4:00 p.m. Easy enough.

The fourth easy step was drinking good quality water. Up to 60 percent of the adult human body is water. All of our cells and organs depend on water for functioning, yet most of us are constantly dehydrated. Generally healthy people should be drinking several liters a day—about 2.7 for women and 3.7 for men (or 11.5 cups for women and 15.5 cups for men).[12] Start in the morning when you are the most dehydrated, and drink more water thirty minutes before every meal. (Recommended daily amounts vary dependent upon underlying health conditions and other factors; please consult a healthcare professional.) Not all water is created equal; most tap water picks up pesticides which have been washed into our streams and rivers, or lead from our pipes, hence it is a good idea to investigate getting a good quality water filter.

Maintaining a proper ratio between acid and alkaline foods in your diet is important to prevent over-acidity, resulting in disease. A rule of thumb is that your diet should have 70 percent alkali (from fruit and veggies) to 30 percent acid (meat, fish, eggs, whole wheat, sugar, dairy, coffee, tea, wine, and beer) to maintain this balance. An easy way to help the body alkalize is to add a green smoothie a couple of times a day and eat raw foods.

I also rearranged my food pyramid in line with my nutritionist's recommendations (see figure 3.2).

At least 50 percent of your diet should be plant-based. It is recommended that you eat all colors of the rainbow every day, and you should think of proteins as your condiment.

My biggest issue was bread and pasta, which are known to have a lot of sugar, so while eliminating these would be ideal, I allowed

HEALTHY EATING PLATE

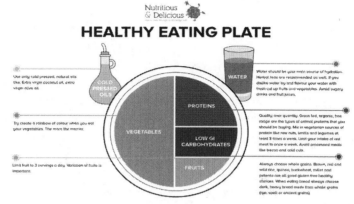

Figure 3.2. Healthy Eating Plate. *Source:* **Courtesy of Karin Reiter, nutritiousndelicious.com.**

myself two days of pasta and bread, and focused instead on better breads (whole wheat). Recently, I even discovered I could make keto bread—which replaces traditional wheat flour with low-carbohydrate, low-sugar alternatives like almond flour or lupin flour.

In general, the closer you are to nature, the better. When buying fruit and vegetables, take extra caution with the "dirty dozen"—like strawberries, apples, and peaches, which do not have a hard shell and hence are more prone to exposing you to pesticides when eaten; these are better bought organic.[13]

Stay away from processed foods, which often contain higher levels of sugar and salt than home-cooked food. While convenient, they have become the curse of our modern-day living. It is well documented that we have taught our palates to consume too much sugar—estimated at a whopping 17 percent of our diet—and that is associated with many of the diseases we experience today, from obesity to cancer.[14] But the good news is that your sweet tooth can be tamed and there are enough of sugar alcohols (like erythritol) that do not spike blood sugar and insulin leading to weight benefits when consumed with moderation.

Touch Is a Natural Healer

My son, Liam, is the best hugger on earth. Liam was born in the summer of 2003, which happened to be the hottest July ever in Geneva. He only calmed down when he was stripped naked and was lying on my stomach. When he was four, I vividly remember sitting in the garden, him putting his little arms around my neck, giving me the biggest squeeze, and saying, "I love you, Mummy." This loving touch has continued deep into his teens. Even at fifteen, when he almost stopped talking to me and moved to barking, he would still "demand" his hugs, and after I gave him a hug he would say, "Okay, enough. Love you, now out of my room, please."

> We need four hugs a day for survival. We need eight hugs a day for maintenance. We need twelve hugs a day for growth.
>
> —Psychologist Virginia Satir

Tiffany Field from the University of Miami School of Medicine summarizes the benefits of touch:[15]

1. Alleviates pain—touch releases opioids, which calm us and relieve us of pain.
2. Helps overcome injuries and is a natural healer. Kids run to their moms for a hug after a fall.
3. Reduces stress and strengthens the immune system.
4. Promotes healthy cognitive development.
5. Drives emotional bonding, increases trust and generosity by releasing oxytocin—the love hormone.

You can see why I was delighted to learn that touch was as essential as food, exercise, and sleep for well-being. Several researchers have proven the above.

The classical attachment theory research conducted by Harry Harlow with monkeys proves that it is touch, not food, that creates the strong bond known as attachment between mom and baby.[16] In this research monkeys were separated from their mothers and given the choice between two mother substitutes: a "wire mother" with a feeding tube, or a "cloth mother" providing contact comfort. The monkeys overwhelmingly chose the cloth mother as a secure base. When they were hungry, they tried reaching the feeding tube while clinging to the cloth mother.

The most impressive research on touch was done among premature human babies. A hospital director was surprised to see huge differences in preemie growth in the baby's weight and cognitive development between his two departments. He was shocked to discover that the reason was that in the healthier department, a nurse would come in at midnight, take out each of the babies, and caress them. That was the only difference.[17]

Living in Asia, I have become addicted to touch therapy—also known as massage ;-)—which has been proven to help not only our muscles but also our entire mental and physical health, helping us to overcome depression, anxiety, and eating disorders.

Go ahead and find five people to hug today!

Rest and Recovery

I have dedicated the next chapter to recovery, so with this section I will focus specifically on rest and sleep.

Researcher Sara Mednick declared "fatigue as the silent epidemic of the twenty-first century; it is wreaking havoc on our health."[18] Together with air, quality food, and exercise, sleep is vital to maintaining both our physiological, cognitive, and psychological health.

Remember the people in the Blue Zones? They are religious about their sleep. They rise with the sun and go to sleep when it is dark. They are getting eight hours, which is often considered the optimal level for healthy functioning.

You can't skip sleep, you can only borrow against it, and too many of us are serious borrowers. Research by Sarah Mednick and others indicates the critical importance of sleep, including several key benefits.

1. **Physiological benefits**. Beauty sleep is real. Proper sleep is important for the skin to rejuvenate and keep looking young for as long as possible.

It helps to maintain our immune system and lowers the risk for asthma, flu, cancer, and heart disease. Research found women with mild sleep deprivation (six hours per night), had a 40 percent higher chance for a heart attack. It helps to maintain body weight. Sleep deprivation sends the body signals to ask for energy, which makes us crave high fat/high glucose foods—processed food such as fast-food burgers and fries.

It's a libido killer. Fatigue is the number one libido killer because it lowers testosterone levels. Among my forty-year-old friends, morning sex became so much more prevalent for this reason because they were less tired.

2. **IQ/Cognitive benefits**. My teenage kids were doing their final IB exams (International Baccalaureate) prep as I wrote this. My daughter told me about so many of her friends "burning the midnight oil" to study. I showed her this research and insisted they get a minimum of eight to nine hours of sleep even, especially during this stressful period. Sleep helps process learning and increases focus and memory, while prolonged insomnia is also proven to lower IQ levels.[19]

3. **Psychological benefits**. I remember my mom used to nap every afternoon. She would come home from work, feed us lunch, and then we would hide in our rooms until she woke up from her happiness sleep. Our minds continue to process not only new learning but also emotions just like if we were writing them down or talking about them with someone. Sleep is our internal therapist and prolonged fatigue is associated with anger management issues and depression.

Movement

In July 2018, I was diagnosed as having a hyperactive brain or Attention Deficient Hyperactivity Disorder (ADHD). The assessor told me my brain takes in two to three times more information than normal, resulting in constant data overload. I never noticed this to be a problem, quite frankly. I'm creative and like making connections with the information I consume. When I shared this new diagnosis with my mom, she didn't believe me, "But you were such a good student! You would lock yourself in the room for hours making your mind map summaries of everything you learned!"

If there was a problem, it seems what saved me from not being able to concentrate or being obsessively productive was physical activity. I was a competitive rhythmic gymnast practicing four days a week for four hours straight and, at fourteen, when I dropped out, I became a coach and trained others. I was constantly on the move. My friends always called me the blonde on the bike, as I would bike everywhere.

This is different for some of today's kids with ADHD. Kids spend more time on screens than on bicycles these days and this may explain some of the reasons for the explosion of kids diagnosed with ADHD, on top of better diagnostics for screening. New research shows that ADHD may be affected positively by physical activity.[20]

Truly, physical exercise is not a luxury but a necessity for a variety of physical and psychological reasons.

In a longitudinal research study conducted for over thirty years in Denmark, researchers concluded that the group which exercised three times for thirty minutes a week outlived those who didn't by six and a half years.[21] This was also confirmed in Dan Buettner's Blue Zone research. The folks in Sardinia were constantly outdoors working as farmers and shepherds, and those in Costa Rica avoided using cars and walked everywhere. It also helps manage weight, diabetes, stroke, inflammation, cancer, and libido.

As we know, the body and mind are connected. Physical exercise is proven to increase memory and concentration through neurogenesis, or growth and development of nervous tissue. Brain expert Dr. Ratey says exercise is like taking a little bit of Prozac and a little bit of Ritalin.[22]

Exercise releases endorphins, which have been shown to elevate mood. Robust evidence suggests that physical exercise can be as effective as antidepressants to reduce anxiety and depression with fewer side effects (while in most patients adjacent programs are recommended).[23]

Most excitingly, research has shown that aerobic exercise three times a week, even if started later in life, is associated with a reduction in risk of dementia among the elderly.[24] As someone who is constantly losing her mind, that is enough to send me to the gym.

What if I don't have time to exercise?

Time is no longer an excuse. Research has shown that even one hour per week, three sessions of twenty-minute HIIT—High Intensity Interval Training—is as effective as five hours of heavy aerobic activity for all the benefits mentioned above.[25] Even the famous seven minutes of Tabata training (a type of HIIT) three times a week, amounting to a mere twenty-one minutes weekly, appears helpful in reducing insulin resistance, which can cause weight gain.

Now to get the full physical and psychological benefits mentioned above, three sessions of thirty-minute light aerobic exercise is recommended—walking, running, yoga, Pilates, dance—as long as you develop a sweat.

One of my friends recently complained I don't have enough time for her, so we recently picked up "Walk & Coach" sessions— a beautiful off-hours stroll in the botanical gardens while doing a coaching session. Nothing like a good heart-filled chat with my friend while working out. I have since started incorporating walk and coach sessions in my practice and encourage walking meetings whenever possible.

What if I don't like to exercise?

My first boss at P&G started off as a gym trainer. In 2009, he led three hundred P&G employees to do their first half marathon. It was an amazing movement and he made running fun. It was a proud moment as I finished my half marathon (13 miles) to be joined by my kids, Mia and Liam, in crossing the finishing line. I know many swear by running, but after that one I had so many injuries that I don't enjoy running as much. What I love about my new gym is that it allows me to try out a variety of activities. I now train five times a week and do something new every day—between Booty Barre, Pilates, hot yoga, and boxing, I am always happy. So it really doesn't matter how you move; just find something you love and incorporate it into your schedule a few times a week. If you sit a lot for work, tune in to YouTube and search for chair yoga or chair exercises so you can keep active even as you work. If you can, purchase a small standing desk or standing desk platform, so you can spend part of your day standing. Find your thing and stick to it.

WHAT IS YOUR NEXT STEP?

During our Tony Robbins's Life Mastery sessions, we were encouraged to jump off a telephone pole. The lessons were twofold—letting go of fear and previous attachments, and understanding change is a journey. Throughout the climb the guides asked us not to focus on the end but simply to focus on what is your next step—one step at a time on the climb.

I've given you a lot of information and this may seem quite overwhelming. My advice is to take back your health one step at a time. As I always tell my coaching clients: *You don't have to have it all figured out to make the first step.*

Start by educating yourself based on what I've shared and then figure out what works for you. Maybe you tackle food and sleep, or physical activity and touch. The important thing is to choose something and begin.

To summarize, here is what worked for *me*:

- I sought medical advice and appropriate testing.
- I did hormone balance testing and started a supplement program.
- I had a food allergies test—and removed cow's milk.
- Hydration—I bought the largest hydro-flask and started drinking a minimum of 32 ounces a day, with 16 ounces flavored with lemon first thing and before every meal.
- Healthy oils—Now I always carry almonds, pistachios, and Brazil nuts.
- Avoid processed sugar—I replaced soft drinks with plain soda with blueberries and got used to coffee without sugar.

After six months, the above changes became habits. I lost eight pounds and was ready to integrate new changes.

- Exercise intervention—I signed up to the gym and simply went to every single lesson to find what I enjoyed most. I love the variety and now am religious about two to three sessions of cardio a week, two machine Pilates classes, and my Saturday morning hot yoga classes, which I do with my daughter, Mia.
- Intermittent fasting—Dinner is the most important time, and we are devoted to enjoying family dinners together every night. I've found that finishing food consumption by 8:00 p.m. and starting the first food of the day at 11:00–11:30 a.m. typically works for me. But you can test out what works best for you.
- Green smoothies—I became passionate about green smoothies (see an example on page 58).
- I got a good water filter.

The key is, I took it one step at a time, adding a new intervention every month. With these interventions, I managed to get to my target fifteen-pound weight loss goal in six months and have maintained that weight, feeling younger and stronger than ever. After a few months, my husband joined me; we bought an ice plunge bath and started a daily plunge, meditation, and naps.

Most critically, I was clear on *why* I was getting healthy—the why cannot be driven externally, it must be based on your own desires and goals. For me, my goal was more energy. This was enough to make me understand that my body is my temple, and I should treat it with respect, so I have enough energy to do what I dream of in life.

One year later I got my annual post treatment checkup: see table 3.1, "Health Report."

My doctor was overjoyed, especially with my sugar intake, which was my Achilles' heel. I have an incredible sweet tooth and hereditary diabetes. I am now back within normal ranges on all measures. I was previously out of whack and now even my hormones were back in balance, so no more aggressively emotional crazy lady! There's still some work to be done, especially on portion control and caloric intake, but I'm on my way to being more educated and mindful about the most important currency of my life, my energy.

Leading like a girl is being able to listen to your body and treat it as your temple, to put the oxygen mask on yourself first so that you can be a better leader to others by modeling behaviors that encourage your team to realize that the ultimate wealth is health.

Table 3.1. Health Report

	Before 16/04/2018	**After 18/01/2020**
Sugar	96 (Prediabetic)	85 (Normal)
HDL Cholesterol	42 (Borderline)	50 (Normal)
Hormonal Balance	Testosterone High/ Estrogen High	Testosterone Normal/ Estrogen Normal
Weight	Pre-Obese	−8KG within Norm

ACTIVITY

Here is my health routine (table 3.2), which I created and pinned on my fridge. Create your own.

What habit changes resonated with you which you can start adopting tomorrow?

Add a new habit every month to create your own fat-to-fit plan.

Table 3.2.   Dalia—Healthy Living Schedule, Nov. 18

7:00	Water with lemon 1/2 liter
7:15–7:45	Priming breathing, gratitude 10 min. + 20 min. yoga
8:00–12:00	Focused Work *(complex mental tasks)* (+ flask of black coffee + 1/2 liter water)
11:30–12:00	Green shake plus MCT oil + supplements
12:00–13:00	Gym + 1/2 liter water
13:00–14:00	Lunch 70% veggie and 30% fish/chicken/meat with Udo oil *(30-min. nap or nature walk if possible)*
14:00–18:00	Work—Meetings *(collaboration/social/coaching tasks)*
16:00–17:00	Green shake plus MCT oil + 1/4 cup nuts
18:00–18:45	Gym *(if I didn't go over lunch)* + 1/2 liter water
19:00–20:00	Dinner with family—soup and salad with MCT oil *(Highlight of my day—never to be missed!)*
20:00–22:00	Digital detox—Kids, husband, friends, massage 1x week *(Night meetings/work limited to 1x per week)*
22:00–23:00	Journal magic moments and read
23.00–7.00	Sleep 8 hrs.

Super Easy Green Smoothie

Ingredients:

1 cup leafy greens, usually spinach

1 pod of fresh frozen spirulina

1 green apple or berries (for the kids I also add 1/2 greenish, frozen banana)
1 teaspoon MCT oil
1 teaspoon chia seeds
1 teaspoon flax seed, preferably sprouted

Other additions:
Sprouted broccoli
Vitamin D (one pill)
A probiotic pill or powder

Method:
Place all the ingredients in a blender with coconut water or almond milk and blend until smooth.

4

MINDFUL RECOVERY: THE SCIENCE OF DOING NOTHING

I have talked about the importance of goals. A few of my friends came back and challenged me on how my commitment to goal setting fits with my yogi approach of living in the here and now. My best friend told me, "I loved your focus on goal setting, but this whole notion of goals stresses me out, as I know I will never tick off everything on my list."

This chapter aims to answer exactly this dichotomy—how the idea of goal setting, and the science behind it, sits with the exact opposite notion—the science of mindfulness and the importance of living in the here and now. How striving for goals is more important than attaining them and how important it is to be able to also do absolutely nothing sometimes.

I have always been known as a busy bee, an overachiever, a constant doer with a hyperactive brain.

I do have early memories of being very reflective—whenever I was not feeling well enough for school, my mum, who was a personal assistant to a shipping tycoon, would take me with her to work—which was a beautiful home on the shores of Haifa Bat Galim in Israel. She would allow me to go down by the beach where

I spent precious time sitting on the stones, listening to the sound of waves, and reflecting.

I even remember having deep thoughts about regret and how I made a promise to myself then and there to always dare, so I would never have to live my life regretting that I never tried. Those were very deep reflective thoughts for an eight-year-old.

My mom loved to read child psychology books, especially Dr. Spock, and talked about the concept of "healthy neglect"—leaving your child alone to develop their own creativity. And so, when I was younger and she was still working part time, she would ask me to stay in my room between 2:00 p.m. and 4:00 p.m. and "entertain" myself. In the beginning I felt like a prisoner in my own room, but soon these *schlafstunde* (Yiddish for nap time) evolved to be the most glorious Barbie and Playmobil parties—and while sometimes I was overly creative, like cutting my doll's hair and making her a new dress out of my cut-up sheet, my mom and I both got the benefits of this "healthy neglect."

But as time went by, I grew busier and busier. By the age of ten I made the national team for rhythmic gymnastics. I would come home from school at 1:00 p.m., quickly eat, pack my bag, and at 2:00 p.m. our team taxi driver would pick me up for a ninety-minute drive to Wingate where we would practice for three hours and drive back arriving home at 9:00 p.m., and straight to bed. And so from elementary school, to high school, to the army service, to university, to P&G in Geneva, Moscow, and Singapore, to raising three kids and having an entrepreneur husband, it was all *go*. My mind was constantly running on a spinning wheel—planning work, planning launches, planning team events, planning family vacation, planning kids' parties, planning Friday dinners, planning, planning, strategizing, and planning.

And somehow in the process, I became so active and task-oriented, I forgot how to enjoy time doing nothing.

Inactivity was my enemy and so was silence. I filled in every spare moment with activity, with words, and over time I forgot to listen to the world, to others, and to myself.

Did you ever realize the word *listen* has the same letters as the word *silent*? You need to be silent to truly listen. So much has been written on how people will be better off doing less and listening and reflecting more.

The word *stress* is enough to stress us all out. We are all over-stressed. But stress is good for us—if we have the right mindset toward it and if we know how to recover properly afterward. Recovery is essential to stress management.

I remember once my very committed and hard-working employee Sowmya came to me and said she just had too much on her plate and was totally stressed out. I asked her what specifically stressed her out and why. It boiled down to the fact she had been planning to have a vacation with her sister, which she had to cancel due to the visit from her global functional manager and team.

I always used to tell my folks, "Only you control your overload. Is it good overload that is energizing you to perform, or bad overload that is overwhelming you and hampering performance?"

I helped her understand that it was her choice whether she wanted to be there for the visit, and helped her reframe her thinking about the visit from "stressed'" to "excited." She decided to stay and delayed her holiday by ten days. The global visit was a huge success, but even more importantly, during her delayed vacation, something amazing happened to her—not only did she get her much-needed rest, she ended up meeting the man of her dreams, and a year later I took my whole family, all in full saris and kurta pajama, to her traditional Indian wedding in Chennai. She often said it was this sense of choice toward her source of stress and reframing her state from stressful to excited that made all the difference.

Stress at a manageable, controllable level is good for us—it releases adrenaline, glucose, and dopamine, which increases energy, heightens alertness, narrows focus, improves cognition, and even strengthens immunity. The key as shown in the Yerkes-Dodson law is maintaining moderate arousal levels and avoiding prolonged stress.[1]

But having this positive mindset to stress makes all the difference. In a research study at a banking firm amidst a crisis, Dr. Alia

Crum divided the firm into two—to one group, she gave a lecture on the positive effects of stress, to the other, she gave no intervention.[2] Despite them going through the same external experience of stress, the first group was not only happier but also performed better in the crisis. It is the mindset toward stress that matters.

The other critical element in managing stress is the need for recovery. Nothing better exemplifies this than the amazing story of marathoner Derek Clayton, who shook the world and changed how athletes and coaches think about recovery. In 1967, Derek worked hard toward a marathon in Japan, trying to break his personal record of two hours, fourteen minutes without success. But it seems he worked too hard: he injured himself and was forced to take a month off to rest. He was cleared to run again just one week before the race, so he decided to attend but declared the race a practice. To his, and the world's amazement, he stopped the clock at 02:09:36.4—almost five minutes faster than his personal best. A new world record. A few years later, the same thing happened again. He was again forced to rest post-injury, but when he went back to run, he achieved a new personal best and a new world record of 02:08:33.6. Stress with recovery is good for you—it is the rest that builds muscle and resilience. Lack of recovery from stress is what leads to burnout.

The most successful, happiest, and healthiest people in the world experience stress just like everyone else; they just know how to listen to their bodies and dot their days, months, and years with adequate recovery, be it a mindfulness or walking break every hour, Churchill's famous day naps, ensuring a good night's sleep of a minimum seven to eight hours, or taking real vacations.

> The key for creation is recreation.
>
> —Tal Ben-Shahar[3]

So the enemy is not stress, it is the mindset that stress is bad coupled with lack of recovery.[4] But rest, recovery, and contemplation help in so many ways.

Mindfulness has proven to be an extremely effective way to reduce stress. But it takes practice. It is like the gym for the brain. Daniel Goleman and Richard Davidson[5] suggest that mindfulness changes the structure of a brain, something that is known as neuroplasticity. The test group that engaged in daily mindfulness practice showed significantly more activity in the area of the brain in the frontal cortex, which is associated with having a happier, more focused, and more disease-immune brain. This in as little as eight weeks of daily practice and as little as ten minutes a day, regardless of whether it was planned meditation or informally just taking time to notice the beauty in the mundane tasks.

Mindfulness also helps with emotional regulation; meditating on emotions helps tame their toxicity and creates psychological space to reframe the situation.

No wonder that some companies like 3M, Pixar, Google, Twitter, and Facebook have included contemplative practices and disconnected time into their way of working to increase employees' self-awareness, self-management, and creativity. The most effective managers are those who can both reflect *and* act or REFLACT.[6]

Ellen Langer focuses on mindfulness as the act of noticing new things, having a learner's mindset, treating each day as if it were your first, and turning the most mundane task into magic.[7]

> There are only two ways to live your life. One is as though nothing is a miracle. The other is as though everything is a miracle.
>
> —Albert Einstein

In his article "The Hidden Value of Empty Time and Boredom," my INSEAD professor, Manfred Kets de Vries, tells the famous story of Michelangelo and his work on his sculpture of David back in 1466 to show the power of meditation and mind stillness for creativity.[8] Michelangelo started on the statue, but then abandoned the project for twenty-five years. Even when he came back to it, it was rumored that he spent hours staring at the marble, doing nothing. When asked what he was doing, he replied, "I am working." When the statue became the famous *David*, Michelangelo was quoted to have said, "I saw the angel in the marble and carved until I set him free."

Another sickness of the ever-busy mind is multitasking. I love to do the following experiment with my students; time yourself counting from 1–26 and then saying the alphabet from A–Z. Then try multitasking between the numbers and the letters (i.e., 1A, 2B) and you will see it will take you twice as long. Multitasking always takes longer. In a study conducted by Glenn Wilson, a psychiatrist at the University of London, multitasking was equivalent to a drop in ten points of IQ, a drop similar to that seen after a full night of sleep loss.[9] For both men and women "single tasking" yields higher productivity. In a follow-up study by Harvard among Boston Consulting Group employees, forcing employees to do a digital detox one day a week increased productivity by 74 percent.[10]

In a world which has become ever so busy and prone to distraction, silence and stillness terrify us. We protect ourselves by adding activities, and this can become a developmental trap. We are so busy making a living that we forget to make a life.

Mindfulness has proven to reduce stress, helps with emotional regulation, and increases focus, curiosity, and creativity. It seems that my mum was right; boredom, mind stillness, and doing nothing are found to be extremely valuable in nurturing our creativity. I still remember one of my best campaign ideas—Be the star you are—which came to me late at night while lulling my children to sleep. As Manfred Kets de Vries explains, creative associative processes do not thrive under conscious direction. They will come into consciousness only when our attention is directed elsewhere.

We need to always ask ourselves every day, "Are we busy about the right things?" Are we constantly linking our activities to our purpose and goals or just ticking off items? And that is where goals come in.

Happiness is not about attaining our goals but about the process of working toward them: constantly growing, stretching ourselves, and having a direction. And it is that direction, that energy of the pull, that liberates us to enjoy the here and now and embrace the stillness.

A workaholic who doesn't stop to smell the coffee is as bad as a fully present wanderer who has no direction.

We need goals to reduce the anxiety about the future so that we are liberated to enjoy our present.

But it doesn't matter if you ticked off every single goal on your list, as long as you are making progress and enjoying the ride. As Tal Ben-Shahar concludes, goals become the means while the present experience becomes the end. The destination is the journey.

After twenty years in the rat race, I felt I needed a long break. I needed to strengthen this forgotten muscle of mine—the muscle for doing nothing, observing, listening, reflecting, being present. I decided not to set off traveling—which is what I often did for work— but spent that time at home with my kids practicing being present in the day-to-day tasks.

I am still a busy bee—learning, creating, writing, consulting, teaching, speaking, training, volunteering—but my goal for myself is to slow down my racing mind and to practice being present so that it becomes a habit and I enjoy fully the things I am already doing.

Don't kid yourself, I am not talking sitting on a beach with a book. I am talking about being still *while* being active, which is much harder than it seems, especially for an alpha hyperactive person like myself, but it is a muscle that can be strengthened by practice and so I hope to become still, so that the angel in the stone presents itself before me.

My motto has the two sides to it: Have an idea of where you are headed (your goals), but be mindful and enjoy the view on the way. Be still, observe, and take it all in.

Do you take real vacations? I will never forget, when I was a young associate brand manager (ABM), our P&G CEO John Pepper sent out a note to all the employees that read something like this—"I am leaving on a real vacation. Gone to sharpen my saw. I will not be accessible during this time. I have an amazing leadership team and I trust them to handle any crisis in my absence. I wish you all to take real breaks this holiday season."

And then he shared the story that explains the phrase "sharpen my saw":

> Two woodcutters were hard at work, chopping down wood. They both rose at sunrise and finished at sunset—but one of them was especially hard working and went at it nonstop, while the other kept stopping, sitting by a tree. To everyone's amazement, the "slacker" managed to chop almost 50 percent more than the "hard worker." When they asked the "slacker" what he was doing, they realized every time he stopped, he would sharpen his saw and so when he went back to work, he could achieve more with less effort, and thus was more effective.

From that day on, my out-of-office message became "Out to sharpen my saw, see you when I'm back."

ACTIVITY

Confucius is thought to have said, "Learning without reflection is a waste," so why don't you try putting all this into action starting tomorrow?

1. Take a few mindful breaks during the day. Practice 4, 4, 8, 4 breathing (four counts in, four counts out, done four times, then four counts in and eight counts out, done four times). If you need to, try setting an alarm for a few mindfulness breaks each day, or wear a red bracelet to remind you.
2. Try mindfulness in action. When things get hectic or emotional, try to step out of the situation, go to the mental "balcony" and observe yourself observing.
3. Work smarter. If I only achieve one task today, what is it? Then accomplish that first thing in the morning. Eliminate nonessential meetings, skim nonessential emails.

4. Force yourself to take on a single task instead of multitasking.
5. Before going to sleep, write down what happened in those elevated moments of awareness. Start to observe those magical moments as they unfold, the angel in the stone being set free.
6. Try a technological detox evening at least once a week.
7. On your next vacation, sharpen your saw and let your mind wander in wonder.

III

PERSPECTIVE AND MENTAL PERSEVERANCE

Perspective and mental perseverance means understanding our limiting beliefs and embracing these as an opportunity for growth by cultivating the mental resilience to be able to bounce back and grow from hardship.

5

OVERCOMING FEAR AND
OUR LIMITING BELIEFS

When I was eight years old, I earned a spot on the competitive artistic gymnastics team. I loved it and was extremely hard working. I was considered very good and my coach had very high expectations that I would win the national championship. The day of my first national competition came. My whole family joined me and maybe a few of my neighbors were roped into attending as well. The competition went very well. I was getting great scores and was in the lead. My strongest apparatus were ball, ribbon, and clubs, and the last routine was the rope, my weakest apparatus, but I did very well. I looked up at my coach and saw the huge smile on her face, but then, in one of my last moves, I got stuck in the rope. I lost half a point and came in second.

My coach came in screaming, "What happened—you never get stuck—you should have taken the championship—I am so disappointed!"

Just then my mum came in and I remember her physically standing in between us and saying, "What are you talking about? This was her first competition, and she already came in second. We are going out to celebrate—are you coming with us?"

And just like that my failure was reframed. It was my first competition and I already came in second!

I continued with the national team until I was fourteen, and then became a coach. That is the only "failure" I remember in my childhood. My mother taught me to be a good sport, to compete internally but not externally—it didn't matter if I won or lost as long as I did my best and enjoyed the game.

But that said, I remember the feeling of disappointment from my coach, and I went on to excel in everything I did.

I was a very good student and won the best-in-grade award every year for the whole twelve years of studies, from first to twelfth grade. I was invited to the Knesset (Israel government) to be awarded a special education award given to the top one percent of students. In the army, I received the best soldier award during the commander's course. In university, I was awarded *summa cum laude* and the Dean's Award.

I wasn't the smartest in my class—I had smart classmates who all now hold prominent roles, but I had grit and a strong drive for results. I knew where I was heading, I was self-driven, and I worked hard—the gymnast and army stamina meant I kept working until I felt I gave it my best. I was not going to disappoint again. I wasn't externally competitive as much as I was internally driven. I never gave up. Close the door on me and I will crawl in through the window.

Going back to that *Harvard Business Review* data I shared in the preface, women score better than men on taking initiative and being results driven. We women crawl in through the window . . . if we need to. Daring to lead like a girl is this drive, the drive to achieve against all odds. But there is a danger to this mentality, which is the desire to avoid disappointment. We need to avoid sinking into what has been described as the "wounded feminine"—being overly dependent on *praise*.[1]

Using my friend Nilima Bhat's model, we can split emotional reaction into four areas:[2]

1. Positive feminine reaction is reacting from a point of empathy, teamwork, common goals.
2. Positive masculine reaction is reacting based on logic, assertiveness when boundaries are crossed.
3. Negative (wounded) feminine reaction is becoming dependable and defensive.
4. Negative (wounded) masculine reaction is becoming aggressive and asserting power OVER another.

Somehow, I became a junkie for praise. What other people thought of me was everything to me. I started associating praise with love and with being alive. It is not that I didn't get any criticism, but it was always balanced, always a part of my growth. Until one day I learned my lesson—a boss who was determined not to praise me admitted that he didn't know how to praise. For me, that meant total failure. I didn't know who I was without external praise.

Despite the tough environment, I succeeded. I built a strong team, and together we turned around the business to be more consumer focused. We created campaigns that won awards for the first time ever. But my boss felt I was too positive and that he had to criticize me to keep me balanced. As a six-sigma black belt (a management decision tool that focuses on learning from past mistakes), he felt that compliments were a waste of time. His role was to fix me. I was also so obsessed with changing his mind and gaining his support that I spent all my energy defending myself. Slowly I started to believe him and lost my spark. I allowed one person's view of me to determine my view of myself.

Being the high stamina person that I was, I refused to quit and I persevered. And after making my mark, I chose to leave. I often wonder if I really did succeed in that role. Did I fail? Objectively, I succeeded as my results for the business and the people were great, but I felt I only delivered 10 percent of my ability because I was too busy defending myself. I was too focused on external validation and in that sense I failed. That was a strong lesson—I understood that I had a deeply rooted fear of failure as I didn't want to disappoint.

Fear of Failure

Learn to fail or fail to learn.

—Tal Ben-Shahar

Sara Blakely, one of the youngest self-made billionaires, tells the story of her father who, from her early childhood on, didn't ask her about her great scores.[3] He would instead ask every week seven words which changed her life—"What did you fail at this week?" And when young Sara would answer, he would high-five her. He taught her she was still loved and that her failures were to be celebrated as a critical stepping stone toward growth.

Carol Dweck in her book *Mindset* talks about the importance of keeping a growth mindset.[4] Those with a growth mindset like Sara see failure as a stepping stone. They don't take feedback personally and believe they can learn anything they set their minds to do and as a result develop a healthier and happier approach to life. No need to keep up the façade of perfection.

Martin Seligman talks about 3Ps that enhance this pain of failure. When we take something **P**ersonally, we believe it is **P**ermanent and **P**revalent.

Don't overclaim failure.

During one of my classes at INSEAD, one of my classmates was telling a story about a failure he had had. The professor then encouraged him to be specific—where exactly did you fail? What skill did you fail to acquire? It is not denying you failed but ensuring that it is pinpointed and hasn't become prevalent. Yes, you failed in acquiring Skill A, but you are not a failure as a whole. So remember, a failure is just an event to learn from, not a badge to carry! Make sure you reflect, learn, and *move on*.

Learn to forgive yourself and see failure as an essential stepping-stone to success. Many companies have since embraced this idea. I remember walking into Google offices in Palo Alto back in 2016 and seeing at the entrance to the building a "graveyard of failures." Teams were encouraged to fail forward, to state their failure and pinpoint what they learned from the experience. Giving your employees permission to fail is giving them an opportunity to innovate. *There is no innovation without failure.*

> I have not failed. I've just found 10,000 ways that won't work.
>
> —Thomas Edison

Ensure you are not using a limited view of reality.

I recently heard the story shared by the mother of president Bill Clinton. He would walk into a room full of admirers but would only notice and pay all his attention to the one person in the audience who didn't like him, versus the hundreds who did. It is clear I was overly focused on trying to be liked by everyone and, unlike the growth mindset, I prioritized approval over development.

Introduce the word "yet" into your vocabulary.

"I haven't failed. I just haven't gotten there *yet*," explains Dr. Carol Dweck in her book *Mindset*.

Our beliefs toward failure will determine whether we have a growth mindset or a fixed one. Those with a growth mindset as opposed to those with a fixed mindset believe they can learn, change, and grow—they don't seek approval but seek development, and they don't see failures as a disaster but merely as opportunities for growth. Change your language to add the magic word "yet."

No Regrets

We often regret more those things we didn't try.

> The greatest mistake you can make in life is to be continually fearing you will make one.
>
> —Elbert Hubbard

My eldest daughter is cautious, so she tries to play it safe. She is afraid to fail and so doesn't put herself out there. She made it on the swim team but refused to compete. She just doesn't like the stress, she said. My husband, the coach, and I did everything we could. She spent six years practicing with the school team but refused to compete.

Then one day, her lesson came in the form of a drama perfor-mance—her drama teacher kept encouraging her to audition for the school play. She promised him to try out but kept finding excuses. During the first parent-teacher meeting, he asked her again, "I have the perfect role for you—please audition for this upcoming play." But again, Mia managed to be sick the two days of the auditions. The play was a huge success and all of Mia's friends were in it. One of Mia's best friends had the main role. Mia felt huge regret. The next parent-teacher conference, the drama teacher asked Mia again, "What happened? I really wanted you for the MAIN role." Mia broke down into tears. She was so angry with herself. She cried and cried the whole way home. Finally, I told her I was so happy this happened, and she should never forget this deep feeling of regret to ensure it never happens to her again.

> You miss one hundred percent of the shots you don't take.

> —Wayne Gretzky, made famous as used by Michael Jordan

The following year, she took the leap, auditioned for the play *Chicago* and got one of the main roles. Before the first night she told me, "Mom, I am not scared. I am excited." She took the shot and nailed it!

Fear of Success

However, a surprising revelation for me was that I also had an inher-ent fear of success as well!—the main reason being fear of jealousy. Looking back at my past, I could see where this limiting belief came from. I was once shunned at school. My ex-boyfriend was jealous and turned the class against me—that experience was very painful. Work-ing with a therapist, I realized my subconscious held on to the faulty, limiting belief that being successful makes others jealous and can end in pain. The painful consequence was that I avoided playing all out.

I learned success is painful and we should be successful but not too successful. I didn't play all out to avoid jealousy. A coach of mine once told me a sentence which helped me a lot: What other people think of you is none of your business, and how others choose to react to you is their choice. You are a sun—some may choose to be burned by you, but others will choose to sunbathe or, like a sunflower, grow from your light. What they do is their choice—you can't stop being the sun.

Impostor Syndrome

Another common limiting belief is *impostor syndrome* (IS), which is described as an internal experience of believing that you are not as competent as others perceive you to be. It leaves you feeling like a phony—you feel as though at any moment you are going to be found out as a fraud. You tend to over-internalize failure and attribute success externally—you had a great team or just got lucky.

The term was first used by psychologists Suzanne Imes and Pauline Rose Clance in the 1970s. When the concept of IS was introduced, it was originally thought to apply mostly to high-achieving women. While more common among women versus men, it is estimated that 70 percent of all people will experience at least one episode of this phenomena in their lives.[5]

To overcome impostor syndrome, you might want to go back to your strengths as well as take a closer look at your core beliefs—especially those limiting, often irrational beliefs.

Leading like a girl is being aware of these limiting beliefs and doing the internal work to eradicate them. Let's review how.

Limiting Beliefs and How to Eradicate Them

We all create these irrational, limiting beliefs. They are created in our infantile subconscious in childhood and unless we address and dispute them, they can come back to haunt us in adulthood. According to Rational Emotive Behavior Therapy (REBT), founded by Albert Ellis, people do not get emotionally disturbed by unfortunate circumstances but by how they evaluate a situation—their perspective toward it.[6] The A–B–C–D–E model is used to help understand this (figure 5.1).

Activating event—A triggering event happening in the present.

Belief—Our evaluation of this event given our sometimes unconscious limiting beliefs rooted in the past.

Consequences—The negative impact this belief has had on your life thus far and could have in the future.

Dispute—Expose the irrationality of this belief.

Effective Exchange—Exchange with a new more empowering belief and design experiments to strengthen that new belief.

It is not the Activating event itself that affects us emotionally, but rather the Beliefs we construct leading to the Consequences in behavior and emotions. You need to Dispute this limiting belief, effec-

ABCDE Model
To change your emotion – dispute your limiting beliefs

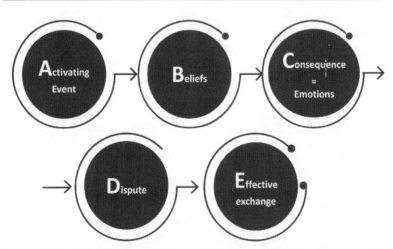

Figure 5.1. ABCDE Model. *Source:* Cognitive Behavior Therapy, Albert Ellis 1962.

tively eradicate it, gain a healthier perspective, and replace it with a new Empowering belief so that new, more effective emotions, and resulting behaviors may emerge.

The irrationality in our beliefs usually falls into one of three categories:

1. *Magnifying*—We tend to over-exaggerate: If I failed and was scolded by my parents, I may have created a belief I am not good enough. If someone rejected me, I will experience any exclusion as total rejection. If I experienced pain when disappointing and gain when achieving, I may have developed an over reliant on external praise. Or if someone was scolded by their parents or made to feel small, they may develop a feeling of "not good enough," sadly the most prevalent limiting belief among many of my coaching clients. Children who had a traumatic experience of interpersonal conflict may have created a limiting belief that all conflict should be avoided at all cost, limiting their coping as adults.

2. *Minimizing*—This is about creating a tunnel view. If one person didn't like me, I conclude I am not likable.

3. *Making up a belief*—For example, if I was constantly praised by my parents, I may make up a belief that praise = love and life and, hence, criticism is death. Or if someone was jealous of me and ended up shunning me, I may experience any envy as painful and hence play small to avoid this expectation of pain.

Using this model on myself, I found that I tend to jump first and defend myself whenever I receive feedback. I realized I had a limiting belief that any feedback is an indication I had failed, which I then catastrophized in my head. Being aware of that limiting belief and disputing it, I was able to launch a series of experiments to be silent and listen to feedback with a true desire to learn and grow, seeing criticism as an opportunity for growth versus a total attack on my self-esteem. In the same way, whenever I do something and someone else says they are envious of my success, I remember I

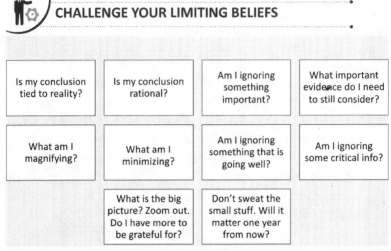

CHALLENGE YOUR LIMITING BELIEFS

Is my conclusion tied to reality?	Is my conclusion rational?	Am I ignoring something important?	What important evidence do I need to still consider?
What am I magnifying?	What am I minimizing?	Am I ignoring something that is going well?	Am I ignoring some critical info?
	What is the big picture? Zoom out. Do I have more to be grateful for?	Don't sweat the small stuff. Will it matter one year from now?	

Figure 5.2. Challenge Your Limiting Beliefs. *Source:* **Based on Tal Ben-Shahar Happiness Studies Academy.**

have a limiting belief around jealousy and remind myself of this amazing quote by Marianne Williamson, an American author and spiritual activist, that sends chills down my spine:

> Our deepest fear is not that we are inadequate. Our deepest fear is that we are powerful beyond measure. It is our light, not our darkness that most frightens us. We ask ourselves—who am I to be brilliant, gorgeous, talented, fabulous? Actually, who are you not to be? You are a child of God. You playing small doesn't serve the world. There is nothing enlightened about shrinking so that other people won't feel insecure around you. We are all meant to shine, as children do. . . . And as we let our own light shine, we unconsciously give other people permission to do the same.
>
> —Marianne Williamson[7]

My biggest leap on this fear of failure and fear of success is writing this book—I wake up in sweat about putting myself fully out there. But then I remind myself that when you let your own light shine, you give other people permission to shine theirs.

So, dare to try, and if you fail, reflect, collect your learnings; then get up, and shine on like the star you are.

ACTIVITY

After creating a vision board in chapter 1, you should spend some time reflecting on what is preventing you from getting there. Are there any limiting beliefs preventing you from living your best life?

How to Identify Your Limiting Beliefs

Activating event—Uncover your limiting belief. Meditate and think about the first pain-related experience of your childhood:

- Write it down—What happened? Who was there? How did you feel?

Belief—What irrational belief did your subconscious create?

Consequences—Detach emotionally and see the negative impact this belief has had on your life thus far and could have in the future.

- What is the downside of carrying this limiting belief? What has it cost you so far?
- What will it cost you in the future if you continue believing this? What is holding you back from achieving? Often we hold on to these limiting beliefs as they served us in the past—you may need to play out the consequences to the extreme to really admit your beliefs might be limiting.

Dispute—Expose the irrationality of this belief. To dispute these beliefs, you can try asking yourself one of the dispute questions in figure 5.2.

- Meditate and reflect on the irrationality of this limiting belief.

Empowering belief—What could be a new more empowering belief? Write it down as an incantation—a statement you repeat every morning. (I am enough; I have everything I need to succeed; I am not dependent on others' appreciation; failing means I am growing, etc.) Design a few experiments that would prove and strengthen your new empowering belief.

6

LEARNING TO DANCE
WITH ADVERSITY

Growing up, I was always considered to have healthy "chutzpah"—
a Yiddish term which means being cheeky and fearless. I was a competitive gymnast and later an army platoon commander, which were
both my crash courses in perseverance and stamina. Doing things
"like a girl" was never an insult in my mind.

It was 1998, and I had just completed my degree in psychology
and business and landed the role of Associate Brand Manager for
Procter & Gamble FemCare in Geneva. For the first six months, I
didn't have a direct manager and so was reporting to the country
General Manager—Jim Lafferty. I was sitting in his office, angry
about a project that hit a wall. My samples for a huge PR event I
was planning for months were stuck in customs. I was so frustrated
about this "failed" launch that, suddenly, tears began rolling down
my cheeks. I was horrified—there I was at one of my first business
meetings in my GM's office, crying. . . . I quickly tried to hide my
tears and regain my composure.

Jim leaned forward, offered me a box of tissues, and, when I
calmed down a little, looked me dead in the eyes and said something
I will forever remember: "Dalia, don't you ever be embarrassed for

crying in the office again. It's a sign of your **passion** and passion is your superpower!" Wow.

Then he added: "And if you ever work for anyone who doesn't appreciate that, walk away—they don't deserve you."

At that moment, I felt so empowered, and for the next 17 years at P&G I had many managers like Jim who nurtured me and believed in me sometimes more then I believed in myself. And I delivered the moon—my career went from strength to strength. I loved what I was doing, I was good at it, and I thrived!

But it wasn't until I reached the lowest point of my career that I realized the importance of what Jim said and how critical it is to BE MY WHOLE SELF AND LEAD LIKE A GIRL.

It happened seventeen years later. P&G needed me back in Geneva, but my husband, Dror, had just opened his high-tech company in Singapore. I felt compelled to "put my money where my mouth was" by supporting our dual careers. I also felt I was ready for the next big CMO role. So I decided to leave P&G. It was not easy—almost like a divorce. I loved everything about the culture. It felt like my second home—but it was time to move on and we parted as good friends.

I was offered many roles in the Fast-Moving Consumer Goods (FMCG) sector, but I decided I wanted something totally new. I took on a role as CMO Asia for a leading white goods (electronics) company. I loved the CEO and global CMO's vision to turn this company from product-led to consumer-led. In fact, I would be the head of marketing and would be helping to transform everything in this department—people, processes, digital, commercial launch, and how we were going to market.

I thought I had landed my dream job.

After two months on the job, my local line manager changed. It took me a week to realize that he and I were—how can I put this delicately . . . like fire and water.

- While I was all about people, he was all about results—even *at the expense of* people.

- I was an outspoken Israeli, where speaking your mind was a sign of respect and a desire to improve things, but he believed in hierarchy and obedience.
- I was all about passion and creativity; he was all about spreadsheets, scorecards, and ROI (Return On Investment).

Most days the culture felt like—ROI or you die!

During one of our first meeting, he bluntly said, "Dalia, I will not give you compliments. I see it as a waste of time. I'll just focus you on what you need to fix," and then he added, "And please don't kid yourself—there is no art to marketing, only science. You just don't get it yet." A stab to the heart—ouch.

You get the picture: we were a match made in . . . hell . . .

One morning I was summoned to his office from another team meeting (he would do that often, like a summons to the headmaster), and that is when it really felt like hell.

He was pounding with negative feedback. Now, I love feedback and enjoy the growth that comes with tough love feedback—feedback that comes from a position of care. But, boy, there was no love in his feedback—it was just tough, denigrating, belittling.

I tried to hold it all in. I was now a C-suite executive—one of the only women on his leadership team—but my anger and frustration mounted.

Then he moved to insulting my team—and that's when I became a lioness. I could hold it in when he was belittling me, but my team? It was so unfair as I knew how hard my team worked! I was so angry and frustrated . . . that I started to . . . tear up.

He smiled and handed me a box of tissues, and, for a moment, I had this warm fuzzy feeling remembering my first boss—Jim. But then I notice something weird, almost evil, in his smile. He turned the tissue box around, and I could not believe my eyes . . .

On the other side of that tissue box was a handmade sticker that he had prepared in advance, which read: "Dalia's tissue box." Gasp.

Have you ever felt belittled, diminished, destroyed because people told you that you were weak? Used your emotions against you?

"Are you kidding me?" I said, with the little self-esteem I had left in me. "I should report this to HR!"

"Oh, come on, Dalia," he leaned back in his chair and said, "don't get all emotional. It's just 'boy banter'—I know you have a sense of humor!"

A few days later I was standing with some of my peers arguing something.

My boss walked up to us and said to them, "You think Dalia is such a tough cookie, an Israeli ex-platoon commander? Did you know she has a tissue box in my office with her name on it?"

Suddenly, all my strengths and values were not only not being appreciated, they were being mocked.

My passion? Seen as weakness.

My commitment to people? Too motherly

My positive disposition? I was seen by him as overly positive. In a meeting where we received feedback, our leadership team was too negative and I suggested to run positive psychology workshops for the team—he turned to me and said, "Thank you 'Miss Kumbaya,' that won't be needed."

Unfortunately, I allowed this to get to me, fear crept in, and I began to lose my confidence.

Within a few months, the two friends I made, the human resources manager and the vice president of product, left. During the time I was there, half the leadership team left or was fired. It took me a full three years to categorize this behavior as bullying. Why so long? Maybe it was my stamina, or how I was raised to never give up, that made me choose to persevere there for three years. Maybe it was my cognitive dissonance—could I, the head of the P&G women's network, be a victim of bullying? Or maybe it was my innate desire to be empathetic and try and coach him?

Those three years of adversity were very challenging but, in a weird way, this book was born based on what I learned from all my experiences, including these more challenging ones.

Year 1—Fight

When under attack, my natural instinct is to do one thing—*fight.* I felt the culture was wrong, and I felt compelled to fix it. I focused all my energy on the external environment and tried to change it. I tried to "coach" my boss—I thought I was being brave and proactive by providing open feedback and what's even worse, I became very defensive to feedback—every time my boss gave me negative feedback, my fairness radar went on and so I tried to argue it.

BIG MISTAKE.

This was a lose-lose strategy. I was investing a lot of energy in changing the external environment and it was perceived as me not listening, which then provoked my boss to be even more negative and mean in an effort to balance my positivity and shake me into obedience. This was the dance of death, as we both wanted to be heard.

I learned you cannot change someone who doesn't want to change: you can only change how you react to the environment.

Year 2—Flight

I told myself, *you are a coach, there is a lesson here for you, shut up and listen.* I focused on changing myself, changing everything my boss felt needed "fixing." I was determined to give my boss what he asked for—and hired a data scientist to complement me and his almost obsessive need for data. I was determined to get his appreciation, even if it was spending day after day formatting presentations to the global team exactly as he had requested. But whatever my team and I did, it seemed it was never enough. I was so focused on fixing myself, that I ended up losing myself—so much so that at the end of that year I fell physically sick. I was drained and burnt out.

I realized I had allowed his feedback to soak in and noticed a new emotion I'd never felt before in my life—fear. Every summons into his office sent chills down my back. I knew I would be criticized and belittled. Every email I sent, I had to reread ten times. Under these conditions, I found my brain simply wasn't functioning properly. In one meeting, I mixed up currencies and my boss mocked me mercilessly, saying "Marketing doesn't know their numbers." When I answered that I was actually a math and physics major and summa cum laude in business, I was mocked. "Don't mess with the rocket scientist." I tried to build my resilience, but sadly, the more resilient I became, the worse it got. Over time, I started believing the criticism that was leveled at me; I was losing my spark. I felt I was not allowed to be myself—that I had left my heart and my art at the door.

It was death by a thousand paper cuts.

I learned that when you try to change yourself beyond your values and suffocate your strengths, you end up losing yourself and this misalignment creates havoc in your body and soul.

At the end of that year, I happened to attend a P&G alumni event. Walking into that room and listening to all the presentations on culture, servant leadership, and collaboration made me realize I wasn't crazy; the examples given were what normal culture feels like. I was just in a toxic culture. I knew I had to leave, but, being the results-driven person that I am, I was determined to regain my spark and deliver everything I had committed to the global CEO so I could leave with my head held high, knowing I didn't quit and had delivered on my commitments.

Year 3—Learn to Dance with Adversity

I decided to change strategy and focus on win-win—how can I meet my boss's needs without sacrificing my own? My boss wanted science, and I was determined to bring back my art and my heart to the workplace. I decided I had to drop that crippling fear, stop trying to change to what other people thought I should be, and instead go back to my strengths: people and creativity. That was my turning point.

I invested in creating a best-in-class team and in being the leader I wanted to have. Knowing I was going to leave at the end of the year, I focused on grooming two potential successors. We created the strongest marketing community. My team rated our culture as a family—a tribe. My greatest pride is that I was able to shield them from the toxicity most of the time and cultivate our own marketing subculture of a family.

To bring back my art, I decided to create a campaign that was extremely data-based but also very creative.

My boss was reluctant and so was the product line VP, so I tamed my natural passion and just let the data speak—and in the leadership meeting, showed the consumer reaction, the risk assessment, and then invited the sales clusters to share their point of view. The sales manager in Australia was standing in for the country manager and knew nothing of the leadership team politics. He just gave his raving support and the other clusters followed. My boss reluctantly agreed, and the campaign was launched.

The campaign ended up being a huge success. It transformed our equity, turned around shares, and delivered all the hard numbers, but through heart and art. I learned the magic of the AND instead of the tyranny of OR and that only when I went back to my strengths was I able to succeed.

I knew I had delivered everything I came in to deliver. I got my spark back and was ready to move on. My successors were ready to be promoted. I knew my team would be in good hands.

At the end of the global talent review meeting, the visiting global HR was furious with how my boss had spoken to me. The amazing thing was that I had thought he was on his best behavior because of her presence. I realized I had become completely numb to his denigrating style of communication; I had become a frog in boiling water. It was time to move on.

Interestingly, when I did my thesis and interviewed other victims of office bullying, many used this phrase—a frog in boiling water— to describe how we tend to numb painful experiences which prevent us from acting on them and sometimes need a breaking point to jump out of the water.

My breaking point was the annual meeting. My team and I worked intensively that year to deliver and the scorecard reflected that. I believe in giving credit where credit is due, so I asked my boss to have my directors join in this review to present their results. I was sure this would be an opportunity for my boss to give some positive encouragement to the team that had worked so hard and delivered against all odds. We worked determinedly to ensure that everything about that presentation was well thought through and addressed every single issue that he had expressed in the past so that he couldn't find any fault. I was proud of the team, the work, and our results as well as how the presentation went. Yet at the end, when it was my boss's turn to provide his thoughts, he only shared one thought: "I think your targets were too low."

We were all broken—my team experienced first-hand some of his harsh behavior and I felt as if my world was crumbling. I could take the abuse when it was just against me, but when it was directed at my team, I felt helpless. If at the start I had felt I couldn't leave as I had to protect my tribe, now, when I was no longer able to protect them and I was the cause of this harsh behavior, I came to the conclusion that removing myself was the best option.

The last step in my decision process was the need for courage—the courage to leave a high six-figure salary when I was the main breadwinner, financing the kids' school and house as my husband's high tech company developed, and the courage to move on and be happy. I found this courage while walking on fire during an "Unleash the Power Within" workshop in February with Tony Robbins which I bought myself as a birthday gift. And so, when my boss wasn't able to acknowledge the huge progress my team had made during the sales meeting presentation the following week, I decided to leave—six months earlier than planned—without even securing my next role. It was super scary, but I decided to trust the universe and take the leap.

My boss seemed relieved that I had decided to leave. Yet, even in that meeting, my desire to coach him still emerged and I said, "You have an amazing HR head, why don't you let her do her job?" He replied, "And risk losing control? Are you crazy?" You cannot change someone who doesn't want to change, so stop trying.

Those three years weren't easy, but they helped me realize what was important to me and they inspired me to realign my purpose.

Despite some incredible offers that followed, I decided to take a break from corporate life. I took up a master's in organizational psychology at INSEAD business school and dedicated my thesis research to "me-search." I focused on one major question, *Can you coach yourself out of a toxic environment?* My conclusion was *yes* and *no*.

YES, you can, and you should build your own resilience, and my 5P model helped me survive, but when it comes to highly toxic environments, often the more resilient you are, the more you bring on bullying—so, in that sense, NO. In the case of bullying, resilience strategy is ineffective. There is really only one strategy that works, and that is zero tolerance.

During my research, I discovered that what happened to me is, sadly, all too common in the workplace, which I would argue is currently too masculine and needs to be changed, not merely for the sake of women's advancement but for the sake of all employees' advancement, well-being, and performance.

Let me share the brief thesis findings here.

EMPLOYEE ENGAGEMENT

Gallup employee engagement research (2018) found that 87 percent of employees are unhappy at work, working for companies that don't appreciate them as human beings, and 18 percent of employees are so unhappy they are hostile. This goes straight to the bottom line costing the economy about $7 trillion in lost productivity and stress-related disease.[1]

Bullying is more common than people realize, with some research showing one in two employees complaining of office bullying (even in the United States).[2] "Bullying at work means harassing, offending, socially excluding someone or negatively affecting someone's work tasks. [However a] conflict cannot be called bullying if the incident is an isolated event or if two parties of approximately equal 'strength' are in conflict."[3] In other words, to be labeled as bullying it needs to be persistent (in repetition and duration) and show ill intent and a power imbalance in which there is illegitimate use of personal power by the bully.

THE 5P MODEL FOR MANAGING TOUGH SITUATIONS

Leading like a girl is remembering the 5P model, even in the toughest of times. This is how we build resilience over time and, as I discuss in the last chapter, also how we grow from trauma. Let me reflect on how each of the Ps were used in this situation.

Purpose, Value, and Strengths

Always make sure you are clear on your values and strengths, even when your strengths seem not to be valued. Your strengths bolster you and give you energy to deal with the rest. Only when I was able to get back to my strengths was I able to perform. When in the most challenging environment—make sure to use your strengths in new and creative ways!

Physical Power

When facing anxiety at work, you quickly lose energy. You stop sleeping and exercising, and that affects mental performance. The key is to keep up healthy routines as described in chapter 3 so that you have the energy to deal with the aggression.

Perspective and Mental Perseverance

Start by listening to the other's needs before jumping to change them. When people are emotional, it is usually because one emotion is out of check—*fear*. Why the aggression? What is the underlying fear? And how can you diffuse it? Remember—listen and silent are anagrams of each other, so keep quiet and *listen*. Once you understand others' needs, focus your energy on meeting those needs to establish trust. Don't waste your energy defending; listen, take it in, and prove your value.

Adopt a growth mind set. Step out of the drama to understand the movie. Don't get caught up in emotions. As will be described in chapter 13, it's important to create space between the stimulus and the response, to *center* your emotions and *respond* rather than *react* in a way that focuses on the win-win.

People and Relationships

Don't keep it to yourself. Reach out to friends and mentors. When I reflected upon my bullying situation, I realized it was the first time as the only C-suite woman in the room that I didn't have a strong network. I should have made more of an effort to reach out for support.

Positivity and Emotional Bravery

CENTER your emotions (**C**ontain–**E**xplain–**N**ame–**T**ame–**E**mpathize–**R**eframe). Breathe. Try to understand what triggered you so much in the other's words. Physically remove yourself from the situation, creating space to evaluate your emotions. For example, you can say, "I am sorry, but this discussion is becoming too toxic. I suggest we continue tomorrow when you are ready to have a respectful dispute." And then simply walk out. . . . Women tend to underplay anger, yet anger is an emotion that gets a bully's attention.

Convert CONFLICT into CONNECTION through CURIOSITY and CONVERSATION.

Leading like a girl is not being afraid of tough conversations. Done well, conflict means something is important to you and to the other person, so if you focus on curiosity and conversation, you could, actually, come out with deeper connections. Here are a few tips on how to do this:

- Situation-Behavior-Impact: Explain the *situation* (where, when, who was there, what was said), the *behavior* that triggered you (share what you saw, create a dialogue versus jumping to conclusions), and share the *impact* using "I" statements: I felt humiliated, denigrated, etc.
- Avoid persuasion: There is no black and white—your objective is to understand the triggers on both sides.
- Avoid problem solving: Remember every conflict is an invitation for deepening connection through curiosity and conversation.
- Listen with curiosity and empathy.
- When someone is rude, it may be due to other things happening. Diffuse it by asking "Is everything okay?" Then reflect empathetically:

  What is the other side's story?
  Why am I emotionally triggered?
  What are they afraid of?
  What am I afraid of?

- Make sure to name and label your emotion(s): The objective at this stage is to manage your emotions so that you can choose the appropriate action. In an argument, especially with a toxic personality, being smart is more important than being right.
- And finally validate the other's emotion—for example, acknowledge them: "You seem very passionate about this." Empathy means you understand even if you don't always agree. Help the other feel seen and heard. This understanding shifts conflict into conversation and can end up deepening connections.

This is about understanding your emotions, centering but not suppressing them, and finding the right avenue for expressing them. Being passive will lead you to passive-aggressiveness, which is the least beneficial response. Suppressing your emotions will wreak havoc on your body and soul.

After reflecting on the 5Ps, and CENTERing your emotions as I will explain in more detail in chapter 13, the final step is to choose how you *A-C-T* (versus react). When choosing how to ACT, there are several elements to keep in mind:

A Stands for Active Control—Dance with Adversity

When you are punched, the natural response is to fight, flee, or freeze. The key is to be active versus passive, but what if instead of fight or flight, you learn to dance with your adversary? Regain control by finding the win-win. This is how this could look:

- Understand what the other person's needs are.
- Step alongside the aggressor instead of facing them in attack.
- Now, try to use the power of their punch to lead the aggressor in the direction you want to go, thereby creating a beautiful dance. In my case, by understanding my boss's need for ROI and digital transformation, I was able to use the power of the punch, get his support for resources, and invest in a campaign that was both very data driven and ROI focused but also very creative—that was how I was able to dance, meeting the others' needs without sacrificing my own.

Another critical point is how you communicate, knowing that 93 percent of the perceived message is *how* you say things versus *what* you say. When you are caught in emotion, your message is simply less effective. In his book, *The No Asshole Rule*, Robert Sutton talks about the importance of calmly and effectively responding to misinformation.[4] When you have a beef with someone (a term I learned from my teenagers means conflict), use a **BIFF** response:

Brief (three to four sentences),
Informative (not defensive or emotional or counterattacking, just the info as you have it),
Firm, yet Friendly.

This is especially useful when you are being attacked or shamed via email using misinformation. If the original email was public, the advice is to send out one BIFF email publicly and then take the rest offline. The reason is that you want to set the record right with the same people and send a signal that you cannot be messed with. Avoid being dragged into a public tit-for-tat that will lower your credibility. Ensure there is no counterattack. Your objective is to share information. For example: "Thank you for raising this issue. There might be some misunderstanding here, so I wanted to clarify the facts and share some info you may not have. If you have any questions, I suggest we continue this conversation offline. Wish you a great weekend and good luck with that presentation."

C Stands for Clear Boundaries

When interviewing people who successfully came out of a bullying situation, I realized this was one thing I could have done much better! Set very clear boundaries early on. *How* and *when* boundaries are set is extremely important. When setting boundaries, stick to:

1. What are the rules, policies, and the law—don't make it personal. For example, "This comment is against company ethics, so I'd appreciate it if we could stay professional." Don't point a finger at the person, but at the rules. Create a sense of "we." For example, "We have a situation that needs to be resolved. Upper management made this a priority."
2. State the consequences if the rule is violated. "You may not realize it, but this violates company ethics and I will need to complain if it persists." Avoid being emotional.

T Stands for Talk and Report

When I was younger, I volunteered for a year in a home for victims of domestic violence. I was shocked by the women's denials of their situations and their reactions to being labeled victims. This is a natural defense mechanism. The word "victim" is immediately associated with being weak. And the stronger and more confident you are, the harder it is to accept, as the word creates a cognitive dissonance.

It's not that I was afraid to speak up, it's that I kept thinking I could coach my boss. After six months on the job, when global HR came down to interview us, I shared with them my honest point of view, which I then also shared with my boss. As I told him, I would never share anything behind his back that I wasn't brave enough to say to his face. I thought I was acting with integrity. I also went ahead and told local HR about the tissue box story, but she too was a victim of bullying and it never reached the right people with leverage. It was only after one of my directors noticed what was going on that they suggested I write it all down. I sat down that night and poured my heart out. I wrote down every single insult and snarky remark and when I finished, I sent it to two people—my mentor and first boss, Jim, and my husband. Jim was fuming. He wanted me to seek legal counsel for gender-biased harassment. I did, and it was clear I had a case. But I decided to sit on it. I really didn't want to get into a legal battle. My husband was fuming as well and said, "This is bullying. You must complain and get out." This reflection and labeling were an important wake-up call. I was no longer a frog in boiling water and was able to reflect as an outsider about the situation.

The 5Ps are about leading like a girl and building your resilience in dealing with challenging situations—however when it comes to prolonged harassment and toxic environments, my findings indicate there really is only one strategy that works and that is *zero tolerance!*

A year into the role, I met with a very senior headhunter who had placed me in the position and knew my boss very well. She said to me, "Yes, he is known to have a reputation, but only you can change him." Her intentions were good, and I had taken pride in being successful in coaching up many previous managers in my prior job. But this case was different, and there is only one way to change someone who doesn't want to change. Use leverage. Go to your boss's boss, and get the boss to focus on something that is critical for them—like their career. File an official ethics line complaint. An official complaint forces the company to make tough decisions, versus sweeping issues under the rug.

You must "Talk and Report," as hard as it is. You cannot change someone who doesn't want to be changed and you cannot coach yourself out of bullying—you will not solve it yourself. You need to apply a zero-tolerance strategy and report the abusive behavior.

And if they let *you* go? Well, you're better off than staying in a toxic environment.

In summary, leading like a girl means that when attacked by a "wounded masculine," as my friends Nilima Bhat and Raj Sisodia[5] refer to a bully—man or woman, we need to first remember our strengths and step into our "healthy feminine" traits—apply the 5P model using empathy, build our resilience, and seek the win-win.

When doing so we need to be aware so we do not drop into our wounded feminine, becoming defensive and overly dependent on external praise and validation.

However, effectively leading like a girl also means that when none of that helps, then we need to step into our healthy assertive masculine and *ROAR!*

Or, as Muhammad Ali put it:

Float like a butterfly—sting like a bee.

—Muhammad Ali

IV

PEOPLE

People is about investing in relationships and redefining "ROI" to mean "Return On Interaction" instead of "Return On Investment." It's about bringing out our typical female gathering skills in a holistic view as partners, parents, and leaders, fostering teamwork, inclusiveness, and personal growth for all.

7

"SELF-FULLNESS": YOUR RELATIONSHIP WITH YOUR SELF

Imagine the following scenario: your best friend calls you up and tells you she was up all night sick. She is shaking all over and has a presentation that morning. What would you advise her to do?

Years back, while at P&G, I was lucky to be on staff for an amazing course called "Women Supporting Women," created by Denise Andrews. This was an incredible course which focused on the importance of social support in the workplace. During the course, we asked participants this very question and their answers were often, "I would tell her to stay home and go to the doctor" or "I would remind her that no work is worth risking your health for and that she is better off rescheduling this presentation than going in her present state."

We would then ask, "Now imagine if this scenario happened to you. What would you do?" Most replied that they would suck it up and go into work. I remember answering exactly that myself.

Why?

Why would your advice to your best friend—to be kind to herself—be so different from your advice to yourself?

Why are we so harsh with ourselves, falling into habits of extreme self-criticizing and self-loathing?

The objective of this exercise was to encourage us to be as kind to ourselves as we are to others, to be our own best friends. This concept stuck strongly in my mind and is one of the most powerful strategies I have adopted in my life.

We often refer to this idea as the oxygen mask principle. While on a flight, the attendant will remind you that in case of an oxygen drop, you should put the oxygen mask on yourself *first* before attending to others. The rationale is simple. How can you attend to and help others when you can't help yourself first?

> To say "I love you," one must first know how to say the "I."
>
> —Ayn Rand, American philosopher

As a working mom, I remember thinking about this idea one day. I had just picked up Mia from kindergarten and had baby Liam with me. We walked into the house. I was starving and so were they, with Liam crying to be breastfed. I could have sat down and fed him immediately but then I would be so hungry and restless for the next forty minutes of feeding. Remembering the oxygen mask principle, I took one extra minute to give Mia some cornflakes, make myself some tea, and only then did I sit down to peacefully feed Liam. I am sure my calm milk tasted better.

So why do we feel selfish when we are our own best friend?

In this, I want to point out the cultural differences between the East and West. In the West, we have two terms generally believed to be in conflict with each other: egoism, which refers to the concept that self-interest is what motivates all conscious action, and altruism, which refers to an unselfish devotion to the welfare of others, regardless of personal benefit. The idea is that you are either one or the other; you can't be a true altruist if you have some egoism in you. Or, as in that legendary *Friends* episode (which my daughters are addicted to) when Joey challenges Phoebe to create a selfless deed, arguing that every deed has some benefit to the giver and, hence, there is no selfless deed. Well, the question is, should there be?

Eastern philosophy teaches us there should not.

I wrote this while in Bhutan with my family. I was there to complete my happiness studies and to learn a little more about Buddhism. Bhutan is considered the happiest nation on earth, prioritizing gross national happiness (GNH) over the more financial measure of gross domestic product (GDP). One example of this? Both health care and education—even higher education in a foreign country—are paid for by the government.

Our guide was Dr. Karma, a former Buddhist monk (he chose to marry and gave up his monkhood). While my kids were enjoying the sightseeing, biking, and rafting, I was fascinated by his teaching of Buddhism.

The story goes that when the Dalai Lama started working with people in the West, he was surprised with the concept of self-hate and concluded this is because the West sees selfishness and selflessness as two opposing concepts—either/or. If selfish love comes at the expense of love to others, then a conscientious person would choose selfless love or would be ridden with guilt every time they cared for themselves.

In Buddhism, there is no such discrepancy. There is only one word for compassion, and it is the Tibetan word *tsewa*, which roughly translated means tenderness, warmth, or compassion—and the interesting fact is that it relates equally to self and to others. It's the ability to extend how you feel toward yourself to others. Self-love is seen as a precondition to compassion and love of others, and this is inherent in the language. Starting with self leads to not only happier individuals but happier relationships and happier society.

> [W]hen you have known who you are, then a love arises in your being. . . . How can you give something which you don't have? To give it, the first basic requirement is to have it.
>
> —Osho Indian mystic

We see this in many religious teachings. One of my favorite quotes comes from Rabbi Hillel:

If I am not for myself, who will be for me? But if I am only for myself, who am I? And if not now, when?

One needs to care for oneself *and* for others.

The Bible (Matthew 22:39, KJV) also states: "Thou shalt love thy neighbour as thyself." Usually what we remember is *love thy neighbor* and forget the part about *as thyself.*

The Lebanese poet Kahlil Gibran[1] uses the analogy of the fruit tree to make this point. He says that like fruit trees, we need to take care of ourselves by sucking from our roots, so that we can give to others. Just like a tree can only flourish and share fruits when it takes up nourishment, so people can share love when they are well nourished.

Selflessness leaves you without a sense of self. Selfishness trumps any chance of positive human relations, a core to productive life. The magic is combining the two.

Tal Ben-Shahar coined a new word, **self-fullness**—acting on behalf of yourself, while still caring for the greater good.

What is critical for giving to others is the ability to give to oneself. Generous people are not selfless. They care about themselves *so that* they can care about others. They sees the two as intertwined. And this is especially important for women in leadership positions.

Leading like a girl is about being intuitive about and listening to your own body—understanding your stress levels and knowing when it is time to take a pause to focus on your self-care. An interesting fact is that women suffer from chronic stress more than men, yet men are 3.5 times more likely to commit suicide.[2] One reason given is that women are more self-aware of their stress and the impact it has on their bodies, so they are more inclined to admit they need help, to talk about it, and to know when enough is enough *before* it is too late.

I do not have to explain why I put my health first. Physical health is mental health.

—Simone Biles

As a competitive gymnast, I am awed by the incredible story of Simone Biles—often referred to as the greatest of all time. Biles, the American gymnast who has four Olympic gold medals and four gymnastics moves named after her, decided in July 2021 to withdraw from the Olympics, prioritizing her mental health. She explained that she knew if she continued, she would risk severe injury as well as risking the team's chance at a medal. While criticized by many for "throwing in the towel"—called weak, selfish, and a shame to the country—Biles will go down in the history for being not weak but exceptionally brave—brave to recognize her body and mind were not in sync and that if she continued pushing ahead, she would harm herself and might end up harming her team. She is an amazing example of an individual who leads like a girl—she has persevered and competed with a broken toe, she has also persevered and competed despite sexual abuse, but she is in tune with her mind and body to know when enough is enough.[3] In her opinion piece, "What Men Need to Learn from Simone Biles," *Washington Post* columnist Karen Attiah enhances this point:

> Biles has shown what it looks like to have the freedom and bravery to protect oneself and others. Let us hope more male athletes will be strong enough to follow her lead.[4]

In his book *Give and Take*, Wharton professor Adam Grant talks about the importance of self-love for effective giving in the following way:

- Takers are self-centered and focus only on what benefits they can get from others.
- Givers are driven by the desire to help others and create success for the group.
- Matchers strive for equally fair exchange with others—if they give, they should receive to the same extent—when they get, they feel compelled to return the favor.[5]

What do we know about the most successful people?

Traditionally we have been taught to believe that to succeed, we must be takers. This assumes the pie is finite and hence we need to compete for our share. Grant's research, as well as historical evidence, shows that a style of giving is more prominent among the most successful versus taking because givers are focused on the common good. Givers believe resource and knowledge pooling is beneficial for everyone, so they use their networks to benefit themselves as well as others. They communicate not in a powerful and domineering way but in a collaborative style, focusing on seeking advice and asking questions. They see potential in everyone they meet, especially unnurtured talent.

Most critically, Grant's recent research showed that givers were not only overrepresented in the most successful groups, they were also overrepresented in the least successful. Givers are both the most successful and the least successful and in the middle are the takers. Generosity appears to sink some individuals to the bottom yet propel others to the top. How is that possible?

The difference between the successful givers and the unsuccessful givers was self-love—givers who give to themselves *and* give to others are successful; these successful "self-full" givers know to identify and limit abuse by takers and focus on seeing the impact of their giving. They know to value the power of giving *and* receiving.

"Self-full" giving is the healthiest form of giving because it is sustainable—the giver gives with joy and the receiver receives without guilt.

What is the bottom line?

Success doesn't need to come at another's expense—we don't give to expect a return, but by focusing on the joy of giving, we do end up gaining pleasure and growth in the long run. When we move from a place of judgment to a place of self compassion, we are able to be our true selves, to fail forwards and grow and help others grow in the process. That is the essence of leading like a girl.

> Friendship with oneself is all important because without it friendship with others is not possible.
>
> —Eleanor Roosevelt

It took me a while, but I created an agreement with all my friends—in our relationships, we do what is right for the other AND for ourselves. If my friend didn't fancy going out, even if we'd agreed to upfront, it should be okay to say we needed to stay at home and enjoy ME time. This will ensure that when we *are* together it is because it is the right thing for both of us, and that caring for each other was 100% out of love and not obligation. We learned to be our own best friends so that we could be best friends with each other.

In January of 2018, the Israeli ambassador to Singapore Simona approached the Israeli community and asked us whether we would help run projects to help mark the anniversary of fifty years of diplomatic relationships between Israel and Singapore. As I had just left the full-time corporate world, I was eager to get more involved in charity work and this project also enabled me to do something for my country, one I haven't lived in for twenty years.

We knew we wanted to do something in technology to celebrate the partnership of Start-Up Nation Israel and Smart Nation Singapore. But we also wanted to do something to give back to the Singapore society, which had been such a special home to us the past ten years. By working with some friends in Israel, we came across an NGO called TOM and loved its purpose. TOM—Tikkun Olam Makers—makers to mend the world—is an Israeli global NGO that brings together people with disabilities with the local maker community to solve daily struggles. It was beautifully aligned with my purpose—to empower people to be the best that they can be.

I took on the role of TOM country manager for Singapore, which became a full-time job for six months as we fundraised and together with an incredible team created the first-ever Makeathon for Singapore.

The nice thing about self-fullness and generosity is that it is contagious, and within weeks we managed to surround ourselves with an incredible group of volunteers who gave their time, energy, and skill to create the event. When we started to advertise it, we were surprised with the overwhelming response from others. There were engineers willing to give a whole weekend of their time to use their tech skills for good and help another person solve their daily struggle.

In Hebrew, the word for "giving" comes from the root word "natan"—it's a palindrome. As giving is a two-way journey—when we give, we also get.

The TOM Makeathon was a huge success. We had ten projects and all the people with disabilities went home with a prototype they could immediately use and that helped change their lives. I personally mentored project Boon, centered around an incredible fifty-six-year-old man. He was a double amputee who'd lost his hands and legs due to a bad case of food poisoning. His team of engineers worked day and night to create a modular 3D printable version of his limbs which could adapt to different tasks. Recently, they shared with me that they all joined him for a rugby game. As one of the engineers told me, he had never had so much fun in all his life.

Because when we give, we get.

ACTIVITY

Are you your own best friend?

Please answer the following:

1. To my close friend I am _____ (attributes).
2. To my best friend, I would never _____, _____, _____.
3. Why should I be a better friend to someone else than I am to myself?
4. How can I be my own best friend?

Write down some of the self-care activities you enjoy the most.

What are some of the negative self-talk and limiting beliefs you have identified in chapter 5 and how have you disputed them?

How can YOU be more self-compassionate and reward yourself with more self-care each and every day?

8

MAKING YOUR PARTNER
A REAL PARTNER

It was July 26, 2018, when I received an exciting historical envelope. But first some background.

Sheryl Sandberg once said, "The best career decision I ever made was whom to marry." She was devastated (and others with her) years later when her husband unexpectedly passed away, but I agree with her completely. I wouldn't have achieved my successful career if it weren't for the support of my husband, Dror.

When we first moved to Geneva in 1998, Dror was studying and we lived on one salary for a couple of years—he always felt uncomfortable with the idea of being on a dependent pass. It was exasperating for him, with me being such a workaholic and him waiting for me in the lobby of P&G as I finished "just one more email." I will never forget the look on his face when a friend we'd just met turned to him and said, "Wow! So, you are actually the trailing spouse." How frustrated he was when we both had to go down to the tax authorities and declare that his wife was the bread-winner, a status not common in Switzerland. Yet, he was always supportive of my career.

When he finished studying and was struggling to find a job, I told him, "Dror, by the age of forty you will be a millionaire and then you will look back and say how grateful you were for having spent Mia's first year as a stay-at-home dad."

I believe these early years of being so involved made him the amazing dad he is today.

Every year our respective managers would ask us, "Who is lead career in your family?" We both refused to answer. "We decide what is right for us as a family," we told our companies.

And so he followed me to Geneva, but later our move to Russia was initiated by him. He followed me back to Geneva, and then again it was he who inspired our move to Singapore. Fast forward a few years and Dror is an amazingly successful businessman.

In 2010, he founded a company called Trax Image Recognition with his partner (I often call him Dror's second wife), Joel, which went on to be the most successful and valued Israeli-Singaporean company. In an interview with *Bloomberg*, he proudly shared his beginnings as a trailing spouse and, ironically, the woman who'd made the trailing spouse comment ended up working with him. They became great friends.

Women in more prominent roles often come to me for advice. Unfortunately, I have seen powerful women lose their relationships because their partner was intimidated by their success. I think part of the success in those early challenging years is that we *always* saw ourselves as *independently interdependent*.

Yes, we were very independent. We each made sure we had a very complete and thriving life independent from each other. In the Venn diagrams of partnership, I always stress the importance of having a circle that is only for yourself, be it his sports time, or my girls' night out, etc. (figure 8.1).

However, we both invested in making sure our time together was meaningful. He knew I loved what I was doing and that my career was important to me, but NEVER more important than him or the kids.

People often ask me, "Can women have it all?" and I say, "*Yes, but not all at once.*" When I came back from maternity leave, I

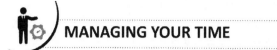

MANAGING YOUR TIME

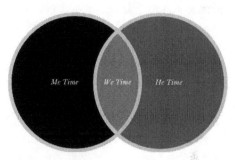

Figure 8.1.   Me vs. We vs. He Time.

worked less than full time and took different, less prestigious assignments. We moved to Moscow because it was the best thing
for both my career as well as Dror's. In 2015, after five years in
Singapore, I was asked by P&G to move back to Geneva and then
it was the time to put my money where my mouth was—Dror was
thriving in Singapore, and it wasn't right for us as a family. After
seventeen years of Dror following my career, it was time for me
to follow his and so I left P&G. Leaving P&G wasn't easy—I still
remember the day I decided to leave. I couldn't get a taxi home
from a conference and walked five kilometers in pouring rain. I was
crying the whole way home and when I arrived, I slept twenty-five
hours straight. When I got up, I handed in my resignation. As my
boss friend Jim used to say—a principle is not a principle unless it
costs you something and on matters of family versus career, family
should always win!

The other part to this question, "Can women have it all?" is even
more important, and it is about not doing it alone. If you want to
make dual careers work, then you need to make your partner a real
partner. What you don't set as normal in the first year of marriage,

the first year of having a child, will not happen. So yes, you might be scared to go out as a young mom leaving him to do that first bath, but if you don't trust him to be an equal partner, he never will be.

And this takes work. My mom once shared an amazing analogy with me—staying married is like going white-water rafting. You are each in a separate canoe, but you need to be rowing together, in the same direction, to ensure you stay on course and don't end up on opposite banks of the river.

I am not a couple's counselor in any way, but recently I found this strategy was backed up by research. Yes, statistics for keeping a healthy marriage are against us—almost 50 percent of couples divorce, and of those who stick together, almost half are disloyal.

Yet research by Dr. David Schnarch and others studying those couples who defy the odds show that contrary to common belief, passion in a relationship can be sustained and even *grow* over time.[1]

How? *Independent inter-dependency.*

Marriage, like white-water rafting, is constantly hard work. We don't enter thriving relationships; we cultivate them over time.

INDEPENDENCE AS EQUALS

When adults enter into a committed relationship, they often seek to get the nourishment and support they received from their parents, or the dependency and support they were craving as children. Trust and being able to count on your partner are critical, but problems begin when an individual becomes completely dependent on another. Regressing to dependence is not a path to a healthy relationship. The more independent we become, the more interdependent we can be.

Relationships develop independence through struggle.

Leading like a girl is being both a supporter and a challenger. Take a lesson from the first girl—Eve. God named Eve *Ezer Kenegdo,* which in Hebrew means "support against him." There should be a natural tension—a spouse helps but also challenges. David Schnarch, in his book *Passionate Marriage: Love, Sex, and Intimacy in Emotionally Committed Relationships*, talks about the importance of having marital crisis but finding the win-win—maintaining self while maintaining the relationship. To build muscle you need some resistance. The same goes for all relationships, as we covered earlier in the book, and especially for marriage—tensions are okay, as they lead to growth when managed properly.

Turn conflict into an opportunity for connection.

Tony Robbins, when talking about thriving relationships, talks about the importance of polarity of masculine versus feminine energy and meeting each other's needs while meeting oneself.[2] He goes on to talk about the three passion killers: the three "U"s for women and three "C"s for men (see table 8.1).

The one I personally struggled with the most is feeling *unseen*—not feeling validated. I do want my husband to notice my new dress, to say "I love you" every day, to appreciate me. But one thing I learned during the Tony Robbins's Date With Destiny conference that I attended was to change my conditions for feeling seen/loved. Let me explain in hopes that it may help you, too.

The need to feel *loved* is very high on my list of "toward-values" (values I want more of). But the rules I had put in place to feel loved were quite hard to achieve, that is, I will *only* feel loved when I am told I am loved every day. The key to happiness is in how you construct your toward-values rules:

Table 8.1. The Passion Killers

Passion Killers for Women (3Us)	Passion Killers for Men (3Cs)
Unseen	Controlled
MisUnderstood	Criticized
Unsafe	Closed off

1. Make them as easy to achieve as possible.
2. Replace the word *only* with *or*.
3. Make them *self*-dependent versus dependent on others.

In my case, if I am waiting for my husband to say, "I love you" every day, I will very quickly feel unhappy. So, I need to create new rules to feel loved that are easy and self-dependent. I have changed my rules to the following:

> *Before*—I will feel loved *only* when I am told I am loved every day.
>
> *After*—I will feel loved every time I receive love, *or* when I notice small acts of love from others (like when my husband makes me my favorite dish or takes my car in to be fixed) *or* when I give love (by saying and showing) *or* when I notice the love in magical everyday moments (even when laughing together at a TV show), *or* when I love myself and do an act of self-care *or* when I feel loved by nature.

At the end of this five-day conference, I went on a diving trip with people I'd just met. For a moment, the sun caressed my face, a beautiful double rainbow became visible, and a pod of dolphins came by our boat to play—a huge smile came over me—I felt deeply loved. When I arrived home, I was more mindful and noticed my husband's different language of love—he doesn't say it as often as I would like but he shows it in small, caring acts.

Do I still get excited when my husband says "I love you," or notices my new haircut? Do I encourage him when he does? Of course! But I have grown to be less dependent on it since I have cultivated my internal self-validation. This takes time and maturity, but self-validation is a key milestone in everyone's personal growth journey.

Another learning for me was around my own strength. My husband has always been very proud of me. But when I decided to switch careers, I wanted to become softer and more supportive of his career. So I decided to join him on his next business trip to a conference in San Francisco. He asked me to book the hotels, but due to the conference, all the hotels were full. I decided to book a nice romantic place up Route 1. What I didn't think of is that he needed to be in a meeting at 7:30 a.m. in town and so we had to get up at 5:00 a.m.; the shirt he was about to wear got stained by my makeup that spilled open in the bag; and my first attempts to iron his shirt almost burned it. I was a very poor trailing spouse! That evening, he made a statement that initially really hurt me. He said, "You know, I don't like you like this—weak—I prefer when you are strong and independent."

"But that means you only love me when I achieve?" I pushed back.

That evening, he invited me to join him for drinks with his Google partners. I was talking with them about my career, the work I did with Google in the past, etc. I was in my element and I was beaming. That evening he said to me, "You said I only love you when you achieve—that is not true, but you are just so sexy when you are in your element."

Men feel freedom when you can rely on them, yet don't depend on them to be your best self. And as women we are the most beautiful when we are comfortable in our own skin. Being independent and not desperately relying on others for validation is what makes us strong and sexy.

INTERDEPENDENCE

Leading like a girl is finding the right balance between dependence and independence—in other words, by creating interdependency. Interdependency is about teamwork. Each one of us has unique skills but you need one another to achieve any task successfully. Parenting is a great source of interdependency. We both care about our children deeply and want to see them grow to be kind, independent, and successful. Do we sometimes disagree about how to get there? Of course! Dror is more of a worrier than I am, I am more patient with studies and coaching, and we both see the value of being adventurous and playful with them. Our friends and kids all know—he is the one who dreams up wild adventures but I am the one to make them happen!

One thing we found very useful was to discuss and align the values we would like to see in our family. My husband usually hates these types of things, but I told him it was a task for my INSEAD organizational psychology degree, and he agreed. We chose our top twenty values from one hundred. We argued a lot but, through this struggle, we gained clarity on what was important to us individually and as a couple. I have attached the list of values at the end of this chapter for you to experience.

But raising kids is not the only way to build interdependency—building a house, working together, or just cultivating a healthy life-style—the key is to recognize the value each side brings and work those to the max.

So, invest in your independent inter-dependency. If you are too dependent, find your core; if you are too controlling, maybe it's because you don't have enough "me" time or don't spend enough appreciating the value of your partner and what's important to him.

As a woman avoid the 3 "C"s—don't try to over control and give him space. You fell in love with a strong, free man—give him the freedom he needs to thrive, check whether you support your partner or criticize him, and find ways to surprise and innovate by bringing out your fun, playful self.

As a man, avoid the marriage trap of the three "U"s—don't take her for granted (yes, show her the love *every* day if you can), avoid trying to fix everything, just shut up and make her feel understood (see the chapter on empathy), and whatever you do, be honest and reliable so she feels safe.

These principles of dependent interdependency are as critical for marriage as they are for working relationships—the *Harvard Business Review* research mentioned in the preface[3] shows that building relationships and fostering teamwork is a skill women are better at than men. Teamwork has been proven to be critical not only in achieving business results but also in boosting creativity and a sense of belonging that is critical for employee engagement. This interdependency is one trait that will help both men and women become better leaders.

And back to the mysterious envelope . . .

In the summer of 2018, I decided to leave the corporate world (at least for a while). Dror was now traveling often—any C-suite corporate role I would take would require at least 50 percent travel. My two older kids were going through their final years of school and would be leaving home soon.

I always said my career is important but my family comes first, and again it was time to put my money where my mouth was.

So despite being successful and enjoying what I was doing, I decided to shift my career, both to be fully committed to my purpose and also to enable Dror to do what he needed to do to bring his company to its full potential, knowing I was there to focus on our family. He never asked me to leave, and at the beginning was a little scared about this change in dynamic, but we both agreed this was the right thing for our joint interdependent operation—that it was time for me to move into a portfolio career—still growing and learning but having more flexibility.

Don't get me wrong—while I have genuine admiration for stay-at-home moms (which is as hard if not harder), I still would recommend that my daughters invest in financial and career independence as one key for their continuous intellectual growth as well as their marriages, as stated above. But there is a time and place for everything. And for me, now was a time for a more flexible career. There are times to press the pedal of career and times to let go and focus on family—it's what leading like a girl is all about.

It's not that I helped my kids prepare for their exams, but I was there. From the breakfast on exam day, driving them to school for the midday exams, helping them manage their time or stress, arranging for extra tutoring if needed, or booking joint gym classes to keep it all in balance.

And when, at the end of those three months, my daughter came home with a rock star report card and said this exam period was actually really fun, I felt the love—big time.

And so, in summer of 2018 I received an envelope and in it was . . . my first-ever dependent pass (me being registered on his visa versus him being registered on mine). I was so proud to now be a little more "dependent" on my husband. Proud of the journey we had made together as a truly equal, dual-career partners, being independently interdependent.

Thank you, hubby, for being the best career decision I've ever made! :)

ACTIVITY

Values Alignment in a Relationship

Print out two copies of the following list (table 8.2, also found on my website). Now grab a glass of wine and spend time each aligning your five top values and then having a discussion to align your five family values with your hubby ;-)

Table 8.2. Values Alignment in a Relationship

Abundance	Empowerment	Mindfulness	Thoughtfulness
Acceptance	Encouragement	Motivation	Traditionalism
Accountability	Enthusiasm	Optimism	Trustworthiness
Achievement	Ethics	Open-Mindedness	Understanding
Advancement	Excellence	Originality	Uniqueness
Adventure	Expressiveness	Passion	Usefulness
Advocacy	Fairness	Peace	Versatility
Ambition	Family	Perfection	Vision
Appreciation	Filial Piety	Performance	Warmth
Attractiveness	Financial Freedom	Personal Development	Wealth
Autonomy	Friendships	Playfulness	Well-Being
Balance	Flexibility	Preparedness	Wisdom
Being the Best	Freedom	Proactive	Zeal
Benevolence	Fun	Professionalism	Joker—*Add your own*
Boldness	Generosity	Popularity	
Brilliance	Grace	Positivity	
Calmness	Growth	Power	
Caring	Happiness	Punctuality	
Challenge	Harmony	Quality	
Charity	Health	Recognition	
Cheerfulness	Honesty	Relationships	
Cleverness	Humility	Reliability	
Community	Humor	Resilience	
Commitment	Inclusiveness	Resourcefulness	
Compassion	Independence	Respect	
Cooperation	Individuality	Responsibility	
Collaboration	Innovation	Responsiveness	
Consistency	Inspiration	Risk Taking	
Contribution	Intelligence	Safety	
Courage	Integrity	Security	
Creativity	Inner Peace	Self-Control	

Credibility	Intuition	Selflessness
Curiosity	Joy	Service
Daring	Kindness	Simplicity
Decisiveness	Knowledge	Spirituality
Dedication	Leadership	Stability
Dependability	Learning	Stewardship
Diversity	Love	Success
Education	Loyalty	Teamwork
Empathy	Making a Difference	Thankfulness

9

WORK-LIFE BALANCE
AS A PARENT

One of the most important relationships for many working parents is the relationship with their kids while keeping work-life balance.

While work-life balance is important for both men and women, sadly, women still carry the majority of the load when it comes to housework and parenting. As leaders, women need to learn to balance these many aspects to their lives and accept that "good enough" is a positive choice—in work, yes, but also in parenting.

I have three kids, an entrepreneurial husband, and I've spent the last twenty years in extremely demanding jobs. I often get the question, "How do you do it?" Everyone has their own way of finding this balance, but I hope by sharing some of the strategies that worked for me, it will help you find what works for *you*.

When my son, Liam, was eight, he gave me a gift that changed my approach to work and to life. He was performing in a school play—not a huge role, I think he was a tree in *Peter Pan* or something—but it was very important to him that I be there to see him. Unfortunately, it fell on a day my husband was traveling and I had to present our annual plan to the global CEO visiting from the United States. I begged and pleaded and finally managed to get myself early on the agenda so I could get to school on time. But as seemingly always happens, my CEO's flight was delayed and even as first on the agenda, I was late. I ended up rushing to school—arrived in my high heels, messy hair, sweaty—just as my little "tree" was coming off stage. He saw me arrive late. I was devastated that I'd missed his *big* tree role. I couldn't stop apologizing the whole way home. And then he said to me something I will never forget—"Mom, I know you are not perfect, but I see you really try."

This cute, sensitive eight-year-old taught me to accept being "good enough," a concept that changed my approach to work-life balance and to my endless question of "Can I have it all?"

When we moved to Geneva "sans enfants" (without kids), I was a complete workaholic. It was all about work hard, play harder. I would work ten to twelve hours a day. Some days my hubby, Dror, who was studying at the time, would join me over lunch when we went roller blading in the carpark or water skiing on the lake. Some nights, my colleagues and I would all stay at work till 1:00 a.m.— and yes, there was that one week when our boss, Alex Sabbag, our king of strategic focus, decided we would not waste three months doing the annual business review as usual but condense it into one week. On the last night, we all ended staying overnight in the office, eating pizza and coffee at 3:00 a.m., to get it completed.

My life wasn't really in balance and the person suffering most was my husband, Dror. I loved what I was doing and was in total flow, so immersed in what I was doing that I would lose all concept of time. Dror was finishing his studies and, as a passionate cook, enjoyed making elaborate meals for us, but he often had to call my colleagues because I was so immersed I wouldn't hear my phone and would forgot to come home in time and the meal would go cold. Even worse was during the cold winters. We only had one car and when it was heavily snowing, Dror would come to pick me up but would end up having to wait for me in the lobby as I was "just finishing something." It drove him mad. One day, Dror was losing it waiting for me again, when he met another person losing it—Mark, who was waiting for his wife, Kathy. The two decided to ditch us and go to the local pub together. When Kathy and I both came down to the cold lobby, we found we had been punished and ditched, so we went back up, made ourselves a cup of tea and had our own bonding. Since then, we both knew we had ten minutes to get downstairs or the boys were off to dinner together, without us! Mark and Dror became buddies and Kathy became my first soul mate at P&G.

Then I had my first child, and "work hard, play harder" was no longer an option. I always tell women—*If you want work-life balance, have kids!* Truly, they bring in perspective . . .

I remember being three months pregnant and I was in one of my toughest meetings. My boss was sick that day and I had to handle it alone. The visiting VP (vice president) was being quite mean, so I excused myself and went to the washroom to breathe. Just then I felt my first kick. I remember looking in the mirror, tears of anger about this VP in my eyes, when a huge smile took over my frown. F*ck him, I am bearing life—what can be more important than that?! I went back into the meeting room and was cool and collected, data-focused, and professional. I refuted all his accusations. I didn't care about what he said, I had perspective!

Mia—my firstborn—arrived in 2002 at La Tour Hospital, Geneva. The whole pregnancy and birth were magical. Maybe it was because I was working so hard that I didn't have time for morning sickness. My boss at the time—the brave warrior, Tammy Minick—was also pregnant (yes, pregnancy was contagious!) and she had her third child one week before Mia's birth. I was lucky to have Tammy and the Geneva Women's Network as my go-to for everything motherhood. One of the best tips they gave me was that same "airplane oxygen mask" principle that I talk about in chapter 7.

So, when the birth came, I knew my "oxygen mask" would be the epidural. Yes, Eve ate from the apple and was punished with painful childbearing, but what does that have to do with me now? Dror and I were sitting watching Muhammad Ali and just as one of the actors screamed "The king is here!" my waters broke. My queen was coming! We rushed to the hospital with our prepared bags and CDs. As we drove up to the hospital, I remembered to call up my doc (in between contractions!) to have her get the epidural ready—I was determined to minimize pain. The anesthetic arrived within twenty minutes, they administered the epidural, and Dror was sent home to rest until the birth started at 9:00 a.m. the next day. We spent the next eight hours, Dror and me, listening to our favorite bands, U2 and Coldplay. My queen came out at 4:44 p.m. and when they put that little creation on my chest and I saw those big blue eyes look up at me, I realized my life would never be the same. I was totally in love with this little girl who gave me my most fulfilling role—she made me a mother.

When I lifted my head to look outside the big windows, I heard Coldplay singing "It was all yellow," and indeed, outside the window the mustard fields were in full bloom and it was all yellow—a bright yellow sunshine girl entered my heart.

I remembered that oxygen mask analogy, and every time Mia cried, I would make sure I took care of myself—that I was well fed and comfortable—then put on the music and sit calmly to breastfeed.

Happy wife, happy life—happy mother, happy other.

Every night at eight o'clock, Mia would start her wailing. Nothing would calm her down and we, as young parents, would stress, waiting for the cops to charge in arresting us for child abuse. We rushed to the doctor one evening when Mia wouldn't calm down—but then he told us, "All babies need to exert their last energy of the day and cry themselves to sleep. It's normal, just let it happen." Mia wouldn't stop crying that whole visit as if to show the doctor and us who was boss, but on the way home, something magical happened. Something about the rattle of the engine and the movement did its trick and she fell deeply asleep. And hence, for the next few months, Dror and Mia had their special date night—he would put on the music nice and loud, let Mia cry, and drive up and down the highway until she was fast asleep.

I took a long maternity break of eight months and, as my husband was still searching for a job, we decided to travel the world. And so, Mia became the youngest jet-setter . . . all she needed was my chest, which happened to be attached to me, so we were good to go! In France, we covered her head with a napkin in the little baby carrier as we ate at Michelin restaurants; in New York we agreed to meet up with friends at Sushisamba, not realizing it was a club. Arriving at the door I greeted my friend (male), gave him the baby carrier (as my husband was parking), and ran in to pee. When I came out, he was surrounded by beautiful ladies admiring the sleeping beauty. My friend was in seventh heaven and insisted he keep holding this ultimate "babe magnet." As Mia was still fast asleep, and we were terribly hungry, we went in, placed her on the table, and danced the night away. She only woke up the next morning to earn the title of youngest party girl ever.

My mom once told me, "You can change your life to adapt to the kids or change the kids to adapt to yours." Well, I think I took her advice a little too literally.

Going back to work was not easy, but again the oxygen mask analogy came in handy for me. We couldn't really afford to have a full-time nanny, so we decided to put Mia in daycare. I will never forget the lesson I got there. The first day I put her in, I stayed for a good hour—she happily played with her new friends, but the moment I got up to leave, she started crying and crying. The school-teachers forced me out of the room and sent me to work. I cried the whole journey to work and much into the day. After an hour, I called, and they told me she was back to playing calmly but I didn't believe them and walked around with such a heavy heart until I went to pick her up at 6:00 p.m. She was in good shape, happy and content. I was hopeful the next day would be easier, but again she was happily playing with her friends until the moment I got up, and then she started crying again. Again, I rushed to work, crying the whole way feeling guilty for leaving her behind. When I came in the third day and Mia started crying again as I stood up, I told the directress I couldn't do it any longer. "Come with me," she said, "and hide here in the teacher's room." I could hear Mia crying for a mere second after I left, and then she stopped and went back to play with her friends.

"You see," said the directress, "kids are very adaptable. Do what is right for you and they will adapt. Mia has moved on; it is just you who unnecessarily carries the guilt into the rest of the day."

After that, I went back to work for another amazing woman, Regi Aalstad, who was also a wonderful women's advocate—she was chairman of the Geneva Women's Network and helped me find my tribe of working moms. But, some of my best lessons for leading like a girl I actually got from my male bosses—like Stassi Anastassov my new general manager (Regi's manager). I found myself pregnant just one month after going back to work and when I went into Stassi's office, all shaking, to tell him I was pregnant again, his reaction was textbook "Congratulations—having kids so close together will be amazing for them. They will quickly become best friends." And then he added, "Make sure to take good care of your health as this is your *top* priority these coming months—we will readjust your workplan to make sure you are not stressed!" Wow. I was so grateful for his empathy and understanding that I worked double as hard to deliver my plan.

And so, Liam was born in July and, typical to his character, he waited in there one extra week, but when he decided to come out, he shot out in just six minutes, wrapping the cord around his neck, which made him look like a purple frog. When they put his little body on my chest, my heart stopped. It was the best feeling in the world. And I noticed, surprisingly, that the song playing was again "Yellow" by Coldplay—and looking out of the window, this time it was the sunflower fields, which painted the view all yellow. My son brought another sun into my heart and that little ugly frog became my beautiful prince.

Having them so close together was indeed an amazing blessing. Mia became very motherly to her little brother, and Liam, who proved to be very competitive, was determined to do everything Mia was doing. "Come, Liami, I show you," was Mia's cue and Liam followed. When Mia learned to dress alone, he followed her; when Mia was two and decided to leave all her dummies (pacifiers) outside the door at night for the dummy fairy, he followed. She even potty-trained her brother at eighteen months—she would sit on the big toilet while he was on his potty and she would tell him elaborate stories until he completed his business. "A peepee in the potty," she would happily sing to him and award him with a hug.

With my third, Anna, the pregnancy wasn't that easy—three months into the pregnancy I contracted cytomegalovirus (CMV). There was a 50 percent chance the fetus would be sick, too—developmentally delayed, hearing loss, etc. But luckily, my little warrior was born healthy and, again, as she was born "Yellow" was playing. This time I looked out of the window to see that the early autumn leaves had all turned yellow—my third sun entered my heart.

When Anna was three, we went to Liam's birthday party where they had a little bungee jump for kids. Mia climbed up but was scared and wouldn't come down. Dror decided to climb up to persuade her and Anna insisted on climbing with him. The play park was about to close, and we were waiting for Mia to jump. We all looked up as we saw her jump, only to discover this wasn't Mia (nine years old), but Anna, at three, doing her first bungee jump. My bravest "lead like a girl" warrior entered our world.

Being a working parent is not easy, especially when your kids' health is involved, but leading like a girl is about focusing on what matters most—the important relationships in your life. And while being dedicated to the job, know that whenever there is a choice to be made between family and work, family always gets priority. Remember, on their death bed, very few claim they wish they'd spent more time in the office! Leading like a girl is also about investing in the support network that will enable you to stay a kick-ass leader while having the family needs in check.

Here are my top ten strategies for leading like a girl as a working parent.

DEFINE SUCCESS HOLISTICALLY—TOP TEN TIPS

I. What are your five roles?

When Mia was born, my first boss and friend Jim shared with me his "hand principle"—we all have different roles in life, yet research shows you can only do five roles well. So I had to choose and prioritize my five roles. I sat down and wrote them down and decided to focus the little time I had on these five roles.

- Mom (this was always going to be first to me)
- Wife
- Career Woman (although I do admit I sometimes wrongly put that role ahead of wife)
- Healthy Athlete
- Social Butterfly

I know this won't work well for everyone, but being far from my parents, I wasn't a daughter who called home every day, but I did my best when I was there to spend quality time (my mom would say I did not do this very well). I also admit I wasn't as close a sister as I could have been. Another role I had to drop was being a close friend to so many people. I focused on a few main friendships, which I nurtured. Despite not being home as much as other moms, my kids and husband knew when there was a decision between work and them, my family always came first. I wasn't always perfect, but as my son said—I always tried.

2. What does "good enough" look like?

Every maternity leave, I would say to my husband, "I can't go back. I am not the perfect mom I would like to be." And he would say, "Look at the long run—what message do you want to send your kids?" A few years ago, I gave a talk on advertising at my daughter's school. On the way home, she told me, "Mom, my friends told me when they grow up, they want to be like you." I realized the message of balance worked. We need to drop the notion of being perfect and accept what is good enough. This is different from person to person and can change over time. Here was the definition for my top five roles.

Good Enough Parent

When the kids were small, "good enough mom" was to spend a minimum of two hours of "carpet time" playing with our kids. Even in Russia, when the long commute meant we sometimes didn't get home until 8:00 p.m., we would take the kids down to the pool to play and enjoy dinner and bedtime stories—they went to sleep later and slept two hours in the afternoon the next day, but we would keep our two-hour rule. Unless we were traveling, we would have every dinner with them and our weekend brunches at home were an event even their friends staying for sleepover wouldn't miss for the world. Birthday fun days were always a big deal. When they were younger and we had to travel on their birthdays, we'd "trick" them and shift their birthdays to the weekend; but when they were older, we did everything we could to be there. The few times we missed a birthday, we were sure to celebrate the full "fake birthday" at the first possible opportunity.

I also knew I couldn't join the Parents Association but did what I could to be involved at their school. I would volunteer to give a talk at school (be it about advertising or Jewish holidays) and tried to join at least one field trip a year with each, so my kids wouldn't be the only ones whose parents never joined. Lastly, we would spend a lot of time and money planning the most amazing family vacations every year. From hiking in New Zealand, diving in the Philippines, skiing in Switzerland, camping in the desert in Israel, and beaching in Thailand and Myanmar, we learned quickly that you *can* buy some happiness—when you spend it on quality experiences.

Good Enough Wife

This was one that was hit the hardest and, admittedly, there were times when I was so engaged in my job that I didn't do as well in this area. But what helped us at the end of day was our "tea and chat" on the terrace, our weekly date-night, and our biannual "couples only" retreat. We will discuss the importance of these retreats in a later chapter.

Good Enough Employee

My second boss, Stassi, was the king of focus—he would always force me to make a "not to do" list on top of my "to do" list and to work the 80/20 principle to identify the 20 percent of effort which yields 80 percent of the impact. I remember him getting mad at me for doing all the little fun scattered projects versus the one big thing which would make the difference. The other principle that helped me a lot in being "good enough" at work was understanding that single-tasking is more effective than multitasking—so when you are at work, swallow the big frog first (do the toughest task in the morning) and just do one thing at a time.

Good Enough Athlete

I would have loved to do sports every day but had to settle for good enough, which was three lots of cardio at a minimum each week.

Good Enough Friend

I focused on a few of my closest friends and invested in those. My best friend, Tzurit, and I met during our army service. We don't speak every day, sometimes we only speak once a month, yet still have we kept our friendship for twenty years. Once a year, in February, we go away together for our joint birthdays. When we meet it is as if we were never apart. My friends know and forgive me for not having time to speak every day, but they know that when they say the magic words—"I would love to talk"—I will make time to spend with them. It may not be as much as they or I would want, but it has to be good enough. Same goes for my parents—I wouldn't speak to them every day, but I would call weekly when I really wanted to call and they knew I would be there when they need me. They accepted the don't HAVE TO but WANT TO rule even if it meant seeing me less often.

3. Make your partner an equal partner.

As I mentioned in the previous chapter, I wouldn't have succeeded in keeping it all in balance without the support of my husband, Dror. Especially with parenting, it is important to make our partners real partners—from bathing the baby to taking up some of the house chores—remember, *what a new father doesn't do in their first year of parenting, they will never do.*

4. Make time for the "big rocks."

You all know the story taught in *The 7 Habits of Highly Effective People.*[1] A professor calls up his students and asks them to fill a jar with tiny stones, then to add small stones, which they manage to push in, and then he gives them big rocks—but the students can only fit half the larger stones into the jar. He asks them to read what the big rocks left out represent—health, love, relationships, etc. He then asks them to start with the big rocks, then the smaller rocks, and finally the tiny stones and, surprisingly, almost all of them fit in—and what doesn't fit is much less important. The moral of the story is that unless you fit the big rocks into your schedule *first* and only then deal with the smaller tasks, you will not achieve those critical goals. I used to encourage my team to develop their Venn diagrams of big rocks—their roles and goals; you are a partner so ensure alone time with your spouse, alone time with each kid, but also alone time with yourself. But don't be shy about combining a work colleague's night out with your husband night out when you're stranded for time, as long as it doesn't become a regular habit. And don't tell me you don't have time for sports—if that is one of your big rocks, schedule it into your week first, and then manage all the gazillion smaller tasks around it!

5. Look after yourself—put the oxygen mask on yourself first, so you can attend to others.

One of your big rocks has to be you! This is not about being selfish, this is about putting a little energy into ensuring you can give to others. Don't underestimate the drain on your coping mechanism from combined sleep deprivation, separation anxiety, work pressures, etc. Identify what makes you feel good and schedule it into your day—be it time in sports, weekend with girlfriends, a pampering bath—do it.

6. It takes a village to raise a child, so ask for help! Delegate and outsource.

I grew up in a culture where having household help is not very common, and was even frowned upon. But then I attended a lecture with Deb Henretta, President of P&G Asia. She said, "Look at help not as a cost but as investment—so you focus the little time you have on the areas most important to you—time with your loved ones versus folding endless piles of washing." And so I started bringing in paid help. I would interview them like I would any P&G employee and pay and treat them well—after all, they were just responsible for the most important people in my life.

On top of that, being away from family, I surrounded myself with friends who were like family for myself and my kids and who stepped in for my kids as they would their own (and we were there for their kids too, of course). My sista Efrat, who was called to the house urgently because my eldest, when she was eight, locked herself in the empty house as she "heard noises." My sista Neta (as my husband and hers are partners, we were practically married), who not only would invite my kids to join hers for trips and outings when we were away but stepped up more than once to sit with my youngest at the hospital through an asthma attack. Her husband Joel, who called late at night to pay a restaurant bill as my eldest's credit card was not working. And my friends Kobi and Anat, who adopted Mia for the year she was in Israel alone. It takes a village to raise a child and I am so very grateful my kids felt they had many aunts and uncles to turn to in times of need.

7. Ask! Don't assume your manager knows what is best for you.

When I started as global director in Singapore, I was really burning the candle at both ends. I had global calls every night (US morning) and often early in the morning, but I would still come in at 9:00 a.m. Singapore time for my daily work, with no time for proper sleep, sports, or life. I was close to burning out when my friend and ex-boss Regi Aalstad told me, "You are in a global role; you need to do night calls, but no one expects you to work double shifts—*take the time back*!"

That was such an amazing relief. I wrote to my boss, Edgar Sandoval, and we aligned a new plan—I started coming in three times a week at 11:00 a.m. I would have breakfast dates with my hubby and work out. I am not a morning person, so I released my US peers from my early morning (their night) and focused our meeting time at 8:30–10:30 p.m., which was a comfortable 8:30–10:30 a.m. for them. Finally, we declared 6:00–8:30 p.m. (their morning) as a black zone so I could spend quality time with my kids. We also banned Friday night calls. This became the standard for US-based teams working with their Asia-based partners and all sides were happy. The US folks were happy we were willing to talk with them during their normal workday and we were happy with the additional flex. Suddenly my team was *the* place to work versus the burnt-out folks in other Asia-based global teams. Your manager often doesn't realize what you are going through and, if they're not a "dick," they should be willing to flex a little to enable you to deliver your best. So don't assume they know what you need, but ask for what you need.

8. Align expectations upfront.

I didn't always have easy-to-manage bosses. Mid-career at P&G, I moved to work under a woman—a tough, single mom who was known to have fired almost everyone working for her and promoting no one. Her favorite sentence was, "Pressure makes diamonds," so you can understand my fear, as I had two young kids at the time. With advice from my mentor and people-expert, Jim, I sat down and wrote an expectations alignment letter: who I was, what she could expect from me (strengths and where I would appreciate her help), and what I expected from her (see worksheet in the next chapter).

I took her out for lunch and first just talked the points through to understand her alignment and sense where she would have some issues, and then a week later, I sent it to her as a kind of living work contract. We ended up having a great working relationship and she even promoted me to associate marketing director. I have used this document to align expectations with every manager ever since and have also used it with my direct reports; we all have our strengths and opportunities—being transparent and understanding each other's needs is the first major investment in a joint emotional bank account of trust.

9. No guilt.

Eight months after going back to work for the first time, I had to go on my first business trip and, to make things worse, Mia became sick just before I left. I had to leave her with her dad in a less-than-ideal state. The trip was to attend a Pampers focus group in Russia. There I was, in cold and gloomy Moscow, listening to the moms talk about how important it is to them to stay home from work a minimum of two years as they didn't want to miss a moment of this critical growth. I was sitting in the back room, ridden with guilt and started sobbing. One of my colleagues—the incredible Nada Dugas—grabbed me by the shoulder and said, "Dalia, if you want to make it as a working mom, you need to develop a no-guilt mentality. When you are home, be a hundred percent home, and when you are traveling be a hundred percent here. Do something fun every time you travel to make it all worthwhile!" That night we booked VIP tickets to see the Bolshoi in Moscow and I made it a habit to have fun whenever I travel, minimizing calling home (kids lose perception of time and calling them every night can be very upsetting) and I would only allow myself to be homesick on the flight home.

10. And finally, be there for the moments that count and make the moments you are there count.

- Your kids will forgive you for missing that odd dinner or two, but they won't be as forgiving if you miss their play—even if they were just a tree, so make every effort to be there for the moments that count (plays, field trips, races, birthdays, etc.).
- When you are there, be 100 percent there. Too often, I see parents coming home on time to be with their families, but then spending all evening with work calls or just being worried about work issues. Kids are the first to sense when you are not 100 percent with them. So put that phone away the moment you walk through the door and enjoy a minimum of two hours of quality time—enjoying the most mundane of tasks and elevating them to magical moments through mindful presence!
- Be a single tasker. I see so many parents rushing to leave work early and take their kids to the park to quiet their conscience, but then they are constantly on their phones while rocking the swing. Women tend to multitask ten hours more a week[2] and also least enjoy both tasks. Yet single tasking is both more effective (as you finish both tasks faster due to focus) and more enjoyable.

Bonus tip—can women have it all? Recognize that different roles take priority at different times—when the kids were young, I decided to take a long maternity leave (including unpaid leave) and return less than full time. To enable that, I chose a role that was "smaller," but I quickly learned there are no small roles, only small people, and this compromise enabled me to be successful in my multiple roles. There were also times where my job was more demanding, and my husband and children had to compromise a little. So, when I am asked—"Can working moms have it all?" my answer is:

Yes, leading like a girl means **we** *can* have it all, but not all at once!

ACTIVITY

My Work-Life Balance Coping Strategies

Make a list of the strategies you would like to adopt in the coming year to better prioritize your five roles; define the "good enough" deliverables. Write them down here.

What I am conscious of dropping? What is my "not to do" list?

Table 9.1. My Work-Life Balance Coping Strategies

My 5 roles	My good enough minimum to deliver	My coping strategies
1.		
2.		
3.		
4.		
5.		

10

BECOMING AN INSPIRATIONAL PEOPLE LEADER

My first boss and people-manager guru, James Michael Lafferty, used to say, "People rise to your highest expectations—or sink to your lowest."

They say the number one predictor of your success in a company is your first boss. You are probably going to be a first boss to many employees. It is a huge responsibility and not to be taken lightly. Too many bosses today are merely managers, but to convert from manager to leader is a whole different ball game. Leaders are managers who have followers. And to have followers, you need to put the hearts of others at the heart of what you do. It's as simple as that. And that is really the essence of "Leading Like a Girl."

Jim Lafferty is not just considered a great people leader, he also became somewhat of an icon for people leadership at P&G. When he left the company, we organized an event where he gave all of his keynote speeches and workshop over one week. The hall overflowed with people; some even came back from maternity leave with their babies to hear Jim's last P&G training. One of these trainings was a course called People Development for New Managers. At that stage in my career, I was a seasoned trainer myself, so I dared to ask if I could colead the course with him. It was an epic moment and many of my people development skills were inspired by learning and then training others in this course. I consider myself very blessed to have had many incredible bosses like Jim, each making me a better leader and, more importantly, a better person. But I only had one first boss. That's why I invited Jim to coauthor this chapter.

I have told you so much about myself. Allow me to share a little more about Jim.

Jim was a physiologist and track coach by training. He coached at-risk African American youth in Ohio. Before working for P&G, he worked part-time at the P&G gym as a contracted trainer. He brought his passion and commitment, and the coaching skills he acquired in his youth, into the corporate gym with great success. One of the brand managers he was training asked him one day, "You have such great people skills, why don't you apply to P&G?" and so he did. Legend goes (and is now confirmed) that at first, Jim was rejected. He was so disappointed that he decided to write HR a note on why he believed they'd made a mistake. Someone in HR liked the courage he showed and decided to hire him after all. He went on to become general manager and had an amazing twenty-five-year career at P&G, later becoming a country CEO for Coca-Cola, and now CEO of Fine Hygienic Holding, all while he was an active business columnist, speaker, and Olympic coach. There are a lot of things you could say about Jim (and he did have quite a few challengers, especially in HR with those who found him at times too "outspoken"), but he always put the hearts of others at the heart of what he did and he had a trail of followers. This chapter aims to summarize our common wisdom on what in our experience is key to transforming a manager into an inspirational people leader: vision, focusing on strengths, creating a psychologically safe learning environment, and coaching for growth.

Being gatherers, women tend to prioritize relationships at work. Developing others, inspiring them, motivating them, and collaborating with your team is collectively the primary skill women should be most proud of and really embrace. It's also an area where men can learn from women. Jim shared that early in his career he was often criticized for being "too good to his people." I've even had several men, like my friend Paul Haury, tell me that they've been told they lead too much like women. The issue is not really about women or men but about the system failing to recognize that people skills are what differentiates leaders from managers. These *soft* skills are actually the *strength* skills needed to deal with today's volatile and ever-changing business world. COVID, with its remote working and enhanced challenges, made these soft skills into survival skills for the seasonal leader.

The issue usually lies in leaders having low self-awareness and believing "pressure makes diamonds."

The role of Human Resources is critical here in several ways: First, HR should enforce leadership assessment tools—the only people who can determine if you are a good leader are your direct reports, so ensure you over-prioritize Leadership Assessment Tools (LAT) with your people. Second, if you want leaders, reward leaders—in P&G talent reviews, you would get a score for your people skills as well as your business skills and you were only promoted if you were top rated in both! Third, some managers just don't know *how* to become good leaders. Every company should invest in leadership training. This chapter is aimed at summarizing some of the tools on the *how* to lead like a girl and become an inspirational people leader.

I. IT ALL STARTS WITH YOUR WHY

In the first chapter, I spoke about discovering your purpose and aligning it to the company purpose. When it comes to company purpose, many organizations mix up mission with purpose, so let me clarify the terms (see figure 10.1).

Vision, mission, and purpose are much more than numbers—it is about why you are doing what you are doing and what your followers will be gaining by following you.

Jim tells the story of how he rallied his first sports team to practice daily. Many of the students came from hardworking families

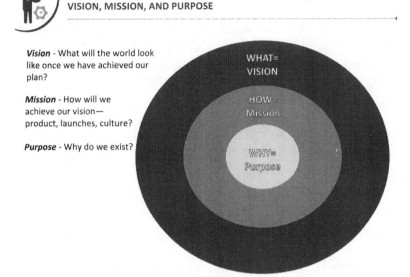

VISION, MISSION, AND PURPOSE

Vision - What will the world look like once we have achieved our plan?

Mission - How will we achieve our vision— product, launches, culture?

Purpose - Why do we exist?

WHAT= VISION

HOW= Mission

WHY= Purpose

Figure 10.1.   Vision, Mission, and Purpose. *Source:* **Simon Sinek,** *Start with Why: How Great Leaders Inspire Everyone to Take Action* **(New York: Penguin, 2009).**

earning low or middle-class wages. It was 1983 and their alternative to track practice was pregnancy and the allure of dealing drugs. Jim didn't focus on winning medals. Instead, he inspired his students to use their athletic prowess as a means to earn a college scholarship and change their lives. This was a much more emotional vision and they followed.

When Jim became my boss, he was appointed head of the Near East team. This included countries that usually don't go together, with the biggest markets being Israel and Lebanon. Jim had a *big* vision. He didn't just want to win in the market, he wanted to also create meaningful change in the Middle East and bring people together.

Jim believed in former Israeli president and prime minister Shimon Peres's "New Middle East peace dream," and he believed Israel and Lebanon were so similar that they had a lot to learn from each other. We were six people on the Israel team, and six on the Lebanese team. While we couldn't, due to political reasons, travel to each other's market, we got to know each other as people, learn about the markets, and see that we were more similar than politicians wanted to admit. Unfortunately, Jim's vision (as well as Peres's) failed when war broke out in the region, but this vision and diversity of thought made us a high-performing organization. All twelve members of the team are successful in their fields, and my counterpart responsible for the Lebanese FemCare markets and I are still friends, making mini visions come true.

When I became a people manager for the first time in the corporate world, it was while I was in Russia and I had a team of six. The team included some very feisty individuals and had a history of bickering. I took them away for the weekend to a dacha (Russian country house) out in the frozen forest to get to know each other as *people*. We spent the weekend sharing our life stories, playing trust-building games, cooking, and enjoying time together. When we came to look at the business, we were able to dig much deeper—who are we serving, what injustice are we trying to solve, what impact did we want to have on our consumers lives? Suddenly each one could connect and link their own life stories and personal purpose to what we were trying to do.

Our vision was clear—we wanted to take over market leadership from historical brand leader Bella. Our mission was to become an icon for high-performing teams in the region, each bringing their personal best and working together to deliver our vision. But it was our WHY that was where our hearts connected—we were determined to inspire young girls in Russia to reach their full potential. I was surrounded by five powerful young women and one young man who all had stories of overcoming personal struggle and they wanted to help consumers do the same.

I very quickly learned that Russians are like coconuts, extremely tough and seemingly emotionless on the outside, but so soft and sweet on the inside. We changed the product and go-to-market strategies and then, in line with our purpose, we created an iconic scholarship program "Be the Star You Are" for girls, transforming our functional benefit of protection to a life benefit of empowerment. Within three years and against all odds, we took over market leadership. I was so proud of my young and talented high-performing team. They were my first high-performing organization, and each of the six are now top of their game. We were changing lives and we changed our own in the process. We had a purpose and a sense of belonging.

Just a few months ago, one of the guys on my team, Tolya, now country manager at Logitech, left a parcel at my doorstep in Singapore. He'd heard I'd pivoted my career to an organizational psychologist and gave me my very own Logitech spotlight slide clicker for presentations. Only when I gave my first-ever lecture at the Singapore Management University did I notice it was engraved with my name. I was so touched. Even though we hadn't seen each other in years, fifteen years later the people I touched (and who shaped me as a leader) were still in my life. As a leader, when you connect from the heart, you not only connect to the hearts of your consumers, you also engage your team in a much deeper way, creating a bond that lasts even fifteen years later.

2. FOCUS ON STRENGTHS

When I reflect on those times, I was in FLOW, delivering to the best of my abilities. My success was not based only on having a clear purpose and setting clear goals. The key ingredient for success in anything you do is the answer to a very simple question that I want you to ask yourself: "Do you have an opportunity to do what you do best every day at work? Are you using your strengths every day?" The majority do not, and yet this is the single biggest driver of performance.[1] Back when I started in 1998, the book *First, Break All the Rules* by Marcus Buckingham and Curt Coffman[2] came out and became a bible for people management at P&G. Based on years of global research by the Gallup group, they challenged what was until then common wisdom. When they asked people, "What is more important for success, focusing on strengths or fixing weakness?" the majority of people across the world said fixing weaknesses. The United States proved to be a strength-based society with 59 percent of Americans believing that to succeed, you need to focus on weaknesses, while a whopping 76 percent in Asian markets, like China and Japan, agreed. And yet, over twenty-five years of research has found that this common perception is simply wrong! When investigating high-performing teams, the most successful leaders do four key things:

1. They select for talent, not experience.
2. They share expectations as destinations without micromanaging the journey.
3. They create effective teams by building on each person's strengths.
4. They motivate people by focusing on their strengths and managing their opportunities.

Yet those 40 percent in this research—those global managers who believed that it is more important to focus on strengths—were disproportionately more successful and happier.

Gallup researchers went on to teach managers around the world to focus on their own strengths and neutralize their weaknesses (using strengthfinder.com). The researchers repeated their research a few years later, and what they found has changed the way we think about leadership.

- Focusing on strengths makes business sense for the individual and the company:

  - People who exercise their strengths every day report a three-times higher quality of life, and were six times more engaged at work.
  - Organizations that apply strength-based leadership see up to a 20 percent increase in sales and a 30 percent increase in profit, as well as higher customer engagement and lower turnover.

- Strength-based leadership is significantly better for organizations and individuals. Yet Gallup research found that only 12 percent of people are focused on their strengths every day.

    - Even worse, when asking about their performance reviews with their managers, the research found that most managers don't focus at all on strengths or weaknesses (40 percent), and if they did focus on any, they focused on weaknesses (36 percent). Only 25 percent of managers focus their performance reviews on identifying strengths.
    - Despite this research being done back in 2001, managers still do not know how to provide strength-based feedback that inspires growth.
    - Only 14 percent of employees and only 8 percent of managers strongly agree that the performance reviews they receive inspire them to grow.[3]

I consider myself very lucky. Throughout my seventeen years at P&G, I had managers who focused on my strengths—some I didn't even know I had! I still remember my first performance review. My boss Jim spent a whole hour with me pinpointing my strengths; they were strategic thinking, goal-orientation, and creative ideas. When looking at my opportunities, he helped me pinpoint how each strength, when overused, could lead to weakness. The feedback went something like this:

Dalia—
You are very goal-oriented and will deliver on your goals no matter what—which is incredible, as I know I can trust you to deliver, even against all odds.

You may want to watch out, however, that in your zeal to get things done, you don't overlook getting the buy-in from your stakeholders. You should spend more time listening and understanding their needs, even if it means slowing down. The goal is important, but the process is just as important. Just take the time to build a good foundation before you paint the roof on the house. You are so goal oriented that I know if you pay attention to this process and results idea, you will nail it in no time.

Bingo! This feedback was very well accepted because:

1. It was balanced.
2. It was delivered with care.
3. I understood my weakness as an overuse of a strength that needs to be tweaked.

Being so goal oriented, I dedicated my time to focusing on my weaknesses. I worked really hard to eliminate them for the following year. But this same issue kept coming up. I shared this with my boss, to which he replied, "Dalia, your weaknesses don't really ever go away; what you do is learn to neutralize them, manage them, but you focus on your strengths. Neutralizing your weaknesses will help you avoid failure, but it is your strengths that will make you soar."

You see, it is human nature for our brain to focus on the negative. Dr. John Gottman calls this the 5:1 Rule. He found that we hear negative input five times louder than we hear positive messages. We need five positive interactions or feedback to negate the impact of each negative one. This ratio has been found to be true in relationships (predicting divorce) as well as the ideal praise-to-criticism at work.[4]

This is why we need to actively search for the positive qualities in the people who work for us. Peter Drucker, father of modern management thinking and author of *The Effective Executive: The Definitive Guide to Getting the Right Things Done*, said,

> Only when you operate from strengths can you achieve true excellence. . . . One cannot build performance on weaknesses. . . . It takes far more energy to improve from incompetence to mediocrity, than to improve from first rate performance to excellence. . . . It is the abilities, not the disabilities that count.[5]

Focusing on strengths doesn't mean ignoring weaknesses; it simply means finding ways to overcome them. This could be by focusing on a "good enough" level of competency or outsourcing for complementary talent.

> The point here is not that you should always forgo this kind of weakness fixing. The point is that you should see it for what it is: damage control, not development. And as we mentioned earlier, damage control can prevent failure, but it will never elevate you to excellence.
>
> —Donald O. Clifton, *Now, Discover Your Strengths.*[6]

It also doesn't mean lowering your standards.

My P&G bosses were extremely demanding and held me to the highest standards. When I didn't perform at my best, they didn't criticize me but instead helped me understand I could do much better. When this happened, I was very committed to not disappointing them again.

Every person has unique strengths—play people to their strengths.

During our people development course, Jim shared a story that stuck with me. It is called *The Animal School*, by George H. Reavis. The story talks about a rabbit who had a nervous breakdown as he was forced to swim, a duck who was forced to stay after school for running classes, and a squirrel who failed flying classes. The moral is clear: every person has unique strengths. Don't try to force people to be the same as you but find and nourish their unique strengths. There is this overriding obsession in big companies today of turning everyone into "jacks of all trades; masters of none." They force people into roles that are not a good fit, and then fire truly outstanding individuals who, when put in the right place, would be absolute superstars. As a leader, your role is to help your people find their strengths and then put the right people in the right seats on the bus, in roles where they are able to exhibit their strengths every day.

3. PSYCHOLOGICAL SAFETY

This term was coined by William Kahn (1990) as the ability of the employee to bring their full self to work "without fear of negative consequences to self-image, status, or career," and that it is key for employee engagement.[7] Harvard Business School professor Amy Edmondson has dedicated her career to this important cultural concept, which she has enhanced at a team level and defined as "a shared belief amongst individuals as to whether it is safe to engage in interpersonal risk-taking in the workplace."[8] In 2012, Google researchers, through their Project Aristotle, found that psychological safety was the underlying driver of high-performing teams.[9] Their research showed that when an employee feels psychologically safe, not only does their engagement and satisfaction increase but so, too, does their performance—all by encouraging an open-learning culture, creativity, and innovation.

Amy Edmondson created the psychological safety team assessment, which is based on four key components.[10]

1. *Attitude to risk and failure*—The degree to which it is permissible to make mistakes.
2. *Open conversation*—The degree to which difficult and sensitive topics can be discussed openly.
3. *Willingness to help*—The degree to which people are willing to help each other.
4. *Diversity and inclusion*—The degree to which you can be yourself and are welcomed for this, creating a sense of belonging. This is such an important topic that I have dedicated a whole chapter to this point (chapter 11).

A leader's role in setting this environment is primarily through concepts like openness, trustworthiness, clarity, and caring candor. The leader's role has a ripple effect and employees supported by the leader through open and clear communication are more likely to reciprocate similar supportive behaviors to their team. On the flip side, just as positive behavior is contagious, negative behaviors from the leader can be equally contagious through the effect of mirroring.[11]

Once the leader sets the stage by creating shared expectations, focusing on strength, and coaching for growth, Amy Edmondson talks of two further steps to enhance psychological safety at a team level.

1. Inviting participation to establish that communication is welcome.
   - A leader must first acknowledge knowledge gaps and invite inclusive feedback.
   - A leader must practice humble inquiry and active listening.
   - A leader must set up systems to enable information gathering and create forums for input and guidelines for discussions.

2. Responding productively to destigmatize failure and welcome continuous learning.

   - How a leader responds to data and suggestions is critically important.
   - Express appreciation—listen and acknowledge contribution.
   - Destigmatize failure by offering help and discussing fail forward learning and alternatives.

How the leader responds to any boundary violation is also critical. If any colleague is disrespectful to another, the leader's role is to immediately set the expectation for nonjudgmental candor with care.

I have included Edmondson's famous "Psychological Safety Team Assessment" (table 10.1), as well as the manager's checklist at the end of this chapter.

4. COACHING CULTURE: OPENNESS—TRUST— CLARITY & CARING CANDOR (OTC)

Once you have a vision and a purpose and have identified your people's strengths and the culture you want to achieve, the question is how to create an atmosphere of coaching.

But the foundation is the relationship between you and your reports. As Jim always likes to say, "Coaching is like medicine—the 'patient' must swallow the medicine! If they 'spit out the pill' then the coaching you give is ineffective." You need to lay a groundwork such that your people assimilate what you teach them. Jim has labeled this OTC (just like over-the-counter medicine). So here is the OTC medicine to create psychological safety and a coaching culture:

Openness

Openness means exactly that—being open. It means being open to people as individuals, and being open to our own biases, which we all have (see the next chapter for a self-test). Being open and encouraging alternative points of view so people speak up and share their views lets people bring their full selves to work.

We must abide by the principle that our people are measured on objective performance and nothing else. If they feel they have to conform to some kind of view of the world that you embrace, they cannot be themselves and they won't be happy or perform at their peak levels.

Great leaders change. You may have to confront your own biases, even those you didn't know you had. You may be judging people on their political or religious beliefs or with regard to personal choices they have made. If you are doing this, I can assure you that you are not as effective a leader or coach as you could be. And honestly, what business is it of yours? Why should we, as coaches, care?

Jim shares the story of the first gay employee who approached him; his response has been consistent for three decades. The employee said to Jim, "You should know I am gay." Jim replied, "I don't care. It doesn't matter to me. What matters to me is your performance in the role you are in and in helping you in every possible way. Your personal choices have no bearing on your career with me. Who you spend private time with and sleep with has zero influence. And when we have corporate events, your significant other is always welcome. We don't judge here. We are a meritocracy."

He always got a huge smile, a thanks, and often tears of joy. *Stay out of it.* A person's private life is their private life. It should have no bearing in the workplace. Tattoos don't matter. Piercings don't matter. Political views don't matter. Sexual orientation doesn't matter. Let this stuff go. Become a coach who focuses on results and substance, not style.

Trust

Without trust, the coaching relationship is DOA—dead on arrival. Trust comes from a few key things. The first is the coach *must be 100 percent honest at all costs, particularly when it comes to career and performance.* There is no room for "positioning" or "selective omission" when it comes to performance or coaching. This doesn't mean we are mean. We should, of course, deliver the truth with dignity and respect for the individual. But our people deserve to know the realities of how they are doing. If they ever suspect or learn that what you say to their face is different from the story you tell about them behind closed doors, their trust will instantly dissipate. You will suddenly be called "a two-faced leader" behind your own back. They will think they cannot trust anything you say. Every time I have seen a leader play the game of having "two sets of books" on performance—one they tell the person and the other they tell management—that leader ended up failing and losing their team's confidence.

People deserve to know how they're performing at work; they deserve to know if they're getting it right, and if there are areas in which they need to improve. Understanding their own performance allows people to make the best decisions for themselves and their families. Too many coaches sugarcoat or lie to their people out of pity or their own selfish desire to be loved. This is a massive rat-hole you don't want to go down.

An additional element of the concept of trust is that your people must know that you have their best interests top of mind. They have to feel that you are in their corner, that you want them to succeed. One of the most toxic work situations I have ever witnessed is when a boss and subordinate are in competition for either a senior boss's praise or fighting for the same promotion! It's toxic. The boss always needs to be the one to take responsiblity. *Never* ask your people to do work, and then put your name on it. *Never*. This destroys trust. Let people take credit for their own work. Let them attend key meetings and present what they did. Doing otherwise just undermines trust.

Clarity and Expectation Alignment

Many leaders today fail to provide clarity to their people. What does success look like? What do you expect them to do? How far can they push the envelope? Give them some clarity and parameters!

This goes beyond a scorecard. It's aligning expectations. I learned this from Jim, and I do it with every new boss and every new employee. At the end of this chapter, I have added Jim's original expectation alignment that he does with team members. I have prepared mine and use it with all my direct reports. It is also a very important process to use with your managers. I shared with you the story of the first expectation alignment document I created. I once worked with a manager who I knew had no kids and who had a very different approach to work-life balance. I had two young kids and was terrified of how we would get along. I prepared an expectation alignment document and insisted in our first meeting that we discuss what is important for her as well as for me. Working with her wasn't easy, but we learned to get along well. After two years, she promoted me. We had clarity. I knew what she expected and I overdelivered. She, in turn, allowed me the flexibility and autonomy I needed to perform at my best.

Caring Candor and Tough Love? How to give feedback

This is probably THE most important attribute of a coaching culture and hence I will elaborate on how to give great feedback. Some cultures (like Netflix) have made feedback core to their culture, but this is still a development opportunity area, especially in Asia, where people avoid conflict to keep harmony. They either avoid giving feedback (which is worse, since bottled-up emotions can cause passive-aggressive behavior) or they seem to prefer to give feedback to the boss versus directly to the person (as I shared with my Korean colleague). This is the worst thing you can do to build trust. Every manager should take the time to learn the art of feedback—clear caring candor, also referred to as "tough love." I call this process D'MAP, 4 stages for feedback: **D**iagnose; **M**ake it pinpointed; **A**ppreciate; **P**rescribe (figure 10.2).

Step 1—Diagnosis

When one of your people is not performing up to your expectations, you need to put your thinking cap on and assess *why*. Don't just

D'MAP- HOW TO GIVE TOUGH LOVE FEEDBACK

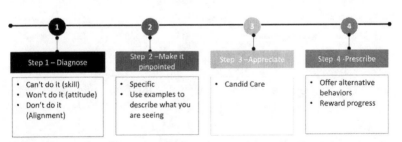

Figure 10.2. D'MAP—How to Give Tough Love Feedback.

jump into feedback! A good coach is like a good doctor. You have a patient (your people). You have an illness (a performance issue). You don't just "give pills"! You have to think and assess and make a *diagnosis*.

Jim uses a "Can't—Won't—Don't" (CWD) initial assessment model that asks, "Why is the person underperforming? Why don't they do what we ask or is required?" There are only three possible reasons:

1. **They can't do it.** This means they lack the skill or knowledge. Or it could be a lack of intrinsic ability. A "can't" assessment most often leads to coaching or special training. If, however, the "can't" is rooted in an intrinsic inability, take for example a weakness in thinking skills or intellectual horsepower, this is usually cause for moving them off the team and into a role that is better suited to their skill set, or otherwise out of the company.

2. **They won't do it.** This means you have someone *choosing* not to do something because they don't want to. This indicates an *attitude* issue and needs to be dealt with as such. Calling it out and dealing with it can lead to an attitude change; or it can lead to termination if the person doesn't take the coaching. When it comes to attitude, it is important to pay attention to those underlying limiting beliefs we talked about in chapter 5. Often underlying bad behavior is some inherent fear.

3. **They don't do it.** It's not a matter of ability (can't), and it's not a question of attitude (won't), they just don't do it. In my experience, this is *the* most prevalent cause of employee underperformance. And it's also one of the causes of employee termination mistakes. *Don't* means they don't know what is *expected* of them! And this comes back to expectations. Expectations are about the end results you seek and ways of working. Have you been doing this with your teams?

Step 2—Make it pinpointed

Whether it is *can't, won't*, or *don't*, there is going to be a need for feedback from you. The more specific, the better. Vague feedback doesn't help anyone! Let's go back to the doctor analogy once again. Let's say a patient goes to the doctor and says, "I have a pain in my leg." This is vague. It will be hard for the doctor to prescribe treatment with this information.

So what does the doctor do? The doctor encourages pinpointing! "Show me with one finger exactly where the pain is." With more information, the doctor can then begin to diagnose the source of the problem. Hip pains are leg pains. Knee pains are leg pains. Ankle pains are leg pains. But each is entirely different and requires different treatments!

When you give your feedback, it is key to pinpoint, and do it with candor and care. It's admittedly an art form. And it takes practice. But anyone can master pinpointing.

Pinpointing, in simple terms, is this: giving feedback that is action-oriented, such that the person will know *exactly what to do* within ten seconds of getting the feedback.

Let's bring this to life with a common example. The number-one performance issue in Fortune 500 companies today is *leadership*— leadership issues and the lack of good leaders are prevalent at many levels in the company. P&G used the 5E model to describe key facets of leadership: **E**nvision, **E**ngage, **E**nergize, **E**nable, and **E**xecute (figure 10.3).

Let's take, for example, a young manager with five years' experience who is put in charge of a big, complex, and important project. She leads the project team. Like any project, it keeps hitting issues and unanticipated obstacles. The team is very quick to give up and claim the project cannot be done. The young manager accepts this at face value and reports this back to her boss, who finds this conclusion unacceptable. So the boss digs in. After pushing here and there, and challenging the team, they finally find a way to get back on track and keep the project moving forward. The fact that the boss has to step in indicates to the boss that the young manager needs

5 E MODEL OF LEADERSHIP

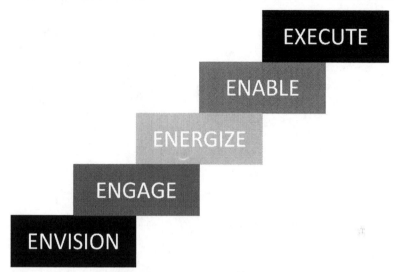

Figure 10.3.   The 5 E Model of Leadership.

some leadership development and coaching assistance. As a result, the boss has a one-on-one with the young manager. The boss gives the young manager useless feedback: "I need you to step up and improve your leadership."

This feedback is unhelpful because it is vague. Leadership is complex. It has many facets. Nobody is good at all elements of leadership, and nobody is a poor performer in all aspects. The boss's feedback would be helpful if it were *pinpointed*. By its very nature, pinpointing indicates the next steps that need to be immediately taken. A generic "you have to lead better" comment helps no one. Use examples to describe what you are seeing.

Many leadership issues stem from the challenge to identify and rally the team to overcome obstacles—the feedback can be pinpointed in this way:

> As you know, leadership is a complex topic. You are a good leader
> in many respects—for example, your ability to *envision* what needs

to be done—but there are some areas in which you need to sharpen your skills, especially in the area of *energizing* and *enabling* your team to look for solutions rather than capitulate. I have noticed when the team came with the issues, you very quickly accepted their POV and reported to me it is not possible. I think you need to halt your inclination to "go with the team" every time they hit a wall. As team leader, I would like to see you rally them to find solutions, potentially creating war games scenarios and brainstorm solutions, instead of focusing on problems.

Now, if you give someone this feedback, they have a good idea of what they can and will start to do differently at the next team meeting. They start to improve!

Step 3—Appreciate with care

Pinpointed candor is key. Another important criterion is that the "patient" understands that the feedback comes from a position of *caring* rather than judgment; that is, you are taking the time to pinpoint accurate feedback as you believe in them and care about their growth.

Step 4—Prescribe: Suggest alternative behavior

Finally, good feedback offers a tangible alternative behavior. This focus prompts a growth mindset, helping your employee gain insight into how they are behaving and how they are perceived. Once you understand the root cause of the issue, you can construct a plan with the employee to take small steps to develop and exhibit new behaviors. Notice and reward these little alterations to allow her to see the value in these new behaviors. For example, in the case above, encourage your employee to seek feedback and to listen before sharing their valuable thoughts. Provide praise of progress to encourage the formation of new beliefs. Listening and then reacting builds more credibility than jumping in.

Going back to my own story, when I received caring feedback, I was able to "swallow the pill" and was constantly growing, but when I received denigrating feedback with no psychological safety or

Openness-Trust-Clarity, even if some of the feedback was valuable, I spit out the pill, as it elicited a fight-or-flight protective response. Sadly, many companies promote managers to become people leaders without this fundamental training, but there is a *huge* difference between a manager and a leader—as a leader, you are no longer managing the business but managing the people who manage your business! This is why it is essential for companies to invest heavily in people skills and, even more importantly, if we want to eradicate assholes from the workplace, to ensure that every employee is measured on the basis of their business performance AND their people performance. HR needs to be clear: you need to be a top performer in both aspects in order to progress. It's as simple as that.

As I am editing this chapter, the Israeli rhythmic gymnast Linoy Ashram just made history by winning the all-round gold in Tokyo. Tears are running down my face. As a former competitive rhythmic gymnast, I have been following Linoy and her coach Ayelet Zussman for a few years now and they really bring to life the principles of people leadership. Ayelet is extremely demanding, but she is also extremely nurturing—her kiss to Linoy before she steps out to do each routine is iconic. She looks Linoy in the eyes and says, "You can do this. I believe in you. Go do your personal best." These women are amazing not just because they are the first non-Russians to bring in the gold in twenty years but also because of their journey. While the impressive Russian twin sisters, Dina and Arina Averina, were clear that they came to win the gold, Linoy and her coach were always focused on enjoying the art—working as a team, constantly calling each other with new ideas. As Ayelet once said, "We work hard as we want to be our best, but the journey is always more important than the medal."

Leading like a girl is about this *and* being extremely demanding and setting high standards but *also* putting the people above everything, being supportive to enable your people to reach these high standards. As Jim used to say: "Take care of your people, and the business will take care of itself!"

That's leading like a girl!

ACTIVITY

WORKSHEET—PSYCHOLOGICAL SAFETY TEAM ASSESSMENT[12]

If your team all strongly disagrees on the first three items in table 10.1 and strongly agrees on the last four, then the team is high on psychological safety. Otherwise, as a manager you need to review what else you could be doing to drive psychological safety (see figure 10.3).

Table 10.1.   Worksheet—Psychological Safety Team Assessment

	Strongly Disagree	Disagree	Neither Agree/ Disagree	Agree	Strongly Agree
1. If you make a mistake in this team, it is often held against you.					
2. People on this team sometimes reject others for being different.					
3. It is difficult to ask other members of this team for help.					
4. Members of this team are able to bring up problems and tough issues					
5. It is safe to take a risk in this team.					
6. No one on this team would deliberately act in a way that undermines my efforts.					
7. Working with members of this team, my unique skills and talents are valued and utilized.					

Credit: Amy Edmondson

PSYCHOLOGICAL SAFETY - THE LEADER'S TOOLKIT

Setting the Stage	Invite Participation	Manage
Leadership Tasks:	**Leadership Tasks:**	**Leadership Tasks:**
Frame the work, emphasize purpose	Show humility, inquire, listen,	Appreciate, destigmatize failure, take risks on new ideas, punish boundary violations
Create Shared Expectation and Purpose	**Create** Confidence That Voice Is Welcome	**Create** Culture of Continuous Learning

Figure 10.4. Leaders' Tool Kit For Building Psychological Safety. *Source:* Amy C. Edmondson, *The Fearless Organization: Creating Psychological Safety in the Workplace for Learning, Innovation, and Growth* (Hoboken, NJ: John Wiley & Sons, 2018).

WORKSHEET SAMPLE I

Expectation Alignment with Employee or Manager

Dear _____:

In expectation of the time we will be working together, I would like to share with you a few general principles based on which I try to operate and based on which I hope to establish the basis of our working relationship.

Integrity, Honesty, and Trust

These are the three most basic principles. They are linked to each other, and they are especially crucial when establishing a working relationship. To me, integrity means having the intention of doing the right thing in everything I do. Being honest is directly linked to that. I don't like politics and I believe that being transparent is almost always the right approach. Showing integrity and being transparent creates genuine trust in people and trust is what can truly transform a working relationship.

What you can expect from me: I will go to great lengths to create a relationship between us that is based on mutual trust. My door is always open to you and you can expect me to be transparent. I will call things by their name. With management, I will be your advocate and will show your results off, ensuring that you are on their radar. I will also absorb some of the pressure from above.

What I expect from you: Be honest and transparent with me in any situation. Ask questions—any question. Have a tendency to over-communicate on your work and plans, allowing me to build trust in you and your abilities. Sometimes, I might make decisions that you don't like. Once the decision is taken, I will ask you to support me and move on.

Strategic Thinking

We are in it for the long run and we must be led by a clear strategy in whatever we do. This is the only way we can build sustainable brands and businesses.

What you can expect from me: I will set the strategic direction for my brand and I will set priorities for the team accordingly. I will strive to eradicate work that is not linked to these priorities. I will base decisions on what is strategically right even if that might be a tough choice in the short term.

What I expect from you: You will be doing a lot of firefighting and you will be working on many projects that have very urgent deliverables. This is often a key part of the Associate Brand Manager (ABM) role. However, I expect you to keep the "big picture" in mind in your daily work. When you come to me, I expect your

POV and your recommendations to be well thought through and based on data.

Leadership

The marketing function leads the business teams. We make things happen. Concepts and strategies are worthless if they are not led through to execution. It is our job to lead and motivate the multifunctional team to deliver that execution.

What you can expect from me: I am ultimately responsible for the brand and, as such, I will be in charge of developing a strategic vision for the business and setting priorities across the team. I will provide you with strategic guidance and give you the big picture, but I will not undermine your authority. Finally, I believe that it is better to take a wrong decision than not taking a decision at all.

What I expect from you: You are the leader of all your projects. You are in charge of them, and I expect you to drive them proactively. Involve me upfront to align on objectives and deliverables and keep me updated regularly on the project status. Do not hesitate to elevate an issue if you are stuck. You will make mistakes along the way, as we all do. I don't expect otherwise but I do expect you to learn from your mistakes and not make them more than once.

Collaboration

This is *the* key skill in the business environment of the twenty-first century. No matter how brilliant you are or how strong your leadership skills are, you need to be able to work well with people from all backgrounds to succeed.

What you can expect from me: I spend a lot of time and effort building strong working relationships with people. I will greatly appreciate and value seeing you doing the same with your team.

What I expect from you: You don't need to be everyone's best friend, but it is crucial that you are able to build real, genuine working relationships with your team. Make people enjoy working with you.

Passion and Ownership

Passion for what we do is what can drive results from good to excellent. We need to develop a feeling of ownership for our business just as if it were actually our own business. With that mindset we will go the extra mile—every time.

What you can expect from me: I will have a huge passion for my brand and how to bring it forward. As such, I have high standards of excellence and I try to challenge the status quo. It would greatly motivate me to see you developing the same kind of passion and I will greatly value your strong ownership for your projects. That is what will let me give you increasing freedom in everything you do.

What I expect from you: I expect you to truly own your projects. You need to feel completely responsible for them. At times, you might find yourself at the end of the line, tying up loose ends and sometimes cleaning up other people's mess. This is part of the manager's role. Know your business better than anybody else.

Focus and Simplicity

It's results that count.

Focus on the 80/20 principle. It should guide our work and we should always aim for substance over style. In large companies we sometimes tend to overcomplicate things unnecessarily. We are not in the field of rocket science. We are also not a charity but a profit-maximizing organization. In the end, it is only the results that count.

What you can expect from me: I am pragmatic and focused on delivering results. I will set clear expectations for you. It is not necessary to impress me with style or words. It's results I value and reward.

What I expect from you: Be focused on your deliverables that are outlined in your project list. This is what I will hold you accountable for. When new tasks arise, discuss them with me before spending time on them.

The Power of Data and Communication

In this company, we work and decide based on data. Data is the only thing that management will accept and value. Our communication has to be clear and simple—both written and verbal. This is what allows our voice to be heard.

What you can expect from me: I will be open to any conclusion or POV you have if it is data based, even if it's contrary to my intuition. I will coach you on a daily basis to be clear in your communication and I will always be open to your feedback on my communication.

What I expect from you: Be clear in your communication. People will judge you not only by what you say but also how you say it, be it in spoken or written words. I expect you to develop a high standard in business writing and I will be picky to help you achieve this. Develop your opinions and recommendations based on the available data.

People

Procter & Gamble is a "promote from within" company. Our life-blood consists of our people. Therefore, hiring, retaining, and training strong people is absolutely key for us. Training needs to have highest priority.

What you can expect from me: As your line manager, I am responsible for your intercompany education and I am dedicated to setting you up for success. I will ensure that you find the time to take all necessary corporate and functional trainings. I will also give you relentless coaching and open feedback, be it good or bad. Expect me to debrief with you after every major meeting or event.

What I expect from you: Have an open attitude to my feedback even if it might be tough at times. Also, I expect you to start developing a sense of building the organization. Find one or several meaningful projects that expose you to this kind of work.

Work-Life Balance

As mentioned, our company is not a charity, and we are not saving the world on a daily basis. It is key to recognize and ensure sufficient time for our private life.

What you can expect from me: I think we have one of the greatest jobs in the world and I am fully dedicated to it, but I also have private priorities that are equally as important as my professional ones.

What I expect from you: Nothing. This is entirely up to you. However, I would advise you not to dedicate your entire life to your work. Make sure that you have a rich and enriching private life to which you can look forward. Enjoy the ride.

—James Michael Lafferty, People Development Course P&G, 2006

WORKSHEET SAMPLE 2

Feedback Is a Gift—Tips for the Manager

1. *People don't drastically change*—Let them become more of what they are versus trying to force them into something they are not.
2. *Focus on their strengths*—Be able to describe in detail what they do well and help them build a plan for what they can do better.
3. *Tailor your approach*—Break the golden rule of treating people as *you* would like to be treated and treat people how *they* would like to be treated. Not everyone is motivated by money. If you don't know what motivates your employee— *ask* when they felt proud.
4. *Learn to pinpoint.*

HOW TO RECEIVE TOUGH LOVE FEEDBACK

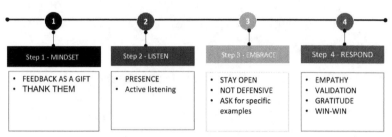

Figure 10.5.   How to Receive Tough Love Feedback.

WORKSHEET SAMPLE 3

Feedback Is a Gift—Checklist for the Employee (or HR Facilitating Feedback)

1. Mindset—Feedback is a gift.
   - First, please make sure you do *not* jump to the negatives. Spend time understanding your strengths—whether in a 360 or a do-it-yourself evaluation. The free strengths finder I use with all my clients is found at https://www. viacharacter.org/survey/account/register.[13]
   - Create a work plan leveraging your strengths. If you are really good with people but don't have a team, how can you do more of what you are good at?
   - Explore whether or not your strengths are overused. What opportunities arise from overuse of that strength?
   - Understand your development opportunity areas. Aim to deeply understand the feedback. If others see you in that specific way, don't be defensive. It is their perception of your behavior.

2. LISTENING = SILENCE—Be silent and really try to understand.

   - If any of the feedback triggers you emotionally, be emotionally intelligent and apply the CENTER and ACT principles explained earlier: create time and space to reflect. Observe your negative emotions with friendly curiosity—why were you triggered? Often when there is a strong emotional trigger, it is a sign there is an underlying fear—what are you afraid of?

3. Embrace

   - Try to really understand the feedback especially when it is consistent, understand why this behavior was perceived the way it was (overuse of strength? ask for specific examples of behaviors), and work with your boss or a coach to understand. What is the *behavior-thought-motivation* behind this perception?

4. Respond

   - Apply empathy and reframing—understand that you may not have meant to behave that way, but something about how you came across gave the others that impression. Seek for the win-win.

   - Clarify your work plan with your manager. This work plan needs to include primary projects that build on and further enhance your strengths while finding solutions to neutralize your weaknesses.

   - Neutralize versus eliminate your development opportunity areas. One of my first bosses once said, "You know, your opportunities won't drastically change over your career." I remember thinking, *Wow, this guy really doesn't self-develop.* I ended up concluding he was right—you never completely eliminate a development opportunity area. You just neutralize it and stop it from limiting your focus on strengths.

11

WOMEN HOLD UP HALF THE SKY

DIVERSITY, EQUITY, AND INCLUSION

Supporting Women's Progression Best Practices

This chapter is intended for the diversity, equity, and inclusion (DE&I) advocate and any leader desiring to create a more inclusive workplace. I coauthored this chapter with my dear friend and women's empowerment advocate Vanessa Steenkamp, Senior Human Resources Manager, Asia Grifols pharmaceuticals.

Vanessa unexpectedly passed away in July of 2021 while she was pregnant with twin girls and before the book was published. Sadly, her girls did not get to meet their incredible "Lead Like a Girl" advocate mom, and so I have dedicated this book to her and her prematurely born girls, Mila and Vivian, in the hope and belief they will continue in her footsteps and be proud of their kind, huge-hearted mom. I am grateful that I am able to capture her legacy and passion in this chapter.

In writing this chapter, we have also consulted with Hanan Heakal, former Global Diversity, Equity & Inclusion Leader for P&G, and current co-founder and managing director of Next-Level

Inclusive Leadership. Hanan spent an impressive twenty-eight years with P&G where she was global DE&I for over fifteen years.

My goal is to share the successful best practice tools that we've discovered in the organizations we've worked for over the years. We also offer some practical worksheets to help you on your DE&I journey to encourage more women to bring their best self to work and lead like a girl.

As women who started our careers in a corporate setting and rose up the corporate ladder, we've seen just about everything in the workplace: the good, the bad, and the very ugly. We hope to help expand the good and eliminate the ugly.

This book is about being brave by using a decidedly feminine approach and leading like a girl. To do this, women need to be supported in the workplace for their uniqueness and authentic feminine leadership style. This can be done in several ways. But first, let's talk about bias, the root of many ill practices.

THE UNCONSCIOUS BIAS

A father and son are in a horrible car crash and tragically, the dad dies. The son is rushed into the hospital and wheeled into the operating room and suddenly the surgeon says, "I can't operate on this boy. He is my son."

How can this be?

If you got the riddle right, you are among a very tiny few, because the mind model most have about surgeons and doctors is that they are male. But this surgeon was the boy's *mother*.

Unconscious bias is a simple and unintended preference or stereotype that affects behaviors and decisions that are formed by our socializations, beliefs, or personal experiences and are deeply ingrained in our memory. These active filters help us make quick assessments and categorize individuals based on visual cues such as gender, ethnicity, profession, culture background, height, religious identity, body size, etc. In other words, by default and without rationalization, we will find affinity or aversion to people, and then label them based on the way they look.

In fact, it's proven that our corporate decisions related to recruitment, performance appraisals, networking, and career advancement can all be highly affected by our own biases. The end result of bias-influenced decisions directly affects the financial results of a company, the company culture, and the level of employee engagement and satisfaction.

You may be surprised to learn that you are biased. Don't be dismayed; we all are. That is why we all need to make a conscious effort to turn it around, together.

Supporting women to be better leaders, managers, executives, and happier people in general starts with getting rid of biases that specifically affect women negatively, biases like: women can only do certain jobs, women of certain ethnicities shouldn't be promoted due to lack of trustworthiness, women who are moms can't handle promotions or heavy workloads, or one woman on a team is enough. These unconscious biases need to be stopped, and it starts with all of us. We must reframe our experiences to be more inclusive and less exclusive.

DOUBLE STANDARDS

On top of hidden biases, our socialization has created expectations on masculine and feminine behavior. Any person who doesn't live up to those expectations is frowned upon. And so we see the troubling phenomenon where men who are connected to their feminine traits are often told they are too soft and emotional, or too caring of their employees.

On the flip side, women who behave in a more assertive manner are seen as "bitches" and unlikable. Some of the double standards I have heard over the years:

Speak up and share your views. / Why are you confrontational?
Be persuasive. / Why are you so pushy?

Make sure to take credit for your work. / Don't over self-promote.
Work hard. / Don't be such a busy bee.
Don't be naïve. / Don't be political.
Anger is a legitimate reaction to frustration; crying is not.

How about: Lead like yourself—lead like a girl!
For a provocative video on these double standards women face,
watch "Be a Lady They Said."[1]

THE BUSINESS CASE FOR DIVERSITY

The business case for diversity has long been established. In their
2015 research study, Diversity Matters, McKinsey & Company
defined diversity as having more women in senior roles and a more
mixed ethnic/racial composition in the leadership of large companies.[2] They go on to say that achieving and maintaining diversity is
not only the right thing to do but has been proven to increase creativity and innovation, and improve company productivity.

How can companies succeed if they are not taking care of half
their workforce, and how can they expect to innovate if they don't
fully understand more than half of their purchasing population?

Psychological safety and inclusion

Inclusion drives business. This has been demonstrated in the research on psychological safety at work, which I briefly covered in
chapter 10. Psychological safety is about speaking up, asking for
another's point of view (POV), listening deeply, and being oneself.

When an employee feels psychologically safe, not only does their
engagement and satisfaction increase, but so does their performance
and, more importantly, their ability to create a psychologically safe
environment for others. The role of the leader is paramount in driving openness, inclusiveness, support, and integrity:

Employees supported by the leader to achieve psychological safety are more likely to reciprocate similar supportive behaviors to their team, and this ripple effect can create a psychologically safe environment for the broader team. On the flip side, just as positive behaviors are contagious, so are a leader's negative behaviors which can spread through the effect of mirroring.[3]

Feminine leadership traits are proven to better fit modern-day leadership challenges

In 2012, researchers at *Harvard Business Review* wanted to evaluate whether men are really more effective than women as leaders. They hoped to try to explain why there are so few women in senior leadership. They found that women leaders are equally as effective as male leaders. In 2019, they repeated the research study. This time they found that not only were women equally as effective as male leaders, women actually scored higher than men in 17 out of 19 leadership traits.

So why is leading "like a girl" still an insult?

What about leading during a crisis? COVID-19 has proven that feminine leadership traits are vital for dealing with today's VUCA world—a world of **V**olatility, **U**ncertainty, **C**omplexity, filled with **A**mbiguity—in fact, seven of the nine countries that have best dealt with COVID-19 were led by women. What these women have in common is the way in which they used their feminine power to lead; they did not declare a premature and early victory with the know-it-all attitude of their male counterparts but rather used their OTC skills (we covered them in chapter 10)—**O**penness, **T**rust, and **C**larity.[4]

- **Openness:** Instead of pretending they know it all, they were humble and consulted experts. They also used technology for free early testing, indicating that saving lives was a priority.
- **Trust by telling the truth:** Angela Merkel, retiring chancellor of Germany, stood up early in the pandemic and calmly told the people that this was a serious bug that would infect up to 70 percent of the population. "It's serious, take it se-

riously," she said. There was no blaming or sugarcoating, which helped create trust and transparency even without having all the information.

- **Clarity and decisiveness:** Female leaders were clear and decisive in their communication, imposing the earliest lockdowns and explaining clearly why it was needed and why the nation should follow precautions. This inspired a feeling of a shared destiny through teamwork.
- **Candid candor and empathy:** They all combined clarity and decisiveness (typically seen as more masculine traits) with down-to-earth motherly empathy. For example, Norwegian prime minister Erna Solberg and Danish prime minister Mette Frederiksen both held live broadcasts to address their nation's children, in which they expressed that it was legitimate to be scared and that everyone's support would be needed to overcome the crisis. This, in turn, elicited unprecedented support for following instructions as well as comradeship.

HOW CAN COMPANIES LEVEL THE PLAYING FIELD?

1. We get what we measure

Set clear diversity and inclusion goals and cascade them to *all* leaders. Everyone in the organization should have clear expectations with regard to the importance of diversity and inclusion in their sub-unit. British consumer goods company Reckitt Benckiser has openly shared their DE&I policy and the goal to double the number of females in senior management positions from 20 to 40 percent by 2020. Most companies today have some similar DE&I targets.

2. Look beyond the numbers to foster a culture of inclusion

Setting goals is important, but there is much more to diversity than just determining numbers. As hiring managers and executives, you must ensure the right person gets the job, for the sake of both women and men. Targets only make sense if you have two equally adequate candidates and you select the woman. Forcing hiring of unqualified women just to meet the numbers is not a good strategy and just causes frustration among both women and men. Choose the best person for the job.

In addition, ensure more women get hired *and* cultivate the inclusive culture to adopt their somewhat different POV; having one woman on the board is not enough if you don't create the psychologically safe culture required to encourage them to speak up and have their diverse point of view *heard.* If you want their voices to be heard, at least 30 percent, but ideally 50 percent, of your leadership team should be women; their unique points of view should be not only respected but sought out. Don't try to change them or expect them to behave like men. Be inclusive. Encourage them to lead like the women they are. That is what diversity is all about.

3. Raise awareness of inherent biases

As mentioned, we all have biases. Be open to evaluate for competence, not style!

As Sheryl Sandberg puts it in her book *Lean In*, "Success and likability are positively correlated for men but negatively correlated for women."[5] Socialization has taught us that men should be tough and women nice.

In her book, she points out the lack of confidence women experience, often suffering from a phenomenon called impostor syndrome, which is a psychological term that refers to a pattern of behavior wherein people—even those with adequate external evidence of success—doubt their abilities and have a persistent fear of being exposed as frauds. This has been proven to be more common among women.[6]

Sandberg refers to research showing that men reach out for opportunity more than women—men will submit themselves for a role with as little as 50 percent of the skills while women will wait until they have 90–95 percent of qualifying skills.

Knowing this, you can act as an ambassador for gender equality. Reach out to women you think may qualify and push to ensure an even split among men and women, even if more men than women apply, and even if it means having to fish for good female candidates. The women may not get the role, but they should be encouraged to put themselves forward. The more qualified women step forward, the better chance you have of reaching your goal of 50 percent women.

Because gender bias is real, help your team by running a bias test to help raise their awareness to their own blind spots—for example, Harvard's Project Implicit Social Attitudes.[7]

4. Senior DE&I leadership

Most great leaders understand the relevance of DE&I practices; however, they also understand that DE&I leadership is a journey that involves the sponsorship of their top management. It also requires educating teams to be aware of and to resist unconscious bias. Finally, it is about making every leader responsible for educating and eradicating unconscious bias-led decision making. Procter & Gamble was selected for many years as the best company to work at—and it all started with top management making DE&I a top business strategy.

5. New manager's training

At P&G, we ran new people manager training for anyone who recently became a people leader (within three months of promotion). One of the women's network initiatives was to include a section on DE&I in this training. This started with the most senior leader talking about a strict anti-harassment policy, what it means to be a working mother, and the appropriate response to avoid biases. For example, the *only* appropriate response when your employee tells you she is pregnant is—"Congratulations." The appropriate response to anyone crying in your office is to recognize that it is as a sign of their passion, not weakness, etc. Empathy is elicited when all managers understand the world through their female employees' eyes. Establishing DE&I as an expectation of every young leader helps make it common practice at all levels.

6. Women's networks

We wish for a day when there will be no women-specific challenges. But until then, we have found that women's networks and support groups in the workplace are a great way for young professional women to hear from more senior women role models. These frameworks help expand women's connections and help them feel supported and provide a sense of belonging through sisterhood support. The format was very simple (an example of our P&G women's network workplan is shown in table 11.1 at the end of the chapter). Once a month, the women's network would convene to hear a speech from a female senior manager, or a He4She manager (see following discussion), or a panel on a given subject. Hearing these different stories helped women identify with different roads to success and adopt the habits that would help expand our toolbox of coping strategies.

If your company doesn't have an internal women's network, seek to create one, or search within your professional community for one to join.

7. He4She advocates

Diversity cannot be achieved with just a minority point of view. As Chimamanda Ngozi Adichie said, "We should all be feminists."[8] Without men caring just as much about women's rights and appreciating female leadership traits, we will not be able to lead to the change we need in the world. Many women's networks ask, "What do we do about the men?" We always reply with encouraging them to invite men and to secure as many men as there are women in a leadership team, at a minimum of 30 percent. These passionate partners can then be appointed He4She advocates who can provide other men with a better understanding of the issues that face working women, role modeling for the rest of the organization.

8. Mentorship programs

Many companies are starting to adopt mentorship programs. A mentor at work is someone (not your line manager) who advises, guides, teaches, inspires, challenges, corrects, and serves as a role model and as a voice of experience and wisdom. A mentor cares both about the business and the individual. The mentor should *not* be directly involved in career decisions, nor does he or she replace a coach. The mentor is there as an experienced guide to:

- Act as a challenger.
- Encourage reflection.
- Share personal experience and company perspective.
- Help identify strengths/weaknesses.
- Be politically savvy enough to connect the mentee with other valuable resources inside and outside the organization.
- Research has shown that employees who have mentors are twice as likely to stay in their job and have higher job satisfaction.

One way to get this started is by getting senior leaders to register online as mentors and providing the online setting in which mentees can approach them. Accepting a mentee would then occur on a first-come-first-serve basis. At P&G, we also held annual "speed dating" events to encourage all young employees to seek a mentor.

But what if your company doesn't have an official mentorship program? If so, why not set one up as a personal organizational project? I always encourage young managers to be bold and approach a senior leader with whom they have a good connection and ask them to be their mentor. Consider that the worst-case scenario is that they will say they are too busy, but many others will be flattered and take you on.

The key is to remember that mentoring is a two-way relationship. It is vital that you as the mentee take the lead on making this mentorship relationship work. Think of ways you can add as much value to your mentor as they add to you. For example, help them with digital transformation, introduce them to a new app, give them cool vacation ideas, or simply be their younger ears to the ground. Just like any relationship, a good, long-lasting mentorship has both individuals contributing to the relationship! See a mentoring guide in the next chapter.

Lastly, it is important to seek at least one female and one male mentor. This is important in order to understand different approaches and POVs.

9. Policies

The best way to ensure that top management culture permeates the organization, is to ensure supportive policies. Here are some of the most important policies that worked for me:

Maternity policies

In some cases, P&G went against local country laws, extending maternity leave in Asia to equalize with that in Europe. One of the biggest successes of the women's network in Europe (and why it was loved by both men and women) was its inclusion of paternity leave policies. It is well documented that the more a father is involved in his baby's first year, the more capable and supportive a father he will be; therefore, society and companies should encourage both men and women to take time off to attend to their babies and ensure that men and women share the load of child raising. It is also important to discourage managers from putting pressure on mothers and fathers to come back too early. Being a new mom is a very special experience. I am saddened to hear that many managers still encourage their female employees to "return early" or give them "some work to keep busy." Mothering a newborn only happens once with each child. A young mother will be a better employee in the long term if she is enabled to fully devote her time to her newborn during maternity leave. Finally, having a tip book for new mothers is always helpful. A "Managing Maternity Checklist" (tables 11.2–11.4) is included as a bonus at the end of this chapter.

Flex work arrangements

As a young mom in Russia, I was really struggling with the commute, which could take as long as three hours during winter. One day, I plucked up my courage and asked my general manager if I could work from home one day a week. My manager, Daniela Ricardi, looked at me and said, "As long as your results are delivered, I don't care if you work from the moon." She also added, "I actually would like you to role model this behavior and write about your experiences."

It turned out to be such a success for the company that it led to our adopting flex work arrangement policies. For me it was a lifesaver. I found that uninterrupted, I was so much more effective. I would often sit there in my home office, in my pajamas, from 7:00 a.m. till 5:00 p.m., sometimes forgetting to eat. As an employee, it added value because this was often my reading and inspiration time. I was able to focus on reflection, learning consolidation and reporting. Too often, we are in such a rut working on a problem that only when we take a break from our regular routine are we able to solve it. I also found that my team was more productive. While I was always available to them, not having me physically there encouraged them to be more independent and solve many of their issues themselves. As a mom, I would sometimes take my lunch break to eat with my husband or be available for my kids when they woke up from their afternoon nap. Sometimes I would even take off a full evening so that we could spend time together as a family. I often worked more hours on these Fridays at home, and I was definitely more productive. It was a win-win. From then on, I worked from home one day a week for the rest of my time at P&G. I also believe that that was my most important coping mechanism as a young mom.

But, working from home is a huge privilege. It exemplifies the trust a company has in you, so I always made sure to live up to this trust. While I occasionally stepped out of my home office when the kids came home, I would indicate I was on lunch break.

I know COVID-19 has forced many parents to balance working from home and taking care of children. Ideally that would be an exception and working from home should not be a replacement for childcare. I hope and expect that hybrid models of home and work will become a norm post-pandemic, but it is a privilege not to be abused. In my case, I was lucky to have a nanny at home while I worked. I never took this privilege for granted and, of course, would cancel on days when I knew it was important to be at the office (i.e., top management visits). When I provided my team with this privilege, I emphasized that this is a huge privilege based on trust. You will be amazed how committed employees are when they feel trusted.

Less than full-time/job sharing

Many companies allow young parents to come back less than full-time for a temporary period after childbirth. The common understanding is that most jobs can be adjusted to an 80 percent schedule (but the manager must be committed to having a work plan suited to 80 percent to avoid an employee being paid for 80 percent but working 130 percent). If an employee wanted to reduce their workload to 50 or 60 percent, P&G would usually design a new role (temporary assignment) for up to twelve months. Some companies also tested out job sharing (two women leaders doing the same job each at 50 percent) with some success. I, personally, went back to an 80 percent workload for three months with my two older kids, and worked on a special finance and marketing project at 60 percent for six months with my youngest. This flexibility was tremendous and helped me ease back into the role.

Return to work policies

Some parents decide they want to stay home for a few years when kids are young. I personally do not like the term "stay home" (we all know kids do not stay put and the role of a stay home parent is often extremely demanding!), with a more appropriate title being "COO of domestic affairs." How we recruit and enable these parents to return to work is critical. Invest in up-skilling as needed, allow the flexibility, but don't underestimate the incredible new skills acquired from project management to conflict resolution—you will surprised by the transferability of these skills to the work place.

Maternity rooms

With more and more women planning to breastfeed their newborns for longer, P&G and other companies created maternity rooms. These relaxation rooms were equipped with special nap chairs and changing tables and had state-of-the-art breast pumps. My lunch-time naps during my last few months of pregnancy were a lifesaver. When my kids were born, I often had my nanny bring my babies to me during my lunch break, for a feed and cuddle. The room was also equipped with a fridge (to avoid having to walk back to the office with breast milk). The room also encouraged spouses of employees to bring their babies to visit their fathers at work. This was a small investment that went a long way, showing employees the company's commitment to parenting and work-life integration.

10. Zero tolerance on harassment

Every company should have an ethics hotline where misconduct complaints can be submitted anonymously. Most critical is a zero-tolerance policy for cases of harassment and sexual abuse. In a clear case of misconduct, an employee would be immediately removed and the case dealt with as transparently as possible for other employees and managers to see.

I have given quite a few examples from P&G, as it has been ranked as a best company for women for many years, and because I have personal experience there. But I am committed to expanding this list, so please do reach out to me with other ideas you saw working at other companies. The more we share, the more we can help great companies create better standards that enable women (and men) to feel psychologically safe and bring their "full self" to work to the benefit of all!

I am often asked, "Why are there so few women in leadership positions? And what are the mistakes women make in the workplace?" These questions indicate the reason lies in mistakes *women* make, but I believe, that while women may tend to have more limiting beliefs and tend to suffer more from lack of confidence, the main issue is with the workplace environment. It is too masculine and exclusive of the different yet valuable input women bring to the workplace and the unique needs of women. I hope the research and success of women during the crisis of COVID-19, as well as this toolkit, will help leaders understand that instead of expecting women to behave like men to succeed, pushing them to adopt fake confidence, there is value in the inherent strengths women bring like empathy, intuition, and teamwork, and a successful leader will be one that will adopt a more balanced approach of positive feminine and masculine traits. Opening your minds and hearts to DE&I is a needed skill from any leader—it is the right thing to do and it is good for business, creating a more inclusive, creative, and productive organization.

Women hold up half the sky: How are you enabling and role-modeling this in your organization?

ACTIVITY

WOMEN'S NETWORK CHARTER P&G ASIA 2013

WOMAN—Women of Marketing Asia Network *Team Charter*

Purpose: Connect, Inspire, Educate, and Grow the Women of Asia Marketing

Equity: A sisterhood of like-minded women empowering each other to be the best they can be.

Objectives of the WOMAN Team

1. Better diversity of women at all levels.
2. More flexibility recognized and "role modeled" as a key enabler.
3. Awareness of programs and resources to help specific challenges for women at work.
4. Support/mentoring for career through life stages (beyond just work)—including mentoring up.

Rules of Engagement

- R&R among team leaders: Divide and conquer each topic led by one person from core team plus three passionate activists.
- Meeting Drumbeat:

  1. Core team monthly connect/annual FTF (Face To Face).
  2. One time per quarter with leadership team.

Table 11.1.   WOMAN Action plan 2013 key focus areas

1. Being successful while managing life changes—key pillars

(Panels and best practices sharing)
• Managing maternity (Mama)
• Career and family planning
• Managing flexibility/work-life balance
• Dual career/location free
• Split family
• Managing elderly parents
• Singles club

2. Women sisterhood and mentoring

• Annual speed-dating mentoring event
• "Just coffee" ongoing mentor database for mentee outreach

3. Bringing the Outside In: My top 10 tips to being a working women—role models

Format: Monthly meetings led by WOMAN for women but open to men who wish to join.

MANAGING OUR MATERNITY: CHECKLIST PLANNER

Ownership of this process is twofold: It is a shared responsibility between an individual and the employee's last supervisor or assignment planner or the respective successor.

Mutual Owners of the Process

*Name of Employee:*_____

*Name of Supervisor/Assignment Planner:*_____

Table 11.2. Maternity Checklist: Before Maternity Leave

BEFORE MATERNITY LEAVE	Action	When	Who
	Inform your direct manager.	When comfortable	Employee
	Inform the team.	When comfortable	Employee
	Inform Employee Service Center/HR about pregnancy.	Immediately	Employee
	Take care of employee during pregnancy; align on priorities for the remaining period and set clear timetable.	Start immediately and finish as appropriate	Supervisor
	Start discussing plans for later parental leave and desires to return to work.	Timing as appropriate	Supervisor/ Employee
	Develop a timetable and a backup plan for the period of maternity/parental leave. (Please note quite often absenteeism increases due to pregnancy. Be prepared for this.)	Start of maternity leave minus 6 months	Supervisor
	In case you are looking for a replacement, forward job description to Employee Service Center for potential job posting. Please take into account that you cannot replace the maternity leavers until childbirth.	Start of maternity leave minus 6 months	Supervisor
	Receive written maternity plan from HR.	2–3 months prior to maternity leave	HR
	Set an appointment with nurse to discuss childcare possibilities.	Ideally first trimester of pregnancy	Employee
	Important: Write annual performance plan indicating last supervisor, last area of responsibility, key skills and last rating in order to facilitate return/onboarding when returning from m/p leave. Forward original annual performance plan document	1 month prior to maternity leave	Supervisor

BEFORE MATERNITY LEAVE	*Action*	*When*	*Who*
	to Employee Service Center for filing. Important: Write interim letter of reference to document current performance of employee (if timing is too short for an annual performance plan).		
	Work to finalize logistics (computer/office/parking).	Last working weeks prior to maternity leave	Employee
	Agree with maternity/parental leaver how to stay in touch during leave.	Last working weeks prior to maternity leave	Supervisor/ Employee

Table 11.3.   Maternity Checklist: During Maternity Leave

DURING MATERNITY LEAVE	*Action*	*When*	*Who*
	Notify HR and fill in e-form to activate maternity leave plan.	2 weeks after childbirth	Supervisor
	Stay in touch while maternity/ parental leave. Talk at least every 3 months—continue to show employee on the organization chart ("on maternity leave"). This is mandatory. Examples of staying in touch: • invite to trainings • invite to Christmas lunch/ social events • provide update on organizational change	During maternity/ parental leave	Supervisor or Successor
	If supervisor or assignment planner changes, please notify: • maternity/parental leaver • your successor (including thorough onboarding on this process) • Employee Service Center	Immediately	Supervisor

DURING MATERNITY LEAVE	Action	When	Who
	Important: Inform supervisor and Employee Service Center about return to work.	3 months prior to planned return to work	Employee

Table 11.4.   Maternity Checklist: Preparing the Return

PREPARING THE RETURN	Action	When	Who
	Plan assignment (check last annual performance plan which organization, which job, full time/part time, etc.). If you need help on this, contact Employee Service Center. You can also get background information on Flexible Work Arrangements from Employee Service Center.	3 months prior to planned return to work	Supervisor
	Organize childcare. Since this is a difficult subject, this step requires time and the employee might need support from your supervisor and Employee Service Center.	3 months prior to planned return to work	Employee
	Develop onboarding plan.	1 month prior to planned return to work	Supervisor
	Fill in required documentation (for child allowance and P&G reimbursement).	ASAP (minimum of 1 month before returning)	Employee
	Welcome maternity/parental leaver and start of onboarding program.	First working day of maternity leaver	Supervisor

TOOLKIT FOR DIVERSITY AND INCLUSION (DE&I) IN THE HR CYCLE, *VANESSA STEENKAMP*

HR Cycle Processes: Attraction; Staffing; Development & Performance Management

Table 11.5. HR Cycle Process: Attraction

ACTION	Human Resources	Managers	CEO
Create an Employee Value Proposition (EVP) that incorporates diversity and inclusion.	Design and implement together with the top management and a trusted consultant the EVP that will drive the talent strategy for your company in the next 5 to 10 years. *Key question: What is the talent needed to deliver the business strategy?*	Actively share your thoughts about the best talent profile that will drive your results from good to greater.	Sponsor and advocate for diversity.
Publish your EVP in your company website.	Partner with the Corporate Communication Department to set the tone. *Key question: What is the best channel to attract the talent in your market (website, ATS, social media, university fairs, etc.)?*	Be an ambassador of your company employee branding. Remember you represent your company at all times. *Key question: Do you act as an owner?*	Make one action that shows your commitment to your D&I work plan. Prepare your speech and deliver the messages so they can cascade down. *Key question: Ask yourself, if you had a daughter who could inherit your position, what kind of culture do you think she would need to succeed in corporate life with continuity?*

ACTION	Human Resources	Managers	CEO
Represent your company at all times.	Represent your company at all times.	Represent your company at all times.	Represent your company at all times.

Table 11.6. HR Cycle Process: Staffing

ACTION	Human Resources	Managers	CEO
Involve your staffing team, HR team, and People Managers on your D&I Policy.	Implement focus groups or workshop to ensure everyone is in the same page.	Speak up about your concerns and ideas that can contribute.	Allow time in the agenda of your team members to see this as a high priority.
Training/Refresh Interview Skills	Engage with an expert of Culture Change so you can have a smooth delivery on the concepts. *Key questions: How do we attract the candidate? Do you think someone will not be comfortable? Who can be your champions to influence the audience?*	Be open and curious but do not ask overly personal questions re motherhood plans. *Key questions: How do we attract the candidate? Do you think someone will not be comfortable? Who can be your champions to influence the audience?*	Opening the session will show that you are serious about it.
Screening Interview	Prepare a list of questions that are a reflection of your company values and behaviors. *Key question: If the candidate name was not in the resume or cover letter, would the profile go into the next step of the process?*	*Key questions: How would you feel if your younger sister or your daughter was requested to share her motherhood plans in an interview? What do you think about the company?*	

ACTION	Human Resources	Managers	CEO
Ensure your talent pool covers your D&I policy.	Explain and align with recruitment partners the expectations on the candidate pool. *Key question: What kind of publicity do I want my recruitment partners to do for my company and D&I policy?*	Check your KPIs in D&I and take the recruitment opportunity to balance for better. Remember you can choose the best and still be fair during the process. *Key question: What kind of diversity do my teams need to deliver the best results?*	

Table 11.7. HR Cycle Process: Development and Performance Management

ACTION	Human Resources	Managers	CEO
Performance Management	Introduce D&I rule during the performance calibration. *Key question: Is the quality of the examples the same while describing performance for women and men?*	Prepare the key facts about the performance of your team members. Try your best to separate the gender from their level of deliveries. *Key question: Do you have a personal preference for any of your team members?*	Ask your team members to meet the higher performance in your company. *Key questions: Is the high achiever selected by your management the one you consider the right bar for the future? Are they too tough or too soft?*

ACTION	Human Resources	Managers	CEO
Compensation and Benefits	Analyze to ensure that performance and merit increase are aligned **regardless of gender.** *Key question: Do you have equal pay for equal job?*	Assign the merit increase only looking at the performance rating and without looking at the name of the employee. *Key question: If there was not a budget, would I ask for something extra?*	Review together with the compensation team how competitive your salary is and benefit of your key players every year at all levels.
Promotions	Analyze your rationale on promotions during the last 3 years. *Key question: Can you detect any difference in career advancement for women versus men?*	Promote and celebrate the good results among your team but also with other key stakeholders. *Key questions: Are you promoting equally and providing the same exposure to your direct reports? Has the promoted employee worked with same manager all the time or can someone else validate the promotion?*	Send the promoted employees a thank-you note for their contributions. *Key question: If the Communication Portal publishes the promotions, does it look even in diversity or you can identify a consistent trait?*

ACTION	Human Resources	Managers	CEO
Talent Management	As you go through the conversations regarding pipeline, analyze if there is any preference toward gender. *Key question: Do you have an even proportion of women and men identified as High Potential or Key Talents?*	Choose one or two key talents from your team but, most importantly, promote and invite someone from another team to work with you. That shows your commitment to develop talent. *Key questions: Am I giving them the same kinds of projects to deliver? How different is the delivery according to the environmental circumstances?*	Casually meet the talent pool. You will always want to engage them to retain them. *Key question: Does this sample of employees that represents the talent align with your D&I policy?*

12

POSITIVE POWER:
BECOME POLITICALLY SAVVY

The quality of our relationships determines the quality of our
lives.

—Esther Perel

This chapter is dedicated to improving relationships with colleagues at work. In my recent transition from director to vice president, I was suddenly confronted with a totally new skill—the need
to evolve from focusing on coaching and managing my team as a
leader to managing my colleagues as a C-suite member. Managing
politics became a core part of my job, but I don't think I was very
good at it; so this chapter is not about what I did well but what I wish
I would have done better.

I have always thought of myself as having good interpersonal
relationships. In the early days of my career, I had a good working
relationship with my peers, but this was much harder later on.

Actually, in my first three years of work, I believed I worked in
an HPO—high performance organization. Each one of us was in
charge of their domain, the role boundaries were clear, yet we were
also a very tight group of friends. We all moved to the headquarters
in Geneva at the same time so we lived close to each other, spent our

weekends together, and we became each other's second family, even traveling together recreationally and also for work. Our boss would often arrange really fun activities. In the summer we would take our lunch break to go water skiing on the lake, and in winter we would go rollerblading in the new parking lot being built. There was some natural competition of course. In the *olden days* (as my kids like to say), back in 1998, we would receive printed share reports into our inboxes and rush to see how our brands were doing. If our brand's shares were up, we were heroes for the day, but no matter who won, there was always a strong team spirit and we always stepped in to help each other no matter what brand we were working on. We were all high achievers, but we were also friends. More than friends, we were family.

I am going to cover four aspects of relationships at work that I found most critical: Best friends, support networks, mentorship, and being smart about office politics.

I. DO YOU HAVE A BEST FRIEND AT WORK?

Gallup[1] conducted their famous research on the key elements that drive engagement and satisfaction at work (as measured by retention, productivity, profitability, and customer satisfaction). They had a total of twelve questions (hence the Q12 of the engagement questionnaire). These included questions on clarity, purpose, etc. However question number ten raised eyebrows among many CEOs.

"Q10—Do you have a best friend at work?"

Quite a few senior managers frowned upon seeing this question. Many believed that employee chitchat and/or long lunch breaks wasted time, and that having close friendships was detrimental to productivity.

Gallup's research surprised everyone by showing a very strong correlation between answering the question positively and good performance. Only 20 percent of surveyed people answered this question positively; but in organizations whose employees answered this question positively at a rate of 60 percent, profit was up 12 percent, engagement rose by 7 percent, and workplace accidents plummeted by 36 percent.

This was found true for both men and women, but most drastically among women. In fact, women who agreed they have a best friend at work showed double the engagement at work than women who didn't have a best friend at work.

Interestingly, when Gallup softened the word "best" to "good" or just "friend," the impact on productivity wasn't as high, indicating a *close* relationship is a key dynamic among high performance organizations. Leading like a girl is being active about fostering these friendships, for oneself and for one's teams.

Having a best friend at work is not only correlated with better performance, higher profitability, and greater satisfaction, it also leads to higher retention rates. Smart employers know that employee loyalty to each other is often stronger than organizational loyalty. Employees know their peers will help them during stressful and challenging times, sometimes even more than any outsider best friend could understand. Those who have a best friend at work also show significantly lower levels of stress, a critical coping mechanism in today's rapid-fire environment.

As I reflect on my career at P&G, I notice that I spent a lot of time building deep emotional connections and that, at different times, I had three best friends in the organization. These were my ultimate go-to friends for professional advice, and for better understanding people and politics.

When I was a young, newly promoted manager, I had the pleasure of leading what I consider to be a breakthrough P&G training course called Women Supporting Women. This program was so successful in driving friendship and emotional bonding between peers at work and creating a sense of belonging that the regional president decided to convert this program to become a co-ed People Supporting People. After several successful workshops, I flew in to Moscow to be on the P&G staff of a pilot training program for the sales community in Russia.

This was somewhat of a traumatic experience. On day two of the program, we take employees through a process called Life Map—where each employee is requested to share their highs and lows in their life. This process usually leads to "peeling the onion," and is a turning point for employees. But with this cohort, things were different. Things are going okay and then this guy throws a wrench into our spokes—one of the regional managers stood up and said bluntly, "Please stop with this psychological bullshit, I separate my work and personal life, and do not want them to mix." He refused to take part in the exercise. This prompted a senior manager, known to be a fierce iron lady who many feared, to say, "I haven't told many of these stories to my closest friends, why would I share them with a total group of strangers?"

Despite these comments and attitudes, the course director and general manager, Daniela Ricardi, whom I mentioned earlier, decided to push on with the process. By the end of day two, we started to see the ice melt, and by day three we saw the same amazing closeness we observed in other workshops. People put down their guard and started to see their peers as people. Many friendships were formed as people got to learn about others' life stories and understand what makes them tick.

This is when I learned the importance of cultural sensitivities. As I mentioned earlier, my Russian friends were like coconuts—hard and protected from the outside, but ever so sweet inside.

A few months later I decided to make a brave career move and I relocated to Russia. That fierce Russian manager became my direct boss, and the regional sales manager my peer. I don't think I would have survived that assignment if not for the personal connections I made thanks to the People Supporting People course.

My new role in Russia came with a promotion to brand manager where I tried to reapply everything I had learned. I shared earlier how I took my team for a weekend at a Russian dacha—we shared our life stories and what inspired us, as well as our individual and common goals.

I am proud to say that that little team of six became my first HPO. We not only turned the business around, we also stayed in touch, attending each other's weddings and sending each other family pictures, and all of my six Russian stars went on to become amazing managers, each now holding VP/CEO roles in key international companies.

What is the role of the leader in promoting friendships and a sense of belonging at work?

As you transform from manager to inspirational leader, your core role becomes about creating a high performing organization of team players. This is *not* about forcing people to be friends, but about creating a culture of collaboration and inclusion. Doing this requires:

1. Psychological safety—promoting open communication and collaboration, even during conflict. This is especially critical when people are not located in the same location, as during the COVID-19 crisis when people were working from home. As a leader, this requires going out of your way to connect personally with your employees and not limiting your interactions to work transactions.

2. Creating ample opportunities for people to get to know each other *as people*. The life map exercise is still my favorite as I form up new teams.

3. Role modeling and rewarding expected behaviors. Culture begins at the top. If a leader keeps their distance and doesn't take part in social events, why would their employees want to spend time at these events? If a leader bad mouths or accepts bad mouthing in their presence, or gains power through divide-and-concur type of behavior, then how can they expect a collaborative culture?

Leading like a girl is about being active in creating this sense of belonging at work.

2. DO YOU HAVE A SUPPORT NETWORK?

I still remember the first woman I met at P&G. Her name was Sandrine Montsma. It was at the P&G recruitment event at Tel Aviv

University, where I was studying. She went onstage while nine months pregnant and said something I will never forget: "I am here on stage with this huge belly to prove to you that you can have an immensely successful international career and be a mom." She made such an impact on me that I carried her words for years to come—I had met my first woman role model.

A few years later I joined the first-ever Geneva Women's Network (GWN) led by my first female boss, Regi Aalstad, a mom of four. I didn't have any kids back then, so some of the topics were less relevant to me, but these amazing role models had a profound impact on me, especially with regard to the plausibility of becoming a working mom at P&G.

I joined the GWN in 1999; in 2002 I was on the organizing committee; and in 2003 I issued, on behalf of the GWN, the booklet "MOM: Managing Our Maternity" to help summarize policies, tips, and advice for women going on maternity leave, as mentioned briefly in the last chapter. I watched with great pride as women in different countries approached me asking to translate it; it was translated into twenty-six languages across Europe, with the P&G president for Western Europe, Mr. Paul Polman, awarding it the diversity initiative of the year.

When I moved to Russia as a young mother manager, I established RWN (Russia Women's Network) and later SWN (Singapore Women's Network).

I led this in parallel to my "day job" and we kept our meetings light-effort as we learned that just bringing women together on a monthly basis to discuss current issues and hear stories from different successful role models was extremely inspiring. We also created annual mentoring "speed dating" events, which later became online mentoring programs.

The results of this work were measurable. Despite Switzerland being one of the countries where a return to work after maternity was the lowest globally, our women retention rate in Geneva was among the highest in the industry and P&G was consistently selected as the best company for women for a decade.

In contrast, years later, as the only woman in a C-suite of men, I wasn't as good at seeking this network outside of the company; there was not enough time and not enough senior women who could give me advice, though that is when I needed it most. Leading like a girl is being active about creating a support system for yourself and for others.

3. DO YOU HAVE A GOOD MENTOR?

Even though I led P&G's formal mentoring program, I didn't find my mentors via the speed dating events (although these were still very useful for people with less exposure). Many of my mentors were former bosses—people who know me well, have seen me working, and know my strengths and potential pitfalls very well.

I have learned so much from each of my amazing mentors and would not be where I am today without their "tough love." They helped me understand the "political buzz" about me, defended me when I wasn't in the room, and gave me amazing career advice.

These mentors were there for me at critical points in my life.

When we got the offer to move to Moscow, we went to visit. Everything we saw was depressing, but my former boss and friend, Jim, said to us, "an expat role with two young kids will be the *best* thing for your career and will set your little family on a totally different course financially." We trusted him and decided to take the role, which set life on a totally new trajectory.

Over a casual dinner with another mentor, Stassi, my husband shared his dream to move to Asia. While sitting in a talent review, Stassi became aware of an opportunity in Singapore and helped me get the role.

And they were there for me beyond my career: at my wedding, helping my husband find a job, providing parenting advice, helping me manage my work-life balance—heck, one of my former bosses and mentors, Alex, even gave my husband and me a weekend hotel voucher so that we could spend more time together (as he mentioned he had more hotel points than time to use them).

In most cases, these mentorship relationships occurred naturally, but in some cases, I did approach a person to directly ask them to mentor me in a specific role or skill I felt lacking.

Leading like a girl is not only about being proactive about establishing mentorships, you also have a very important role in nourishing these relationships and especially remembering that these must be two-way relationships. It's important to identify what you can give back to your mentor, not only what your mentor gives you—see the worksheet example at the end of this chapter.

4. ARE YOU POLITICALLY SAVVY?

Before I start with this section, I would like to acknowledge and thank Jane Horan for allowing me to base parts of this chapter on her presentation at the Eve 2018 Conference, as well as her doctoral research, books, and practical experience.[2]

Leading like a girl is fostering relationships at work to create a sense of belonging—building a tribe of like-minded role models and mentors. But a fourth dimension of relationships at work is actually one where women typically feel they are lacking and that is managing office politics.

Organizational politics was an aspect of managing relationships that I did not understand for years and it was only in my most recent job, where I was lacking psychological safety, that I realized its importance. My prevailing thought was, *I will just focus on doing a damn good job and my results will speak for themselves.* Big mistake as I later learned. I was also really lucky to have had managers who did a great job protecting me, in talent reviews and in random conversations. Your equity is what people say about you when you are not in the room, and I had enough friends and supporters to get by without the need to learn how to be politically savvy.

Despite this, I was hurt once when I came back from maternity leave to find that one of my colleagues was presenting my campaign and received all the credit for it. My boss called me in the next day and told me, "Don't worry, the people who are important know this work is a hundred percent yours." It happened again with my work on "Touch the Pickle" India, which I shared in the first chapter. I launched this campaign in July 2015, a few months before I left P&G. In June 2016, it won the inaugural Cannes Glass Lion Grand Prix Award, the new gender-neutral category spearheaded by Sheryl Sandberg. The Glass Lion "trophy aims to recognize ads that explore ideas of gender and specifically address issues of gender inequality or prejudice"[3] in the ongoing effort to shatter the glass ceiling. I was already outside the company, and so the local director was there to accept the award. This was 100 percent my creation, together with my brand manager and the agency, and while many reached out to congratulate me, I felt forgotten and frustrated that I did not get the credit I deserved. When Sheryl Sandberg kindly agreed to write the foreword to this book on the merit of that campaign, I felt justice was retrieved. Universal justice.

But in 2015, when I joined a quite judgmental and politically cutthroat team as the only woman, I realized that while as a young manager you may be able to get by with relying on your bosses to protect you and "sell" your achievements, as a senior C-suite executive, learning to be politically savvy not only isn't a rude word, it is a requirement to getting things done.

I knew from teaching Stephen Covey's "7 Habits" that I should spend more time building an emotional bank account, thinking win-win, seeking first to understand rather than to be understood—but I didn't do it as well as I should.[4] Why?

Well, first I was constantly strapped for time. I always used to skip lunch or have it at my desk (but I learned, as the Singaporeans say, "*Lunch is the most important meeting of the day*").

Second, my peers were quite individualistic. Once, when we did a team assessment as part of a leadership development, I discovered that, unlike myself, most of my peers scored very low in "need belonging at work"—they would prefer eating with their one or two friends, and my invitations for lunch were often met with a cold acceptance. This became quite evident when we had to stay the weekend in New

Zealand. *This will be a great opportunity for bonding*, I thought to myself. I suggested we do a hike together, but my peers preferred to walk alone; one decided to leverage the weekend to do a motorcycle trip and the other leveraged the time to pop over to his family in Australia. I remember coming back to the hotel, feeling completely alone.

So I focused my energy on creating a sense of belonging within my direct report team—turning the marketing community into a tribe, which gave me the relationships I was yearning for—and I did not invest enough in creating real friendships among my peers.

Third, this individualism expanded to the business, creating siloed departments where each section head focused on defending their own interests versus the greater good. This was often "aided" by our leader, who not only didn't make any efforts to create team collaboration but would also frequently pit us against each other in a "divide-and-conquer" style in order to maintain control.

Add to this to an Asian culture that tends to be conflict-averse, and what you get is a lot of behind-the-scenes feedback instead of direct confrontation, or, if there was direct feedback, it was often extremely judgmental—no psychological safety and no care in the candor.

One day, a colleague of mine called me to complain about a person on my team. I told him I was happy to have a three-way chat, but I thought it was important my employee had an opportunity to hear the feedback directly as well as a chance to explain the situation. My colleague refused. In his culture, he explained, feedback is not given directly, as that would be even more confrontational, especially when given by a senior leader of another department. As shared in a later chapter, lack of direct and open feedback is the fastest way to lose people's trust.

On top of all this, I am quite an outspoken person with an acute sense of justice, so when anything feels wrong, I speak up. One of my peers gave me a helpful piece of advice that I carry with me still today—choose your battles—*don't always be right, be smart.*

My biggest turning point in becoming more politically savvy was when I had to convince upper management to proceed with a project that was very close to my heart.

In the first chapter, I shared that my boss was very science-driven and even told me once, "Dalia, there is no art in marketing, it is only science." I was determined to prove him wrong and bring back my strength of creativity (i.e., *art*) into a very left-brain product-focused organization.

We were losing share in our core category of fabric care, and competition was outspending us 10:1. I knew we needed to do something dramatically different if we were to break through the clutter. So we created a campaign that was driven by deep consumer insights elevating the functional benefit of cleaning clothes into the emotional benefit of looking and feeling great. It was also very creative for the category, shot as a fashion catwalk. But it was also scientifically sound, with robust consumer research and a very scientific, conversion-led, go-to-market media strategy to ensure initial appeal would convert to sales. We started with an emotional right-brain appeal piece of advertising and became more conversion-led as consumers engaged with the material, concluding with a final hard-sell conversion copy.

My colleague, the product line VP, was strictly against this campaign, and no matter how much consumer data I shared with him, he was concerned there wasn't enough rationale—features and facts in the commercial. I showed him the model which pulled consumers in with emotions (as that is how the brain makes decisions) and then, once they were interested, shared the facts and figures to close the sell. He wasn't convinced. I realized this was much more than a typical right-brain creativity versus left-brain rational argument. There was an underlining fear to try something new—as he once blurted out, "If I don't deliver the numbers this year, I will be fired. We need to stick to the tried and tested approach." He wanted science and I was determined to bring my heart and art back to the business.

My colleague and I were in deadlock. No matter how much data I brought to the table, we couldn't convince each other.

Our boss, the Asia CEO who originally supported the campaign, changed his mind when he saw the product line manager's concerns and stalled the decision by asking me to bring even more analysis and data—he was not willing to make the leap of faith needed to try something more creative.

I was confident moving ahead was right for the business, but the more passionate I was, the more concerned they become; I knew being right wasn't enough, now I needed to learn to be smart. So, in the next pages, I will share some of what I learned.

TEN TIPS TO MANAGE HIGHLY POLITICAL ENVIRONMENTS

It is very clear that the leader plays a key role in defining the culture and psychological safety of an organization—whether people speak up or are afraid to share a diverse opinion, how people treat each other, the level of collaboration, the quality of feedback, the conflict culture of an organization (avoidance, competitive, or collaborative), how open an organization is to talking about underlying issues, and the fear of relying on intuition versus researching every aspect.

First, do not underestimate the culture in an organization. If you sense a severe culture clash, you should consider leaving or recognize that you face an uphill battle. In these cases, it's especially important to become more politically savvy. Now, this is not about encouraging one to synchronize swim in a pool of sharks, like when the leader is power-driven and low on integrity (then the only way through is out). This *is* about being more intentional about managing political blind spots, something I wish I had done better.

Being politically savvy is simply about being smart in achieving desired results. Ignoring politics altogether diminishes the positive value of stakeholder management, makes you naïve, and leaves you carrying a target on your back for more politically savvy people to undermine your success.

Jane Horan's research revealed that 35 percent of top managers leave their jobs because of office politics, yet office politics are a fact of life. Some companies like Disney, INSEAD, and Pepsi recognize this and help their people raise their political awareness. The key, however, is to ensure ethical politics—that is, managing your stakeholders with integrity.

Do politics and integrity sound like an oxymoron?

In their book, *Survival of the Savvy* (2004), Seldman and Brandon define two questions that help define whether office politics are ethical:

1. Whether the targeted objectives are in interest of company *or* self.
2. Whether the influence efforts used to achieve these objectives have integrity *or* not.[5]

The following are some tips and advice I have picked up to help you decide if you are politically savvy or if you have some work to do:

I. Become more politically aware—are you an owl, fox, sheep, or donkey?

Baddeley and James (1987) try to explain the political jungle through a simple model that categorizes an individual's political savviness.[6] They use four quadrants to delineate levels of political awareness and integrity, focusing on company interests or self-interest: the fox, owl, sheep, and donkey.

The owl and the fox epitomize high political awareness and are adept at reading a room accurately. However, the owl prioritizes integrity while the fox has lower ethical standards and prioritizes self-interest. The owl embodies transparency, attentive listening, and principled responses while always working toward win-win solutions.

The fox is cunning, with strong situational awareness and a firm understanding of both formal and informal processes, but is ultimately driven by self-interest. This individual can be very charming and is adept at identifying weaknesses in others in order to exploit them for personal gain while favoring win-lose scenarios.

The sheep, like the owl, is high on integrity but does not engage in strategic networking and thus remains naïve and friendly.

By contrast, the donkey demonstrates both low integrity and low political awareness, craving association with authority while hating being ignored. This individual displays overt self-interest and is not good at disguising it.

I like this model because it's simple and helped me realize I was very much a sheep. I valued friendships, loyalty, and integrity but lacked an understanding of interest groups, often taking matters personally instead of considering shared interest. I believed that all I needed to do was focus on doing my job very well, but that was a mistake, especially in a culture of foxes. Ironically, whenever I advocated for the interests of my department (which often clashed with those of other departments), I was perceived as self-serving by the foxes. The more passionate I was, the more I was seen as self-driven, which made me very defensive and made matters worse. It was only toward the end of my assignment that I came to fully understand political maneuvering—strategic alliance building and prioritizing win-win outcomes that benefited the company as a whole rather than only my department, leading to eventual success.

Thus, I invite you to contemplate your view of office politics and how you can become more like the principle-based, politically savvy owl with the following questions:

- Who are you in this model?
- Who is your boss?
- How can I stay politically aware while acting with integrity?
- How can I better understand stakeholder needs and create a win-win scenario, meeting THEIR needs without sacrificing mine?
- How can I show others I really care for what is important to them as well as how my interests better fit the company as a whole?
- What does success look like not only from your perspective but also from the total team perspective?

Remember, being politically savvy is NOT about playing games; it is about understanding the players in the game and their needs, acting with integrity, and working toward the win-win-win: win for the other, win yourself, and win for organization as a whole.

2. Map out your key stakeholders.

Understand who the true sources of power are, who the social connectors are, your potential allies, your mentors, and your competitors with potentially conflicting interest. (See sample mapping at the end of the chapter.) Put yourself in their shoes and understand their needs, drivers, and political style. Write down all stakeholders and strategize how you can meet their needs without sacrificing yours. Especially if they are foxes, learn to dance—as described in chapter 6—using their strengths to aid you on your journey.

3. Understand your own social defense and emotional triggers and those of your peers.

Identify your triggers. How can you CENTER your emotions as I will describe in chapter 13—Contain, Explain, Name, Tame, Empathize, and Reframe your emotions—so people focus on what you are saying and not *how* you come across. Do not drop into your "wounded feminine" and become defensive; spend time to understand the underlying fear that is triggering the others. As an example, I was seeing the product line attack as a personal attack on my expertise; instead, I would have done better to change the narrative to a more empathetic "He fears being fired."

4. Separate content from intent.

Avoid self-sabotage. If you fill your head with all the negativity around you, you will be filled with anxiety. Don't be naïve. Know to identify when others' intentions may be to hurt you, and only take in the feedback you think is correct and ignore the rest. As my

INSEAD professor Eric van de Loo once told me—you don't need to open all of the letters directed at you.

5. Visualize the plan.

What does a great outcome for all look like? Mentally rehearse. Keep perspective. What is the worst that can happen?

6. Do the prework!

To promote change or innovation, get preliminary agreement from those most affected. Make them your cheerleaders and build your resource base on the way to securing the necessary approvals from higher management. Focus on how the idea meets different stakeholders' needs and agendas.

7. Be smart, not right, about giving feedback.

When sharing feedback with a highly political person, share it in a way they will not "spit out the pill" (e.g., not in public).

8. When sharing results, avoid overselling.

Focus on teamwork and the benefit for the company. I've learned that sometimes, being over-passionate can be a turn off . . .

9. Choose your battles.

Learn when to speak up and when to manage offline or let go, based on reading the room accurately.

10. We are better together.

Identify allies, create networks, and, most importantly, lift others as you rise. I wouldn't have succeeded without amazing men and women cheering me on. Who are your raving fans?

So back to the launch of the new campaign. My colleague was adamant about stopping the campaign while I felt that, based on consumer research, we needed to do something drastic to win in the market.

Our boss, the Asia CEO, decided to call an all-in management alignment meeting.

On this occasion, I did one thing differently—I decided to be smart, not just right, and built a coalition of support. I had my local marketing directors share the campaign and their support for it with the sales managers, as well as the retailers, during their weekly work meetings. The retailers stood up and cheered.

Our local sales manager stood up in the meeting and, unaware of the political drama, shared enthusiastically how the retailers had stood up and cheered and how he believed this was exactly what our declining brand needed. That changed everything.

I only needed one raving fan and everyone else in the lead team chimed in to share their support. My colleague, the product line VP, again shared his concerns about the lack of facts and figures support, but our CEO agreed to go ahead and test it in the market, given the support of the sales clusters.

The campaign went on to win the first-ever Effie Award for creativity and business results and was later adopted by the global team to also run in Europe.

At the end of the year, during a performance review, I cited this example as a great achievement and a testimony to my creativity and courage. I did what I thought was right for the consumer and the business, despite obstacles. My boss, however, felt I didn't handle the product line VP well enough, as my win was at his expense.

We were both right. It was a crash course in office politics, and I had a lot to learn . . .

Leading like a girl is fostering friendships—with peers, mentors, and support networks, but, even more importantly, being politically savvy with stakeholders—keep your friends close and your enemies closer.

MENTORSHIP AS A TWO-WAY RELATIONSHIP

Mentorship Roles and Responsibilities

What a Mentor Does

1. Provides a safe, nonthreatening relationship in which the mentee can ask difficult or sensitive questions.
2. Provides emotional support in times of conflict.
3. Better connects the mentee to the informal system of information and relationships across the organization.
4. Shares personal experiences that address issues the mentee is facing in their career.
5. Shares history, company lore, and "war stories" to make the company's values and practices come alive.
6. Shares information on how the company makes decisions and which people are involved.
7. Makes suggestions on what it takes to get things accomplished.
8. Offers coaching on specific problems or work topics, if asked.
9. Shares perspective on assignments and/or career options.
10. Listens well and is alert to early warnings signifying that the mentee may be thinking of leaving the company.
11. Helps the mentee maintain their individuality while working effectively.
12. Provides faster, more candid feedback.
13. Helps clarify misunderstandings stemming from different communication and management styles.

What a Mentor Doesn't Do

1. Actively advocate or exert influence to get the mentee a career move.
2. Provide specifics on how the mentee should do their job.

3. Obligate the mentee in outside social activities or other commitments.

Responsibilities of the Mentor vis-à-vis the Manager

A mentor can provide input to a mentee's performance development and career discussions but should not be involved in formal evaluations. Normally, performance review data should not be shared with the mentor, unless the immediate manager or the mentee believes there is particular reason to do so.

A pre-meeting between the manager and mentor should be held to ensure their responsibilities are clear (i.e., roles, activities, and time commitments are defined). The mentor and the manager should periodically review how things are going; these reviews, however, should not compromise the privacy of the mentoring relationship.

Mentorship is a two-way journey—you need to be as focused on giving to your mentor as you are receiving (table 12.1).

Table 12.1. Mentorship/Menteeship

What a mentee gives	What a mentee can get
• Shares the real street buzz	• Visibility at critical times
• Teaches some skill like digital	• Access to info and company news
• Gratitude for mentor's investment	• Understanding of politics
A mentee does not come with demands and	• Introduction to key stakeholders
expectations but takes charge to develop a	*A mentor does not directly influence your*
relationship	*career*

EXAMPLE—MAPPING YOUR KEY STAKEHOLDERS

List the ten key stakeholders critical for the success of your projects. Look to see who is missing. Have you covered all important decision makers?

Write their names down on the Y axis of a table, and then reflect on these three power questions for each:

1. What are MY needs of each and how can each HELP ME succeed?
2. What are THEIR needs and how can I help THEM succeed?
3. How can I find the win-win?

Once you have mapped out the important stakeholders, write down their needs and desires, and then try to come up with action items that will meet *their* needs while meeting *your* needs. Think win-win. As Stephen Covey states in his book, "Relationships are like a bank account—make sure to invest by meeting their needs so you have enough allowance for when you will need to withdraw from this account![7] Have casual monthly lunches to stay connected, learn of their needs, and build trust as a leader who sees beyond self-interest and seeks to find win-win solutions.

V

POSITIVITY AND EMOTIONAL BRAVERY

Positivity and emotional bravery is about recognizing our own emotions and those of others as signs of passion, not weaknesses, and about how we can, with ourselves and with our teams, create upward spirals of positivity that broaden and build our capacity for success.

13

EMOTIONAL BRAVERY: PERMISSION TO BE HUMAN

When my TED Talk launched on June 3, it received 15,000 views within two weeks and a related post got a whopping 30 percent engagement rate. Many women, and, importantly, men, wrote to thank me for giving them permission to be human and to move away from the destructive cycle of toxic masculinity (a term used to describe behaviors that men exhibit to prove their masculinity, including suppressing emotions and the inability to show weakness or vulnerability). Leaders from around the world reached out to me, as "Lead Like a Girl" represented to them a much-needed movement to promote a culture that supports moving away from viewing emotions as a sign of weakness toward understanding emotions as a sign of passion.

One man wrote to me saying that the day after he watched my talk on YouTube, one of his employees broke down in tears. This time he didn't judge, and he avoided his tendency to jump in to fix the issue (which is often perceived as dismissing her emotions). Instead, he listened until she finished. Then he helped her reframe her emotions positively by saying, "I understand you are very passionate about this, and feel frustrated others don't share your passion. Let's work together to see what can be done and how I can help." His employee expressed feeling seen and validated and was delighted by his empathy and understanding. He felt that the idea of leading like a girl gave him a tangible tool that he could use.

However, the most rewarding comment came unexpectedly from a man who called me up to say that he had watched my talk and realized that he had not been such a nice person—he even referred to himself as "a reformed asshole." He asked me to continue spreading my message of leading like a girl, to help victims claim their power, but also to help bullies, like himself, save themselves!

I also received one comment that stood out from the rest. It was from someone who did not agree with my theory. The comment came from a very prominent and successful personal branding expert. She specializes in teaching women and men how to keep executive presence and drive personal branding. She expressed that being emotional at work hurts your equity, makes you seem weak, and limits your career progression.

On the one hand, much research (described further in this chapter) has concluded that being open about your emotions, even the negative ones, is *good*. On the other hand, socialization is teaching us that sharing emotions, especially at work, is *bad*.

Expressions such as "boys don't cry" and "leaders cannot be emotional—they need to maintain *leadership presence*" undermine the notion of emotional bravery. In Asia, there is a very strong cultural bias against expressing emotions. In the Japanese culture, expressing emotions is viewed as something which disrupts harmony and puts listeners in an uncomfortable position. In fact, in most Asian cultures, expressing emotions is a sign of poor upbringing.

Back to my tissue box story—my first manager saw my tears as a sign of passion and strength, so I flourished. I was highly respected as an expert in my field and was a sought-after resource. I had executive presence; I inspired trust and demonstrated respect while remaining authentic and passionate.

My tissue box manager saw my tears as a weakness, erratic, and lacking executive presence. I became defensive and wasted a lot of energy continuously defending myself, undermining my executive authority and affecting my performance.

So, what did I learn from this experience about emotional intelligence and executive presence? How do we solve this emotional paradox? Is maintaining executive presence important?

The short answer is—*yes.*

The longer answer is—*yes, and . . .*

This insight came to me when I observed Jacinda Ardern, who, at thirty-five years of age, is the youngest prime minister in the history of New Zealand. Jacinda was confronted with a devastating terror attack on a Muslim house of prayer in 2019. She identified with the pain and wore a traditional abaya Muslim head scarf and shed a tear. It wasn't perceived as weak; rather it demonstrated her authenticity and she won hearts across the world. That same day she declared a war on guns; two weeks later, Parliament passed gun use reforms contained in the Arms Amendment Act into law in New Zealand. It was a very bold decision.

As shared previously, during the COVID-19 pandemic in 2020, seven of the nine countries that dealt with the pandemic most successfully were led by women, including New Zealand. While many male leaders used fear to force people into action, Jacinda and the other female leaders used empathy and love, talking directly to the citizens, to the children, reassuring them that it was okay to feel scared, giving permission to be human by connecting to their emotions, explaining why their support was needed while being caring and providing reassurance on the measures taken. They managed to demonstrate that combining strength with empathy was a critical ingredient for effective leadership in the new era.[1] Kamala Harris is another exceptional example of leading like a girl and being emotionally brave—she is warm, yet poised, showing emotions without seeming erratic.

The issue is that the business world continues to associate showing our emotions as a weakness. This emotional bias is especially true for women, as I explore later in the chapter. I believe it is time for leaders to evolve not only to become emotionally intelligent but emotionally brave. In this chapter, we will explore what this means, why it is important, and what you can do to become more emotionally brave.

1. What is emotional bravery and how does it further build our emotional intelligence?

Daniel Goleman argues in *The Emotionally Intelligent Workplace*[2] that emotional intelligence (EQ) is a higher predictor of one's success than our cognitive ability or intelligence quotient (IQ). In fact, he found EQ accounts for 85 percent of a manager's success versus IQ accounting for only 15 percent. In his research, when senior management at one company had a critical mass of EQ, their divisions outperformed the average by 20 percent.

According to Daniel Goleman, EQ involves four dimensions:

a. Self-awareness—good at understanding their own emotions.
b. Self-management—good at managing their own emotions.
c. Social awareness—empathetic to the emotions of others.
d. Social relationships—good at handling other people's emotions, influence, and conflict resolution.

This model is great, but it didn't give me enough clarity on emotional self-management and finding the right balance solving the emotional bias paradox.

I have hence decided in my teaching to use the term *emotionally brave* instead of *self-management*, which seems to indicate emotions are bad and need to be managed.

Leading like a girl goes beyond being emotionally intelligent to being emotionally brave. It is about giving yourself the permission to be human and being able to center your emotions, then being flexible to zoom in and out to avoid being sucked into your emotions. All this so that you can choose the most effective way to act on them with authenticity and vulnerability, while being respectful to your boundaries in a way that builds human connection.

In this chapter I will dive into how we can master this skill to become more emotionally brave. But first, let's better understand our emotions and why emotional bravery is a critical skill for all leaders.

2. Understanding our emotions—biology, language, and cognition.

Emotions are a mirror to our souls; they help us make decisions quickly (fight or flight) and help prepare our bodies for action, hence being sometimes referred to as *Energy* in *MOTION*. When understanding our emotional state, it is important to understand three main components—biology, language, and cognition. Let me explain how each affects our emotional state.

Biology

Our emotions—energy in motion—often start with a physical clue: a smile (happy), increased heart rate (excited), shallow breathing (scared), etc. Being attentive to our bodily signals and knowing how to interpret and name these bodily signals is critical.

In her TED Talk, "How to Make Stress Your Friend," researcher Kelly McGonigal talks about the importance of reframing the physical input we get with regard to stress. Our increased heart rate is our body's self resilience mechanism, pumping hormones to our brain and sharpening cognition. Our faster breathing is our body's way to pump more oxygen to our brain. So how we interpret our body's signals is what matters.[3]

Interestingly, our brains do not distinguish between what is real and what is imagined. In her famous TED Talk, "Your Body May Shape Who You Are," Amy Cuddy, a social psychologist and award-winning Harvard lecturer, talks about "power posing" as a way to increase the emotion of confidence. While some of the research findings were partially disputed, the principle remains whole, and is backed up by many findings, including the body feedback hypothesis which says that how we carry our bodies can help influence our emotional state.

Try this exercise: Put a pencil between your teeth to force a fake smile. Your brain will think you are smiling and release serotonin, the feel-good hormone. In other words, when your body thinks it is happy, you begin to feel happy.

> Sometimes your joy is the source of your smile, but sometimes your smile can be the source of your joy.
>
> —Thich Nhat Hanh

Language

Words create worlds—language is critical to the way we interpret situations. The way in which we are able to change the way we view something is called cognitive reframing. "I am not scared of the audition; I am excited about the opportunity."

Joe Tomaka conducted research among students by giving the same math exam to two groups. For one group he told them that it was a "hard exam" and they should complete it quickly and effectively, and to the second group he said it was "challenging" and they should just do their best.[4] It was the same event, yet the first group's interpretation was threatening and the second's was more positive. The second group was calmer and got significantly better results. Ask yourself: Can I use more empowering language to interpret my emotions more positively?

Cognition

Above we discussed how our body and mouth (language) affect our emotions, but a third critical dimension to our emotional state is our head—the thoughts and meaning we give a situation.

The main misconception people have is that our emotions are triggered directly by events around us. The reality is that in between an event and an emotion is an important component, which is our evaluation of that event—the glasses we choose to wear to view the event.

In other words, thought (our cognitive evaluation of an event) affects our emotions and hence our behavior—this is at the core of cognitive behavioral therapy first used by Albert Ellis as described in chapter 5 on limiting beliefs and is the basis for coaching with neuro-linguistic programming (NLP) today. At the core of behavioral therapy is the belief that we don't react to the reality of our activating event, we react to our cognitive evaluation of that event based on our belief system.

It's not the activating event that leads to the consequences of us feeling sad, rather our interpretation of the event, the meaning we give it based on our somewhat limiting beliefs. For example: Two people can experience the same activating *event*—the death of a close friend—yet the *evaluation* and meaning they give to this event may be completely different based on their beliefs. The first person might see this negatively as a sign we are all going to die one day and hence might withdraw from life. The other person might see this as a sign that life is short, and we should maximize every second and may adopt a philosophy of carpe diem—seize the day. Same activating event, but two different belief systems that lead to two opposite emotions—one person will become depressed and the other elevated.

So if you want to change your emotional state, start by reassessing your evaluation and beliefs—what you are focusing on and the meaning and interpretations you give to the event.

Before going onto the TED stage, I applied cognitive reframing. I kept telling myself that my heart was beating fast not because I was scared to present in front of thousands of people but because I was excited to share my message with the world. I also focused on the meaning of the event—if I helped one person take action, I was making an impact. I used positive reframing of body signals and positive language to change my evaluation of the event, which changed my emotion from a negative panic to a positive excitement that inspired to make a difference.

Martin Seligman, the founding father of positive psychology, further investigated the secret to feeling more positive emotions. He found two differentiating factors between happy and less happy people:

1. The quality of their relationships, as discussed in the previous chapter.
2. The quality of their *evaluations* of the events.[5]

Happy people don't experience less pain than unhappy people; they just differ in how they evaluate their situation. Happy people engage in what I call the "3P" pain preventors:

1. They don't take things *personally*. As discussed in chapter 5, failure is an event not a badge.
2. They understand that the situation is not *permanent*. Failing this math test does not mean you will always fail in math.
3. They don't develop *pervasive* attitudes. Failing in math doesn't mean you will fail at everything.

An important part of emotional bravery and leading like a girl is being able to reflect on our thought processes to understand our emotions, sometimes referred to as "going to the balcony" or stepping out of the drama of your life, so that you can understand the "movie" and your role in it. Albert Ellis refers to this stage as debunking limiting beliefs: What really is going on here? What are my emotions versus those others are projecting on me? What is "my story" versus what is their story that has nothing to do with me? Am I magnifying/minimizing or making things up? What could be a way to reframe this situation? Could there be other explanations? We have the power to decide what interpretation we give to events and hence modify our emotions. If you want to change your emotion, question your cognitive evaluation of the event—your beliefs.

Sometimes emotions lead to a behavior without thought known as automatic response or an "amygdala hijack," as coined by Daniel

Goleman.[6] Our emotions are stored in our primal brain, and our logic in our frontal cortex. Against common belief, decisions are not made in our logical frontal cortex but in our primal emotional brain. This was evolutionary in order to choose fight-or-flight responses. The key, as thinking human beings, is to avoid an automatic response and create space to act and not react. This self-regulation is not emotional suppression, it is taking the time to become emotionally brave.

3. The issue—the emotional biases against women.

Research on emotions and gender shows that women score overall higher on emotional intelligence tests. Women show higher recognition of emotions in others as well as higher levels of empathy. This is associated with strong leadership. Yet, while this higher EQ should be something men learn from women to become better leaders, women being more emotionally expressive has led to several false stereotypes about both women and emotions which need to finally be dispersed, once and for all:

- *She cannot be promoted, she is too emotional.*

While men and women feel the *same* level of emotions, given higher self-awareness of their own emotions, women tend to be more expressive of their emotions, while men tend to suppress them, believing that good leaders don't show emotions. As researcher Victoria Brescoll points out, "This perception is consequential for female leaders because people infer a trade-off between the ability to control outward emotional display and the ability to make rational, objective decisions, and yet this has not been proven and on the contrary—certain emotions aid in sound reasoning and effective decision-making rather than detracting from it."[7]

"People used to say, 'We don't want somebody's finger on the nuclear button who cries,' I would say, 'Well, I don't want somebody with their finger on it who doesn't!' said Ms. Schroeder after criticism of her tears when ending her presidential bid."[8]

Biology and sociology explain women's expressiveness—women's tear ducts are shallower, so "when men cry, 73 percent of the time, tears do not fall down their cheeks. Men may get misty-eyed, but teardrops don't give them away. With women, on the other hand, almost every crying episode involves runaway tears." Hormones, and especially the female hormone prolactin, mean women are five times more prone to cry compared to men around the time of ovulation. But social conditioning is key—as researcher T. Lutz writes, "It was common in the eighteenth century for upper-class men to cry," and in fact, "they were viewed as brutes if they didn't." It was only in the nineteenth century that the idea of male stoicism emerged, and it was not until the mid-twentieth century that tears were used to suggest that "candidates for public office were not manly or stable enough" to be there, Mr. Lutz said.[10]

This approach may have been relevant at the time of the industrial revolution, when productivity and stoic precision were key, but the VUCA world, especially the dispersed virtual world emerging post COVID-19, demands a different type of leadership where emotions are a sign of passion, empathy, vulnerability, and connectedness—and not a weakness.

- *She is an angry bitch.*

When looking at types of emotions, men and women react differently to frustration. Men tend to become angry while women become sad. This is partially due to socialization. Men are encouraged to portray power emotions like assertiveness and are discouraged from displaying sadness because it is perceived as weaker. The "boys don't cry" mentality creates toxic masculinity where both men and women are penalized for acting out of the norm. As a result, the exact same behavior and same intensity of behavior is perceived differently—when a man becomes angry, he is perceived as assertive, which strengthens his leadership presence; when a woman becomes angry (to the same level), she is seen as erratic and out of control, which diminishes her executive presence. Moreover, whereas men's emotional reactions are attributed to external circumstances (he is disappointed with our performance), women's emotional reactions are attributed to internal characteristics (e.g., "she is an angry person, she is out of control").[10]

- *She is a self-promoting show-off.*

Women are more likely to be penalized for expressing emotions of power like pride. Socialization expects women to be modest, while it accepts male competitiveness. Research experiments have consistently found that people are more likely to penalize self-promoting women than their self-promoting male counterparts.[11]

- *She is too sensitive.*

Because women are more likely to openly express sadness compared to men, and are more likely to openly discuss their emotions at work, people generally believe female leaders are more likely to take criticisms and failures personally compared to their male counterparts—again diminishing their perception as effective leaders.

- *She is too motherly and lets her empathy get in the way of making sound, tough decisions.*

Empathy is a key trait of a good leader and neuroscience has proven women sit with empathy for longer than men, who quickly switch off from empathy into fix-it mode. While compassion is a positive trait, public displays of compassion through bonding can create the ungrounded perception that this may affect tough people decisions.

As Brescoll concludes, simply because men *display* less emotion than women, people incorrectly infer that the emotions men feel have little to no sway over their decisions, thoughts, or behaviors. Thus, compared to men, women are likely to be seen as less rational and objective, less able to cope with critical feedback, and inappropriately soft in their dealings with subordinates.

A core feature of stereotypes is that they cause people to notice and even exaggerate stereotype-consistent information—in this case, because of this deeply rooted bias that women are more emotional than men, women's emotional expression is often perceived as more intense than it really is. Indeed, research found that people rate pictures of happy female faces as containing more emotion (i.e., being significantly "happier") than identically happy male faces across all levels of intensity of expression (from very mild to extreme).[12]

Such inferences are likely to significantly undermine perceptions of women leaders' competence and are not grounded in reality—these are stereotypes that need to be eradicated. "Empathy, vulnerability and emotional connectedness are the elements that define today's leaders; traits that are traditionally associated with women."[13] It is time stoic men catch up with the demands of the modern leader.

Leading like a girl is being aware of these stereotypes and yet choosing to embrace emotions as part and parcel of being human. Being aware of this bias is the first step. Learning to understand our emotions is the next step.

4. Why is being emotionally brave critical today more than ever?

In the modern world, we have a bias against negative emotions with the belief that being happy is about never showing sadness. This is not the case. As shared earlier through the work of Martin Seligman, the happiest people on earth experience pain as much as others and they do not repress negative emotions; they deal with them, recognizing they are temporary and specific. Emotions are a mirror to our souls, a report card to alert us to take notice. If we ignore them, we are missing an important source of information to guide our actions.

The world's digital transformation has led to what some call the *empathy crisis*. Research by Sarah Konrath and her colleagues reveals that today's young adults scored 40 percent lower on empathy tests as compared with young adults the same age, thirty years ago.[14] Today's youth can choose to break up with their girlfriend/boyfriend via text, thereby avoiding the responsibility to hold a difficult conversation, or they can share emotions anonymously. This, as the research above shows, results in less empathetic adults and managers. And yet modern, fast-changing, and often remote leadership demands a higher level of empathy, creating an empathy paradox crisis demanding intervention.

Leading like a girl is bringing back empathy as a business tool, giving employees the permission to be human and experience all emotions, teaching them to self-regulate their emotions so they can choose the most appropriate way forward, and being flexible on how they express themselves and not suppress their emotions.

What worked for me is what I have come to call my CENTER and ACT methodology.

HOW TO LEAD LIKE A GIRL BY BECOMING EMOTIONALLY BRAVE

My proposal for being emotionally brave includes three important steps:

> Stage 1—Permission to Be Human. Don't suppress emotions—
> it's okay not to be okay.
> Stage 2—CENTER, Then ACT
> Stage 3—Developing Flexible Intelligence

Let me review each of the stages: Accept, Center and Act, Flex.

Stage 1—Permission to Be Human

Accept all ranges of emotions.

As Tal Ben-Shahar nicely puts it: "There are only two types of people who do not experience emotions—psychopaths and dead people." So, if you experience emotions, congratulations, it's a sign that you are human! The first step in becoming emotionally brave is accepting all emotions including the negative ones. There is proven research on why this makes sense.

Suppressing emotions just intensifies them.

> The only way out is through.
>
>   —Robert Frost

My favorite children's story in A. A. Milne's collection of Pooh stories is "The Heffalump"—Pooh is scared of a big creature that comes to him in his dreams, and Tigger advises that he speak with him directly. That is when Pooh finds out that the scary monster is actually scared himself. The only way to deal with whatever scares you is to deal with whatever scares you. Do not avoid or fight but confront—then the scary monster becomes smaller, temporary, and manageable. The notion of accepting negative emotions is also found in ancient philosophies.

The Buddha argued that pain is inevitable, yet suffering is our choice when we don't accept the cause of pain. In the work context, expecting no hardship or pain is unrealistic, but if we ignore the pain or the cause of pain within our own reaction to it, we turn this reality into suffering.

> Trying to understand is like straining through muddy water. . . .
> Be still and allow the mud to settle.
>
>   —Lao Tzu in the Tao Te Ching

Lao Tzu, who founded Taoism, continues this thought, and uses the analogy of murky water to describe the impact of rejecting negative emotions. To overcome unpleasant emotions, stay still and allow them to flow through you. Fighting the emotions will just make them worse.

Taken together, we know that pain exists as well as negative emotions. Suppressing the negative emotions is bad as is fighting them as they will just intensify; accept them as a normal part of being human.

Limiting negative emotions limits positive emotions too.

Think of your emotional capacity as a pipeline—if you limit the negative emotions from flowing through you, you prevent the positive ones as well.

> Those who don't know how to weep with their whole heart, don't know how to laugh either.
>
> —Golda Meir, Israeli prime minister

Leading like a girl is not numbing our emotions, neither the painful ones nor the positive ones.

Vulnerability drives relationship depth.

As seen on the TED Talk by Brené Brown, who shared and further expressed in subsequent books she authored, "It is our ability to share vulnerabilities that leads to deeper human connections as we let go of a perfect image."[15] Sometimes by trying to maintain executive presence, you become aloof. But sharing that you, as a leader, are also going through a rough patch actually helps people connect and relate to you better.

Negative emotions that haven't been dealt with limit our ability to learn, grow, and effectively communicate.

Neuroscience research shows that not dealing with negative emotions consumes physiological resources, diverting them from the part of the brain that manages working memory and processes new information. This impairs analytical thinking, creative insight, and problem solving.[16] This explains why managing through fear is ineffective. In my personal experience, I spent so much energy in fight-or-flight mode and being so defensive that I had less capacity toward more productive tasks, hence limiting my professional growth.

Undealt with, emotions lead to communication gaps. How often have you told someone how they made you feel, and heard this response: "Wow, I didn't realize you felt that way—that is completely

NOT my intention"? Your evaluation of the event may have been completely flawed, creating unnecessary pain. By sharing the emotion, you were able to clarify the intended evaluation and clear the air. Suppressing these emotions has a damaging effect on working relationships, productivity, turnover, and the bottom line.

Finally, and most importantly, expressing versus suppressing emotions is critical to avoiding disease.

Freud talked about the link between mind and body. John Sarno was a medical doctor who was astonished to find that people with the same symptoms react very differently to pain.[17] He developed a mind-body concept called Tension Myositis Syndrome (TMS theory) covered in his book, *Mind Over Back Pain*, concluding that repressed emotions in the subconscious that are not expressed will find the weakest link in one's body to erupt and cause physical havoc. One of Sarno's former students, David Schechter, MD, showed 52 percent pain reduction when treating certain types of chronic back pain as TMS, encouraging patients to disclose their suppressed emotions.[18]

A lot of the stress and burnout we experience at work today could be prevented if we first would give ourselves the permission to be human.

Stage 2—CENTER, Then ACT

The second stage is to acquire the skill to become more emotionally brave. I use the acronyms CENTER and then ACT:

C *is for Contain and Claim.*

Contain is about pausing to create space to choose the most productive way to react. Take a deep breath. This is the fastest and easiest way to calm down the racing amygdala.

Claim is about owning the emotion—remembering that you don't get triggered if it is not important for you! For example, you are in a meeting and someone says a very offensive comment. You can contain and claim by saying something like, "Your comment triggered me because this is important for me; I prefer to take a break. Let's catch up on this tomorrow."

As explained with the ABCDE model, you are reacting not to the reality but to your cognitive evaluation of the behavior and you need time to analyze this evaluation before reacting.

E is for Evaluate or Explain to yourself what is going on.

Pay attention to your body signals: your heart rate, your breathing, sweat, etc. Tears are just another body signal that some deep emotion has been triggered. No need to apologize for tears, it's a sign of your passion, not of weakness.

N is for Name the emotion.

Use language to understand your emotion. Do you feel angry, sad, frustrated, humiliated? Naming the emotion forces the neocortex to be active. The amygdala (where emotions are stored) and the neocortex (where rational thought and language are stored) act as a seesaw—when one is aroused, the other is depressed. Naming the emotion activates the neocortex and "forces" the amygdala's hyperactivity to decrease. This is often used with children who don't know why they are acting the way they are ("I understand you are frustrated"), but it is just as important with adults.

T is for Tame the emotion.

Take out the poison and meditate on the emotion. Now is the time to step *out* of the drama to analyze the movie. I sometimes use the waterfall analogy; having an emotion is very different from being consumed by an emotion. How can you evolve from saying "I am angry" to saying "I have anger"? Step behind the waterfall rather than being in the waterfall consumed by that anger. A subtle difference occurs when you take some distance from the emotion, looking at it as an outsider watching a movie. This stepping out of the emotion without rejecting it, fighting it, or being consumed by it is a core part of leading like a girl and being emotionally brave. It helps to put matters into perspective. Merely observing the emotion leads to healing. We realize the emotion is temporary and more manageable.

One safe technique to tame the emotion is journaling. It is said of Abraham Lincoln that whenever he felt angry, he would write an angry note. He would look at it every day for the next three days, and if after three days he felt the same, he would mail it, but he never did. Another way to tame the emotion is to ask yourself, "Will all of this matter one year from now?" If it does, then you should act on it; if it doesn't, let it go.

E is for Empathize.

Try to understand how things look from the other person's point of view (POV). This doesn't mean you agree with their POV, just that you see where they are coming from.

R is for Reframe.

Try to add context to what happened so you can interpret what happened in additional ways—remember, the driver overtaking you might not be an asshole but a loving husband rushing his pregnant wife to hospital. Avoid Seligman's 3Ps that intensify pain—don't take it *personally* and understand it isn't *permanent* or *prevalent*. Try to understand what deeper fear or irrational thought was triggered and the lesson that this trigger is trying to teach you.

> Regret is a seminar on making wiser choices.
> Guilt is a class on doing the right thing.
> Boredom is a lesson on finding flow.
> Disappointment a tutorial on preparation or perseverance.
> Anger is a crash course on setting boundaries.
>
> —Adam Grant[19]

Now that you have clarity on the emotion, evaluate rationally the most effective course of action to express the emotion and get the best result. Again, by no means do I suggest suppressing the emotion—but act on it in the most productive way to achieve the desirable goal.

ACT

After any uncomfortable or difficult situation, make sure to take at least twenty-four hours to process your emotions. After that time, if you still feel the same way, I recommend acting on the emotions. This is very different from reacting immediately because you share your POV while staying cool and collected. Always be active about your emotions. Don't suppress them as they will end up coming out as passive-aggressiveness or even disease. But when you are cool and collected, you increase the likelihood that the other person will listen to *what* you have to say and not be overwhelmed by *how* you are emotional. I had one female boss who advised me to come back and "talk emotions, unemotionally." Make your point clear and concise.

As shared in chapter 7, start with empathy, show you understand the other person's needs, but then share authentically how that behavior made you feel, why you care so much (link back to purpose and values), and then set your boundaries clearly. For example: "I understand your intention was X (empathy), but your comment made me feel Y because it is linked to my core values and beliefs. I am here to work in partnership, and I expect you to talk with respect, otherwise I will need to press an official complaint/ask to be removed from the team/won't be able to meet your needs, etc. Now let's focus on how I can help you meet your needs, without sacrificing what is important for me."

Stage 3—Developing Flexible Intelligence

Be brave and flexible in expressing emotions, from EQ to FQ.

Finally, I would like to propose that being emotionally brave is about the ability to be *flexible*. This flexibility manifests itself in two key areas:

1. Flexible Quotient is about being able to zigzag between zooming in and zooming out:

- *Zooming in* is accepting and being in the moment with your emotions, being authentic, not overly contrived, playful and real, and giving yourself the permission to be human, spontaneous, passionate.
- *Zooming out* is taking a time-out to step out to the balcony to CENTER and ACT, to step out of the drama and watch the movie, understand the emotions, name them, tame them, reframe them, and then go back if needed to explain them. It is okay to share your emotions, but then balance it out with rational thinking.

The emotionally brave among us zigzag, able to zoom in at times to sit with the emotion, but also able to zoom out to center and act.

2. Flexible Quotient is also about being able to choose the feminine or masculine response.

In chapter 5, I talked a little about feminine and masculine energy. Being flexibly intelligent is being able to zoom in and out and choose a response ranging from positive feminine to positive masculine without dropping into either the wounded feminine or wounded masculine.

In other words, it is okay to cry, but there is no need to apologize for it or see it as a weakness. Instead, link it to your purpose and common goals (e.g., "This comment frustrated me as it touches something very important to me which I feel hampers our shared goal").

And when attacked by a wounded masculine reaction, be able to step into your positive masculine and state your boundaries clearly (e.g., "Sorry, but your reaction is demeaning and against company values. I cannot accept being talked to like this. Please state your point in a more respectful manner. I am willing to continue this conversation when you are ready to talk to me in a respectful manner").

In summary, leading like a girl is being emotionally brave enough to accept the full range of emotions, to learn the soul message they are trying to express (in self and others), and to CENTER and then ACT on them in a way that respects personal boundaries and builds better relationships.

In calling this concept emotional bravery or being emotionally brave, I wanted to clarify the word *courage*, as it is often misunderstood to mean making tough decisions others wouldn't make. As I learned from my mentor, Paul Polman, former CEO of Unilever, the word *courage* comes from the word *coeur*, meaning *heart* in French.

Courageous leaders lead from their hearts. This is the core of emotional bravery.

14

POSITIVITY AND GRATITUDE

In an earlier chapter, I shared the story of Michelangelo sculpting his masterpiece, *David*. When doing so, he followed two important processes for self-growth:

- Our ability to see our true authentic self (our strengths, values, and goals).
- Our ability to get rid of anything preventing us from revealing our true glory (our fears and limiting beliefs).

This book has followed a similar process. The last step in leading like a girl and increasing well-being—after discovering your "David" and removing any limitations—is being able to brush and shine that "David" by inserting more positivity into your life. This chapter is aimed at giving you practical proven tools to "shine your David."

When I met professor Tal Ben-Shahar, I learned that much of what I have intuitively believed regarding great leadership is backed by scientific evidence. I've always been given feedback that I see the glass as "half full" and was glad to find out that **it is positive to be positive** (for oneself and for society). Research by Sonja Lyubomirsky shows that happier people are significantly more successful than less happy people.[1] She goes on to specify some of the benefits of being happy and shows that being positive isn't just good for oneself, it is actually good for society. The simple fact is that happiness is a positive-sum game—one's happiness doesn't detract from the happiness of others but actually enhances it.

As the Buddha says:

> Thousands of candles can be lighted from a single candle, and the life of the candle will not be shortened. Happiness never decreases by being shared.

PROVEN BENEFITS OF BEING POSITIVE[2]

1. **Creativity and problem solving**. Research shows that a better mood leads to thinking more broadly and more creatively. In fact, our brains in positive mode are 30 percent more productive.[3]

2. **Increased motivation and energy—upward spiral of positivity**. According to the research quoted in the article, when we feel positive emotions, we experience an upward spiral of positive emotions as positivity means we are more open to new experiences. The way it works—being positive makes you feel better. This then makes you more open to new experiences, which further promotes gratitude and positivity. Positive psychologist Barbara Fredrickson calls this the broaden-and-build theory—engaging in positive emotions broadens our view, curiosity, and motivation, and builds more resources, which, in return, leads to more positive emotions creating an upward spiral of positivity.[4]

3. **Overcome painful emotions**. Positive emotions give us the hope we need to get out of a negative spiral.

4. **Physical health—survival and longevity**. A famous 1932 study asked young nuns to write their autobiographies and goals for the future.[5] These nuns were approached again de-

cades later (when they reached ages seventy-five and ninety-five). Researchers looked for factors predicting longevity such as devotion, intelligence, and physical environment and discovered that a significant level of emotional content, hope, and positivity in their early autobiographies was strongly associated with longer and healthier life.

Throughout the book, I have talked about many strategies I have used and continue to use with my clients for increasing positive emotions:

- Finding flow—immersing in challenging yet rewarding activities in line with one's purpose
- Finding new ways to bring one's strengths to life every single day
- Hope and action—envisioning one's best future and setting goals toward that best self
- Taking care of one's physical health and spending time in nature
- Boosting compassion to self and others, practicing random acts of kindness, and giving
- Accepting negative emotions as part and parcel of being human

These are all important components of leading like a girl and boosting holistic well-being. But probably the simplest and most effective strategy is living your life with an attitude of gratitude.

Gratitude

Gratitude is defined as "a sense of thankfulness and joy in response to receiving a gift, whether the gift be a tangible benefit from a specific other or a moment of peaceful bliss evoked by natural beauty."[6] In fact, gratitude interventions have proven to boost one's sense of well-being even one month post intervention.[7]

Much research is done on the virtue of gratitude:

- Bono, Emmons, and McCullough researched gratitude.[8] They asked their subjects to write five things they are grateful for each day for a week. Those who regularly expressed gratitude:

  1. Were significantly happier.
  2. Had a more optimistic view of the future.
  3. Were more likely to achieve their goals and be successful in their tasks.
  4. Were physically healthier.

- Sonja Lyubomirsky found that expressing gratitude even once a week is good enough.[9]
- Seligman et al. found that writing a gratitude letter and then delivering it to someone has impact both for the giver and receiver.[10]
- Hadassah Littman-Ovadia and Maayan Boiman-Meshita asked couples to spend fifteen minutes a week to reflect on three things they had enjoyed doing together the past week. At the end of three months these couples were significantly happier together versus the control group.[11]
- Gratitude doesn't have to be only reserved to the big events—savoring is about noticing everyday positive moments and has proven to have a significant effect on happiness, resilience, well-being, and overall life satisfaction.[12]

At a team level, much has been researched to show positivity and gratitude from the leader to influence their followers' positivity and boost employee engagement, team effectiveness, and resilience.[13] Teresa Amabile found gratitude works in the workplace as it does in personal life.[14] Workers who take the time to appreciate what they did that day and captured their progress that day were significantly happier.

Interestingly, research shows gratitude to be a female trait—women and those with a more feminine mindset were associated with higher scores on the scales of gratitude and positive orientation.[15] Results demonstrated that men were less likely to feel and express gratitude, made more critical evaluations of gratitude, and derived fewer benefits.[16] In explaining this difference, researchers hypothesize that men regard the experience and expression of gratitude as evidence of vulnerability and weakness, which may threaten their masculinity and social standing.[17]

Leading like a girl is hence also about leading with gratitude and positivity. Given the importance of positivity and gratitude to social relationships and overall individual well-being as well as performance, this is one trait both men and women need to actively seek and include in their repertoire of leadership skills.

Our brains are wired to look at where we direct our focus. If we focus on the hardships and problems in our lives and in our relationships, that is all we will see. However, positive psychology is about wiring the brain to focus on those positive things in our lives, making them increase in value.

Look for the negatives about your partner, and you are sure to find them. Even worse, as I shared in earlier chapters, our brains are wired for negativity as a hereditary survival mechanism—we must notice a bear or any danger in our peripheral view. We actually hear negative input four times louder than positive input: said differently, we need four positive events/occasions of feedback, etc., to negate one negative (see chapter 9 on relationships). When I started applying this, I stopped looking at the fact that my husband rarely says he loves me, and I started to notice how he shows his love in other ways: his love for our kids, his attentive advice, his divine cooking, etc. I started focusing on what was working and appreciating the good in our relationship versus constantly complaining.

A core to being grateful is to be mindful, pay attention, and direct our focus to the magic in the mundane. This is not always easy for an alpha, hyperactive person such as I am but is a critical stage I had to learn in leading like a girl.

I decided to write these last chapters in one of my favorite places in the world—Bali. I was reading Irvin Yalom's excellent memoir, *Becoming Myself*, where he spoke about going on a writer's retreat for each of his books,[18] and then and there I booked my flight.

I chose a Bali silent retreat.

I arrived yesterday and woke up to a schedule of total bliss.

5:30 a.m. I waken to the sound of the brass gong, which calls us to meditation; warm ginger tea awaits me on the veranda overlooking the lush green rice terraces. It's still dark. I sip it slowly as I watch the break of dawn. Another gong goes off, and I make my way to the big tent for forty-five minutes of silent meditation. Every ten minutes the bell rings. In the beginning I am busy counting my breaths between each bell, but after the third bell, I lose track of time, just floating, watching my thoughts go by, and suddenly meditation is over.

Jon Kabat-Zinn, author of the amazing book, *Wherever You Go, There You Are*, which I picked up yesterday at the retreat library (and have intended to read for a while), describes meditation:

> Meditation is not about trying to change your thinking, by thinking some more. It involves "watching" thought itself.[19]

Another way to think of meditation is to think of a waterfall. A continuous cascading of thought. In mindful meditation we go beyond, go behind the waterfall.

We see and hear the water.

But we are out of the torrent.

We may notice we have an emotion of anger but we are NOT anger—we are not in the emotion but observing it: a super powerful technique to tame negative emotions as discussed earlier.

After meditation, we have a ninety-minute yoga practice. The sun is now up and caressing us as we go through our pranayama and asanas.

Another wooden gong goes off at the end of the yoga practice to call us for breakfast. We stopped eating the day before at 6:00 p.m. so by 9:00 a.m., I am ready to eat.

Food is divine.

We are encouraged to practice mindful eating—everyone is silent, we collect small portions and find a quiet place overlooking the rice terraces. We first eat with our eyes—enjoying the many different colors on the plate, then we smell the different aromas, and finally the tastes—slowly we take each bite in and spend time observing each different texture and taste in each dish. The mindful eating sign on the wall calls us to "be mindful of the origin of each of the ingredients, the hard work and love that went into planting, caring, harvesting, cooking and plating this dish." As I am thinking about all these people and their efforts, I lift my eyes and see an old woman holding two pitchers of rice on her head. I remember looking at her yesterday standing at sunset with one task at hand—to whip the flag anytime the birds got close to the crops—a human scarecrow. The kitchen angels bring in dessert—the warm smell of the banana cake, vegan and gluten free, and ever so delicious.

Without my noticing, a whole hour passed; I think of how fast we eat normally and promise to create a new ritual and bring this mindful eating back home, bringing gratitude to each bite.

After breakfast I go find a quiet spot to write this chapter. My spot is a wooden bench at the far edge of the retreat. It starts to rain. The sound of the drops on the banana leaves above me joins the sound of the many birds around to create the best music to go with my writing.

I reflect on one of my favorite pieces by Helen Keller from her paper, *Three Days to See*. Helen Keller, who was both blind and deaf, was amazed when her friend returned from a walk in the woods and when Helen asked her, "So what did you see?" she replied, "Nothing much."[20]

This encouraged her to write *Three Days to See*. She encouraged us to imagine we would lose all our senses in three days and goes on to describe what she would do if she suddenly got back her sight for three days—sit in nature observing everything, looking deep into the eyes and faces of the people she loves, observing art, observing the hustle and bustle of life in New York.

All too often we take things for granted, only appreciating them when we lose them. Helen writes:

> If I were the president of the university, I should establish a compulsory course in "how to use your eyes" and the professor would try to show his pupils how they could add joy to their lives by really seeing what passes unnoticed before them.

Use each sense as if you could lose it tomorrow—see more profoundly, hear, smell, and taste each bite as if you could lose them.

Irvin Yalom has worked with people at the end of their lives and reflects on this notion: these people realize everything they are appreciative of too late, when there is not much left to enjoy. He encourages us—don't wait to be grateful. The key is to share gratitude regularly as a ritual—visualize it, relive it. Experience heartfelt positivity. I added a gratitude visualization at the end of my morning routine. I used a tip I once got to stick a Post-it note with the word "gratitude" on my mirror, and so when I wake up to brush my teeth I have a reminder.

Surrender

Another aspect I learned on the retreat was to surrender—to allow the universe to create its magic. This concept—covered in the excellent book *The Surrender Experiment* by Michael Singer—is not about being passive, but about accepting serendipity as the universe will align with a made-up mind.[21]

After the retreat was over and my book was done, I decided to let it sit on the shelf at this point for a few months, as I took on two other life goals that happened to come my way. The first was becoming an adjunct professor!

Let me share with you what happened next, as it is a great example of what happens when you surrender to serendipity and live your life with an attitude of gratitude. As I took a break from my corporate life (door closed), I decided to volunteer for a beautiful project—TOM (Tikun Olam Makers)—together with the incredible Israeli ambassador, Simona. We were pitching the project to the president of SMU (Singapore Management University). At the end of this pitch, the university president shared that the next year they would be teaching a course on happiness and suffering and asked if she had any good Israeli film recommendations on the topic. Simona knew I was studying happiness and told them about my studies. They invited me to a chat and asked me to consult with them in building a theoretical syllabus of what I would teach in this course. I called Tal Ben-Shahar and he was so happy for me. "Please feel free to use any materials from my course—that is exactly my objective—to spread the happiness revolution—make it your own and soar," he encouraged me.

I sat and built a syllabus combining Tal's teaching, my teaching and experiences at P&G, and my coaching experience, as well as recent mindfulness exercises I had picked up as a yoga teacher. I thought I was just consulting with them on their syllabus, however, at the end of the meeting, the dean smiled and said, "This is an incredible syllabus. You are hired, we would like you to start in August!" And so, from June to August I created my course, which became the core of my new career transition.

My class was overbooked with forty-five students, and I had a blast! We had academic teaching, debates, and reading, but also practical sessions, outdoor yoga, and meditation classes.

One of the most successful practical sessions I taught was about purpose. It was one of the early sessions in September and I took the students outdoors for a deeply immersive find-your-purpose and goal-setting exercise. At the end of the session, one of my students got up and said, "Thank you, Prof.—you have helped me find my purpose. But first I will be a corporate slave for a few years to make money, and then I will do what I love." My hair stood up as I knew it doesn't have to be that way!

The next moment another student raised his hand and asked me about my own goals—and so I shared what was on my mind. I want to:

1. Turn this course into an ongoing course for companies to help their managers build resilience and find purpose and joy in the workplace. (My new career mission was born!) Then I added two more goals:
2. Write a book and have it sell 100,000 copies.
3. Speak at TED and empower one million viewers.

That weekend while I was at one of my INSEAD programs, I got an email from my best friend Tzurit: "They are going to run TEDx Women in Israel—you should apply!"

"Oh no, it's such a short notice. I don't have time to prepare the required three-minute video," I told her. One hour later, I got an email with a five-minute talk I'd given a week earlier to Keynote as part of an International Women's Day audition. I called up the videographer, who was so kind, and he agreed to edit that video to a three-minute version for free. "Good luck with TED," he said, and so I applied.

In October, I flew to Israel for the stone setting of my dear grandmother who'd died six weeks before her 105th birthday. As the plane landed in Israel, I got a text: "You have been accepted to TEDxJaffaWomen, but our first meeting will happen in a week—we will need you to be in Israel for this meeting. Would that be possible?" Serendipity.

During my last lesson at the university, I told them that my goal of speaking at TED was going to come true earlier than I thought. They were so excited they all clapped. We wrote down our goals and agreed to meet up in June to see the progress made toward their goals. As shared in chapter 2 on goals—when you set your subconscious toward a goal, the universe has an amazing way of making it come true.

The following months were intense. We had to reconstruct and condense my story, *Lead Like a Girl*—all the pages you have in front of you—to ten minutes and one message only. While this was a goal and a dream, as the event got closer, the idea of speaking in front of eight hundred people and potentially a few thousand over the internet started to dawn on me, but I made a conscious decision to focus on the positive and enjoy the ride!

So many great friends came to the rescue. They taught me the value of sisterhood. I will finish with four mini-stories of gratitude from this incredible experience.

- The first is about sisterhood and a special woman called BatSheva—she was the Google head of communication who helped us for the TOM event; we became friends. I gave her chapters of my book to read. As a new mom, she felt they were written for her. A few months later she came for dinner and when she heard about the TED Talk, she decided to offer me a three-hour communication workshop. Those three hours became a weekly session—she guided me on everything from how to speak to what to wear. She refused to take any pay and said it was not transactional. She was on maternity, had some spare time and she was getting so much back. Two weeks before the trip she told me she never does half a job so had bought her ticket and was coming to Israel to support me! I was stunned—I was so grateful for her generosity! She even helped me hook up with the two leading women's magazines in Israel—all out of her sisterhood support. We pampered her with an incredible time in Israel—not knowing it was her birthday, but she said it was the perfect gift—she had a much-needed break, saw the beautiful country, and was doing what she loved—prepping talents. I am forever grateful to my own self-elected chief brand and communication officer BatSheva.
- The second is about having the gratitude to trust that when one door closes, another opens. A few months before the TED Talk, I had been invited to speak at a P&G alumni event in November. Then a few weeks later I was taken off the agenda. I felt deeply disappointed, even rejected. But upon reflecting on this rejection, I realized that if I had taken up that engagement, I wouldn't have had the time to take on the TED

opportunity. Same with my decision to take a career pause to figure what's next, which opened the door to teaching at university and developing my new corporate consulting career. I even wrote a gratitude letter to my tissue box boss, as it was that hardship that propelled me to take action to promote mental well-being at the workplace. Living in gratitude is staying open to opportunities and recognizing that when one door closes, another better one can come into play.

- The third is about fear of failure and fear of success. Remember when I shared with you that I not only had a fear of failure but also a fear of success? Going on stage, my feet were shaking but I kept remembering my why—I was there to share my story in hopes it would inspire others to share theirs and live more authentic whole lives.

- The last story is about my supportive tribe—from the moment the tickets went live, my husband orchestrated for all of my family and friends to sit in row three—almost fifty friends and family showed up. And so, as I was standing meditating behind the curtains about to go on stage, I thought about all these amazing men and women I have in my life—my family, friends—new and old—my students, and my mentees, and I knew I *had* to be brave.

Courage is not the absence of fear. It's about facing your fear, remembering your purpose, digging into your superpowers, and stepping out onto the stage.

And when the talk ended, my friends in row three stood up, lifting the whole hall to a standing ovation—wow! I stood there on the red circle, limelight on my face, feeling immense gratitude for taking this leap, and hopefully encouraging others to take theirs and lead like a girl and live their lives with an attitude of gratitude!

GRATITUDE EXERCISES[22]

1. Every morning while brushing your teeth, reflect on three things you are grateful for.
2. Write a letter of appreciation to someone important in your life. Share it with the person.
3. Photographic savoring—you can use an app (e.g., Day One journal), which allows you to capture a picture of something that made you happy that day for which you are grateful—a great way to keep appreciating the good in our lives!
4. New gratitude narrative to painful experiences—closing doors, opening new doors. Think about a time in your life when someone rejected you, when you failed, when you missed out on something important, or when a big plan collapsed. These would be points in your life when a door closed. Give yourself space to process and reflect on the negative experience and don't rush to heal. When ready, reflect on what happened after: What doors opened? What would never have happened if the first door didn't close? Write down these experiences. Seeing the positive silver lining is key to posttraumatic growth (as we will cover in the next chapter). Now think of all the people that helped you open that new door; how can you share gratitude? How can you help others see new positive doors to be opened?
5. As a leader—start each occasion of feedback with what is working and what is good about the employee, and be positive on how they can use their strengths to solve the issues. Don't sugarcoat the negative, but build hope in their abilities to turn it around.
6. As a leader, reflect each week—who on your team did exceptionally well this week? Share weekly messages of gratitude—make this positive feedback personal and specific for others to be encouraged by and learn from. Encourage the other leaders on your teams to do the same.
7. As a team—celebrate success! On a public board, encourage your leaders to call out exceptional employees and celebrate their successes.

15

BRINGING IT ALL TOGETHER: POSTTRAUMATIC GROWTH

Never let a good crisis go to waste.

—Winston Churchill

This book was written before we were hit with the world crisis of COVID-19—a crisis that has affected the health of millions as well as the mental health of the entire world. Statistics show that one in four employees experienced work-related anxiety and mental health issues even before COVID-19. And we have seen a rise in anxiety of almost 200 percent due to the immediate health concerns and job security issues surrounding COVID-19, as well as the loneliness and mental challenges that come with prolonged isolation and childcare under quarantine. Prior to this pandemic, the cost of stress-related diseases to the economy was projected to reach an estimated 16 trillion US dollars by 2030.[1] The good news, as I shared throughout this book, is that anxiety and stress is treatable and adopting the 5P model of leading like a girl can help build personal wellness, employee wellness, and resilience. So, while this model was critical pre–COVID-19, with the leadership crisis and mental health crisis we are experiencing due to COVID-19, adopting these skills be-comes paramount.

The COVID-19 crisis was not only a stress test for my 5P model, it also helped bolster my thesis on the urgent need for feminine leadership. As Stefanie K. Johnson calls out in her *Bloomberg* article titled "2021 Is a Tipping Point for Female Leaders":

> The pandemic accelerated questions about whether a "female leadership style" is more effective than the traditionally autocratic male style. When crisis hits, research shows that the preference for command-and-control leadership wanes and a need for relational leadership increases. And indeed, several countries led by men have bungled the public health effort, while female-led countries like New Zealand, Germany, Finland, Iceland, Denmark, Norway, and Taiwan have fared better.[2]

This is explained with the growing need for relational leadership traits in general and even more so during a crisis.

> Using a computer program to qualitatively analyze the content of 251 briefings between April 1, 2020 and May 5, 2020 the authors found that women showed greater empathy and support for followers' welfare. When people feel that leaders are taking care of them, they become more willing to comply with requests to social distance and wear masks. It is basically the norm of reciprocity. . . . An analysis of 122 speeches made by heads of governments across the globe showed that male leaders used more war analogies and fear-based tactics in talking about the virus. In contrast, female leaders focused on people—families, children and vulnerable groups—with a message of compassion and social cohesion.[3]

The "think manager, think male" stereotype no longer stands alone. As 2021 unfolds, we can add a new one: "Think leader, think lady."

Alone in a quarantine hotel room, I decided to add this last chapter, which talks about not only bouncing back from hardship but how we can leverage crisis and trauma in our lives to GROW.

Ancient philosophers have long argued that a time of crisis is an opportunity for growth. We also find this when studying etymology in ancient languages. In Chinese, the word *crisis* is comprised of two characters—the first means "danger" but the other character means "inflection point" or "opportunity." The same is true in Hebrew where the word for crisis, "mashber," is also found in the Bible to mean the last stage before birth.

This idea is further developed in the work of Richard G. Tedeschi and Lawrence Calhoun, who coined the term "posttraumatic growth" (PTG) in the mid-nineties. They define PTG as "a positive psychological change in the wake of a struggle with highly challenging life circumstances."[4] PTG involves life-altering and favorable psychological changes that can potentially modify the way we perceive the world. It comes with a new understanding of life, relationships, money, success, and health. Posttraumatic growth goes beyond acknowledgment or acceptance of a crisis; it entwines personal strength and self-dependence, and while it may still be painful, PTG provides us with a new way of redirecting that pain and turning it into something useful.

While resilience has been defined as our ability to *bounce back* from a difficulty or challenge, PTG is about our ability to *grow* from difficulties. In their research, Tedeschi and Calhoun highlight five drivers of PTG: spiritual strength, personal strength, new possibilities and goals, gratitude, and relationships. Turning one's pain into purpose is essentially about having a positive perspective, maintaining optimism and hope, and focusing on possibilities.

Reflecting on how my experience of workplace bullying led me to write this book, I have come to realize that I had experienced a level of trauma that I had to work through. Considering the intergenerational trauma already existing in the world pre-COVID, and the various levels of pain inflicted by this pandemic worldwide, I cannot help but reflect on how we individually and collectively process trauma. How do we now turn this pain into purpose, this mess into our message? While we might have preferred not to experience this trauma, we can commit to the learning and growth that comes with this experience and help each other grow from our traumatic experiences.

Throughout this book, I delve into each area of the 5P model and demonstrate how it has helped me overcome my struggles and live my best life. With COVID-19, I was drawn back to my 5P model and gave myself a dose of my own medicine. In this last chapter, I would like to bring it all together and dive deeper into what it means to experience PTG and how *you* can apply the 5P model to dealing with COVID-19 and other adversities that may come your way (figure 15.1).

I have also used the 5P model to summarize what *you* as a self-leader and people leader can do to ensure you build resilience to weather any storm.

> The only definition for happiness is wholeness.
>
> —Helen Keller

The word *health* in Latin, "salus," is derived from *sarvas* which means "whole." You cannot be mentally healthy if you are not whole. Said differently, while we don't need to be scoring 10/10 in each of the 5P dimensions, we do need to be growing and making progress in each of them. You may be very spiritual, positive, and

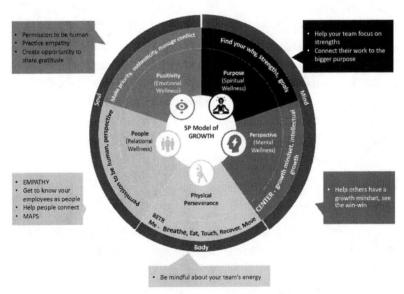

Figure 15.1. 5P Model for Posttraumatic Growth.

adamant about your physical wellness, but one challenging relationship that you ignore robs you of being truly happy. Let's cover the 5P dimensions one at a time and distill strategies that can be applied to build resilience and drive posttraumatic growth.

Purpose

Purpose is about connecting spiritually, having a higher meaning, linking to one's strengths, and looking for new possibilities. It is about focusing on what a person can control versus what they cannot control.

A leader's role is not just managing the business but also managing the people who manage the business. *As a leader*, ask yourself: "Am I spending time understanding my team's strengths, and helping them find new opportunities to bring their best selves to life each day? Do I help them imagine and set goals that focus on creating a better future?" Research during COVID-19 has demonstrated that those who have a purpose and love what they are doing are almost four times more likely to rank themselves as highly resilient.

How has COVID-19 forced or enabled you to pivot your career? What new possibilities were made available to you? What new connections have you made?

COVID-19 hit me just as I was pivoting to build a new career as a speaker and consultant. March 2020 was supposed to be my busiest month ever, with over twenty paid events booked for International Women's Day. One after the other, all those events were canceled and my income from speaking for that month was almost zero and while luckily I was not starving, I felt my world collapse around me. Did I just make a huge mistake leaving the corporate world? In February I was asked by my university to move my whole course online. I was sure it wouldn't work! My students are already so shy—how can we talk emotional bravery online? Yet at the end of that lesson, I sat pleasantly stunned. My students were as participative as ever. In fact, one of my students told a very personal story. It seemed that "hiding" behind a screen had made them much braver.

I felt the huge suffering around me and understood that the computer screen was not a barrier. I was compelled to act, sharing what I have learned about mental wellness with employees. If I could teach them to find resilience and joy at time of deepest anxiety, I would be fully living my purpose and doing my bit to help the intense global post-pandemic anxiety. Success with my students and that challenge encouraged me to turn my course into an online corporate training program, which I called "Building Resilience, Choosing Joy." I started by piloting sessions with friends and word quickly spread. I was invited to give the course to companies and, within six months, I started working with some of the biggest tech companies in the industry.

The extended isolation also encouraged me to reach out to my contacts. During a casual connection with a friend, Oren Appel, I heard about his off-line "Happiness at Work" game. "I would love to add your game to my training," I told him. "But I need an online version."

"I have been planning to create an online version," he said, "but have no time or money for that endeavor. Would you partner with me?" I wasn't planning on becoming an Edu-Tech start-up founder, but this project was an exciting opportunity very much aligned with my purpose. I roped my mentor Tal Ben-Shahar in as a third business partner, deepened and expanded the scientific grounding of the game, created a business model where we would spread joy by qualifying trainers to bring this game to as many companies as possible, and, voilà!—our new company, "Uppiness: Up your game at work," was created. Our first "train the trainer" qualification program went live in January 2022 as well as game booking with some of the most prominent companies like Google and Microsoft. One of the participants mentioned: "This is the most fun I had with my colleagues in months . . ."

Am I successful? I am still only making a fraction of what I made in the past. But despite the circumstances, I am able to live my purpose—to work with individuals and companies to find purpose and joy. I was able to help employees reframe their challenges and teach themselves science-based strategies to alleviate their anxiety. And the online disadvantage became an advantage as, suddenly, companies were motivated to broaden their reach by offering training across locations, and we were able to connect with employees when and where they needed the message most.

I feel privileged to have a stable support system and to know that my worst difficulties during the COVID-19 quarantine were simply about reframing my situation and staying laser-focused on my purpose. During that time, I found a new way to not only survive but thrive. I helped my coaching clients and training participants see new possibilities. One of my clients, whom I was supporting during this period, also received an unexpected opportunity that she welcomed and accepted. While she was shocked that the offer seemed to come in from nowhere, I was not. This is the power of surrendering to serendipity and staying focused on purpose. I believe that the universe aligns with a mind that is made up. I continue to feel blessed and grateful for this ability to stay focused on purpose and help others do the same.

What new possibilities could you uncover from your challenges? *As a leader*, how can you encourage your team to unlock new opportunities?

Perspective and Mental Perseverance

Perspective and mental perseverance is about mentally reframing a situation and having a growth mindset. In the context of COVID-19, someone with a fixed mindset might have seen the situation as a given, their failures as their fault, the news as overwhelming, and being locked at home as suffocating.

As a leader, encourage your team to develop a growth mindset, to see possibilities, to focus on what they can control (versus what they can't), to focus on what they have (versus what they are missing), and to design a better future (versus dwelling on the past). Research shows that the amount of posttraumatic growth is positively correlated with the amount of cognitive engagement and reappraisal.

So on top of my own need to reappraise the situation to turn it into a positive experience, I had a crisis I had to work through as an executive coach when five of my coaching clients were let go from their jobs. This was an unprecedented challenge as many were core breadwinners for their families. We spent the time reframing the situation as an opportunity, clarifying their true purposes, and focusing on how to find new jobs that better fulfilled those purposes. I am grateful and overjoyed to share that, six months later, all five of my coaching clients found new jobs that they are happier with and admit that losing their jobs was actually the best thing that could have happened to them. It forced them to rethink and refocus on what matters most. They all suffered posttraumatic stress from being let go in the middle of a major financial crisis, but the inner work that they did using the 5Ps helped them not only bounce back but actually experience posttraumatic growth.

So what are you doing to build your mental resilience and growth mindset and how can you help your employees?

Physical Perseverance

Physical perseverance was not mentioned in Tedeschi and Calhoun's model. However, given the mind-body link, it is clearly critical in building the energy needed to grow from trauma. Trauma and emotional stress wear you out. In the context of COVID-19, employees are Zoomed out of their minds (Zoom being the online video conferencing platform). The boundaries between work and home are blurred, so employees are overwhelmed from being constantly online. They aren't eating properly, and confinement means they are not spending enough time outdoors. This, together with the concern about job security and isolation and the extra burden from childcare or tending to elderly parents, is creating a mental health crisis that may even rival the physical impact of falling sick with COVID-19. During times of crisis, it is even more CRITICAL that we pay close attention to our energy (as described in chapter 3) and how we can focus on becoming a BETR Me—Breathe-Eat-Touch-Recovery-

Movement. Are you meditating (Breathe)? Are you binge-eating fast food, or are you paying attention to nourishing your body with high quality food (Eat)? Being home alone or with your family, partner, and pets is perhaps something you take for granted. Are you investing in meaningful Touch? Think about Recovery. This is an important one in an always-on world. Are you being conscious about digitally detoxing, sleeping well, and taking the time to play? And finally, Movement. Even in confinement, you are able to move by doing yoga or weights, or within the countries that allow it, are you finding solitude in exercising outdoors?

As a leader, encourage your team to digitally detox and pay attention to their energy levels in order to maintain their mental health. Don't just say you care about the team's mental and physical health. Model it so that your team feels they can prioritize self-care and set boundaries.

I am lucky to have been able to invest in physical wellness transformation during this pandemic. Before quarantine, I had connected with friends who share a similar passion for wellness. In quarantine, we created a monthly wellness experience in our homes where we were able to invite up to five people in accordance with Singaporean social-distancing rules. We experimented with Wim Hof's training. Known as the Iceman, Wim Hof has demonstrated that following his method of using ice baths can increase energy, reduce stress, and potentially strengthen the immune system by significantly reducing symptoms of flu and empowering the body's immune system to fight bacteria and viruses as noted in eight independent university studies.[5]

On top of the ice bath habit, I paid attention to immunity-boosting supplements like vitamins D and C, omega-3, and nutriments like chicken soup (called by many the Jewish penicillin), raw honey, and iron, probiotic-rich, and fermented foods, as well as working out and other physical exercise, whether it was yoga when locked in my hotel room or high-intensity weight training. We did HIIT sessions as a family three times a week while we were confined at home. We also conducted as many "walking meetings" as possible once we were allowed out. My favorite new habit has been a twenty-minute midday nap. And finally, I started free online yoga classes for my community of friends and neighbors.

Some less fortunate really struggled physically, as they fell below the poverty line. Yet many people suffered physically due to a lack of awareness and "Zoom-mania," sitting for long hours.

During a crisis, the area most likely to be neglected is our health and energy—and that is the area that needs the most focus.

How conscious are you about taking extra care of your health and energy, which is especially critical during challenging times? How are you helping your team stay focused on their physical wellness?

People and Relationships

As mentioned in section IV, our quality of life is largely determined by the quality of our relationships. More people have suffered from the isolation that came with COVID-19 than have endured the virus itself. As a manager, you have a responsibility to make an extra effort to connect with your team, especially when they are working remotely. In research conducted by *Harvard Business Review* with Qualtrics and SAP, it was found that nearly 40 percent of global employees said no one at their company checked in to see how they were doing, and those respondents were 38 percent more likely to say that their mental health declined during the pandemic. Seventy percent of employees would have appreciated their managers (and not HR) doing so.[6]

As a leader, try to go beyond asking "how are you?" Really listen. And when someone shares that they are struggling, create a safe space and be compassionate. Then be specific and flexible about how you can help and offer whatever support is needed. Don't make assumptions about what each person needs. Ask them and be flexible to problem solve. Encourage socializing and locate allies with whom they can share the load. Resilience is a learned skill. As a manager, you can encourage your company to invest now more than ever in resilience training. *A leader who isn't investing in their team's mental health should ask themselves if they are really leading.*

One obvious tip is to reach out to friends and family and to your team for daily check-ins. Another one is to have a casual coffee with total strangers. I decided during the pandemic to have one deep meaningful connection with a total stranger once a week. I aimed for a weekly chat with an individual from within my LinkedIn connections. I would usually do these chats while walking in the green corridor (jungle walk in Singapore). Ten of these chats resulted in deep partnerships and collaborations, like the one I mentioned with Oren and the establishment of Uppiness. This did not replace face-to-face interactions, and yet you would be amazed at how deep you can go relatively fast, even online.

Positivity and Gratitude

Positivity and gratitude are about being optimistic and being appreciative of what one has as opposed to what one has lost. Accepting negative emotions as opposed to fighting them is important, as is giving ourselves permission to be human and learning to CENTER our emotions (Contain-Explain-Name-Tame-Empathize-Reframe), before we choose how to act. And finally, positivity is about gratitude and giving. When it rains, look for the rainbow.

As a leader, how can you meet your people where they are, to sit uncomfortably and empathetically with their struggles? How can you share your own vulnerability so they understand that it is okay to feel low sometimes? How can you go out of your way to share gratitude and encourage your team to focus on helping others? Some of your people might be going through real grief from loss of a loved one. Often managers and colleagues don't know how to deal with grief and withdraw when their people need them most. Be there to listen and support but also respect their individual approach to dealing with grief. Key is to be there for them and help them feel truly "felt."

This period helped us as a family connect with our neighbors and with the broader community as I offered free yoga and meditation, and it gave us more time and renewed energy to increase our volunteer work on our different causes (including a school in Myanmar and women's education).

But I would like to finish off with a personal story on how leading like a girl also helps people around you gain perspective and stay positive. In this case I will focus on my eldest daughter, Mia, who is officially part of the graduating class of 2020. It was the morning of April 27, 2020, and my eldest daughter Mia cried for the first time since the beginning of the three months of quarantine. And she had reasons, too: her IB (International Baccalaureate) final exams were canceled, her graduation ceremony was canceled, her end-of-year summer trip was canceled, and she had to spend her last few months in Singapore at home and away from her friends.

In the grand scheme of things, Mia lives a privileged life. Her dreams were put on hold, yes, and so were everyone else's. Still, she was upset, like we all are.

We did everything we could to show her the upside of quarantine life: we had fun family meals every night followed by game nights, she had amazing quality time with us and her siblings before leaving home for good—playing guitar, learning to cook, doing tie-dye art. We had fun family workouts several times a week, outrageous family Tik-Tok competitions, cookout competitions Zoom calls with friends, and on and on . . .

Yet it was on the morning of her eighteenth birthday that she broke down in tears. She would have to celebrate her first legal drink while stuck in quarantine and she could not hold back her tears any longer.

We organized the next best thing—a Zoom party with *all* of her friends and family from around the world, disco balls, a professional DJ, delivery cocktails for her "squad," a funky birthday cake . . . the works. And finally, we organized a surprise "visit" from her favorite singer, who kindly agreed to do a live show over Zoom. We were glad that we were able to support local talent who had lost their source of income while making our daughter happy, too.

In the beginning, the teens felt awkward, but after a while they were dancing their hearts away, dancing as if no one was watching. And when the singer suddenly appeared on our full screen to wish Mia happy birthday, she was lost for words. The next morning, when Mia woke up after dancing all night long, she said to me, "Mom, this was the *best* eighteenth birthday I could have ever asked for. I could have all my friends celebrate with me, not only my Singapore squad—it was so special." Wow, what a growth mindset!

As a result of the pandemic, Mia decided to defer her Ivy league degree. Instead, she chose to enroll in a leadership gap year program where she led a major environmental awareness program as well as volunteered to help the elderly struggling with isolation. Mia shifted her focus from being self-consumed to being focused on others. Her key phrase during this time was "it was so meaningful."

As I watch the pandemic play out all across the world, I know that most children will not get to experience this care, or effort, or luxury. This, however, was our way of teaching our children how to pivot when our expectations aren't met—how to question why we feel we are entitled to some things. As parents, we want to teach our children to build resilience and choose joy. Sadly, COVID-19 provided for an incredible pressure test. Hopefully after this, they will be able to handle anything and will not only bounce back but discover that they have experienced posttraumatic growth.

This is a horrific pandemic. It is as if we've reached the end of the world. With millions dead or sick, natural disasters around the world, the spread of hatred, and the loss of livelihood, the world is definitely full of danger. This crisis has completely redefined what I think of as optimism. Yet, I really believe that this crisis is also an important inflection point for us all to shift our perspective toward what *really* matters. So instead of locking yourself in when faced with adversities, try asking yourself, "What is the universe trying to teach me?" In this case, the COVID-19 message to us is loud and clear for those who take time to listen:

- Be more compassionate—to ourselves, to others, to the planet, as the purpose of living is giving. Kindness is contagious. Leave each person just a little better after they meet you.
- Reach out to people less fortunate than yourself and build solidarity with them. Redefine wealth for yourself and for others.
- Open our eyes to our blind spots and to how poorly we have been treating our planet.
- Stop rampant consumerism—focus inward, focus on the simple pleasures, focus on our families—as most of what we are grateful for is actually free (like nature).
- Learn to accept and surrender—to changed plans and canceled events, and acknowledge that the world continues to revolve around the sun. Find the silver lining—seek what new doors open due to the crisis.
- Learn that true happiness is not getting what you want but wanting and appreciating what you already have!

I don't like the sentence, "Things always happen for the better." I think that it is a passive approach and is on the verge of toxic positivity. I prefer how my friend, Tal Ben-Shahar, has rephrased it:

Things don't necessarily happen for the best, but we can make the best of things that happen.

In other words, we can turn lemons into an amazing lemonade by changing our perspective and by:

- Focusing on what we can do better in the future versus how things were in the past.
- Focusing on what we can control versus what we cannot.
- Focusing on what we have versus what we are missing.
- Focusing on building community, building solidarity, and giving generously.

I dedicate this final chapter to the iconic graduating class of 2020 and to all kids who have struggled through the pandemic, who've had their lives turned upside-down, had their health or their loved ones' health affected, and yet were able to stay focused on what matters most.

When we "Lead Like a Girl" with Purpose-Power-Perspective-People-and-Positivity, we are able to find our rainbow when it rains and not only bounce back but come out of this and any future crisis stronger than ever.

May we stay healthy and happy, always.

ACTIVITY

Drivers of Posttraumatic Growth (PTG)

Posttraumatic growth is about the self-improvement that comes after experiencing life challenges. Tedeschi and Calhoun created this inventory for you to assess how you relate to any given trauma—whether you are able to turn the pain into purpose and experience posttraumatic growth (table 15.1). Each of the twenty statements falls under one of the five dimensions of PTG and is scored accordingly. A summation of the scores indicates the level of posttraumatic growth. Splitting these into five categories enables you to see which areas of self-development need more attention.

Score yourself: 0 meaning "I did not experience this as a result of my crisis" and 5 meaning "I experienced this change to a very great degree as a result of my crisis."

Below is an overview of the test items, along with the characterization of the five factors:

- Relation to Others—Item numbers 6, 8, 9, 15, 16, 20
- New Possibilities—Item numbers 3, 7, 11, 14, 17

- Personal Strengths—Item numbers 4, 10, 12, 19
- Spiritual Enhancement—Item numbers 5, 18
- Appreciation—Item numbers 1, 2, 13

Table 15.1. Posttraumatic Growth Inventory

Statements	Scoring:	0	1	2	3	4	5
1. I changed my priorities about what is important in life.							
2. I have a greater appreciation for the value of my own life.							
3. I have developed new interests.							
4. I have a greater feeling of self-reliance.							
5. I have a better understanding of spiritual matters.							
6. I more clearly see that I can count on people in times of trouble.							
7. I established a new path for my life.							
8. I have a greater sense of closeness with others.							
9. I am more willing to express my emotions.							
10. I know that I can handle difficulties.							
11. I can do better things with my life.							
12. I am better able to accept the way things work out.							
13. I can better appreciate each day.							
14. New opportunities are available which wouldn't have been otherwise.							
15. I have more compassion for others.							
16. I put more effort into my relationships.							
17. I am more likely to try to change things that need changing.							
18. I have stronger religious faith.							
19. I discovered that I'm stronger than I thought I was.							
20. I learned a great deal about how wonderful people are.							

NOTES

PREFACE

1. Marty Swant, "20 Memorable Ads From the Past Decade (for Better and for Worse)," *Forbes*, December 29, 2019, https://www.forbes.com/sites/martyswant/2020/12/29/20-memorable-ads-from-the-past-decade-for-better-and-for-worse/#1e9d76631cdd.

2. Annamarie Mann and Jim Harter, "The Worldwide Employee Engagement Crisis," Gallup Workplace, January 7, 2016, https://www.gallup.com/workplace/236495/worldwide-employee-engagement-crisis.aspx.

3. "Mental Health in the Workplace," World Health Organization, accessed November 15, 2021, https://www.who.int/teams/mental-health-and-substance-use/promotion-prevention/mental-health-in-the-workplace.

4. Donald Sull, Charles Sull, and Ben Zweig, "Toxic Culture Is Driving the Great Resignation," *MIT Sloan Management Review* 63, no. 2 (2022): 1–9.

5. "Mental Health in the Workplace."

6. Ibid.

7. Charles Duhigg, "What Google Learned from Its Quest to Build the Perfect Team," *New York Times Magazine*, February 25, 2016, https://www.nytimes.com/2016/02/28/magazine/what-google-learned-from-its-quest-to-build-the-perfect-team.html?smid=fb-nytimes&smtyp=cur&_r=0&pagewanted=all.

8. William A. Kahn, "Psychological Conditions of Personal Engagement and Disengagement at Work," *Academy of Management Journal* 33, no. 4 (1990): 692–724, https://doi.org/10.5465/256287.

9. Amy Edmondson, "Psychological Safety and Learning Behavior in Work Teams," *Administrative Science Quarterly* 44, no. 2 (1999): 350–83, https://doi.org/10.2307/2666999.

10. Sara H. Konrath, Edward H. O'Brien, and Courtney Hsing, "Changes in Dispositional Empathy in American College Students Over Time: A Meta-Analysis," *Personality and Social Psychology Review* 15, no. 2 (August 5, 2010): 180–98, https://doi.org/10.1177/1088868310377395.

11. Jack Zenger and Joseph Folkman, "Research: Women Score Higher Than Men in Most Leadership Skills," *Harvard Business Review*, June 25, 2019, https://hbr.org/2019/06/research-women-score-higher-than-men-in-most-leadership-skills.

12. James Charles Collins and Jerry I. Porras, *Built to Last: Successful Habits of Visionary Companies* (New York: HarperCollins, 1994).

13. Nilima Bhat and Raj Sisodia, *Shakti Leadership: Embracing Feminine and Masculine Power in Business* (Oakland, CA: Berrett-Koehler, 2016).

14. "Lead Like a Girl," Dalia Feldheim, TEDxJaffaWomen, YouTube, June 3, 2020, https://www.youtube.com/watch?v=nAUIJlAhW5c&t=9s&ab_channel=TEDxTalks.

I. LEAD WITH PURPOSE, LIVE IN FLOW

1. "Mihaly Csikszentmihalyi & Flow," Pursuit of Happiness, accessed July 15, 2021, https://www.pursuit-of-happiness.org/history-of-happiness/mihaly-csikszentmihalyi/.

2. Eva Ritvo, "The Neuroscience of Giving," *Psychology Today* (April 24, 2014), https://www.psychologytoday.com/us/blog/vitality/201404/the-neuroscience-giving.

3. Viktor E. Frankl, *Man's Search for Meaning: An Introduction to Logotherapy* (Boston: Beacon, 2006).

4. Caroline Castrillon, "Why Purpose Is the New Competitive Advantage," *Forbes* (April 28, 2019), https://www.forbes.com/sites/

carolinecastrillon/2019/04/28/why-purpose-is-the-new-competitive-advantage/?sh=205fb56a711f.

5. John Mackey and Rajendra S. Sisodia, *Conscious Capitalism: Liberating the Heroic Spirit of Business* (Boston: Harvard Business Review, 2014).

6. Simon Sinek, "Start With 'Why,'" TED Talk, September 22, 2016, https://www.youtube.com/watch?v=2Ss78LfY3nE.

7. #TouchThePickle, "Cannes Lions Case Study: P&G Whisper Gets 3M Indian Women to 'Touch the Pickle,'" Digital Training Academy, accessed July 19, 2021, http://www.digitaltrainingacademy.com/casestudies/2015/07/cannes_lions_case_study_pg_whisper_gets_3m_indian_women_to_touch_the_pickle.php.

8. Gina Mei, "This Ad Just Won Sheryl Sandberg's Award for Shattering Gender Stereotypes," HelloGiggles, June 23, 2015, https://hellogiggles.com/news/sheryl-sandberg-glass-lion/.

9. #LikeAGirl, "Super Bowl 2015: Always Ad," YouTube, accessed July 19, 2021, https://www.youtube.com/watch?v=F_Ep0O5fWN4&ab_channel=WallStreetJournal.

10. Mei, "This Ad Just Won," HelloGiggles.

11. Jack Zenger and Joseph Folkman, "Research: Women Score Higher Than Men in Most Leadership Skills," *Harvard Business Review,* June 25, 2019.

12. Dalia Feldheim, "Dalia Feldheim," accessed July 15, 2021, https://daliafeldheim.com/.

13. Simon Sinek, David Mead, and Peter Docker, *Find Your Why* (New York: Portfolio, 2017).

2. THE SCIENCE OF GOAL SETTING

1. Tal Ben-Shahar, "The Science of Happiness," Happiness Studies Academy, accessed July 15, 2021, https://www.happinessstudies.academy/.

2. Simon Sinek, *Start with Why: How Great Leaders Inspire Everyone to Take Action* (New York: Penguin, 2009).

3. G. T. Doran, "There's a S.M.A.R.T. Way to Write Management's Goals and Objectives," *Management Review* 70, no. 11 (November 1981): 35–36.

4. Tony Robbins, "Tony Robbins: Rapid Planning Method," Robbins Research International, 2016, https://cdnwp.tonyrobbins.com/wp-content/uploads/2016/11/RPM-Sample-Book2.pdf.

3. MASTER ENERGY, NOT TIME

1. "Live Dirty, Eat Clean: Robynne Chutkan, MD On Everything Microbiome," Dr. Robynne Chutkan, accessed July 15, 2021, https://robynnechutkan.com/featured_item/live-dirty-eat-clean/.

2. Mark Hyman, "ULTRAMIND®: The 6-Week Plan to Heal Your Brain," video, Dr. Mark Hyman, November 25, 2019, https://drhyman.com/blog/2010/08/30/the-ultramind-solution-the-6-week-plan-to-heal-your-brain-2/.

3. Dan Buettner, "How to Live to Be 100+," TEDxTC, 2009, https://www.ted.com/talks/dan_buettner_how_to_live_to_be_100?language=en.

4. Patrick L. Hill and Nicholas A. Turiano, "Purpose in Life as a Predictor of Mortality Across Adulthood." *Psychological Science* 25, no. 7 (2014): 1482–86.

5. David DiSalvo, "How Breathing Calms Your Brain, and Other Science-Based Benefits of Controlled Breathing," *Forbes*, November 29, 2017, https://www.forbes.com/sites/daviddisalvo/2017/11/29/how-breathing-calms-your-brain-and-other-science-based-benefits-of-controlled-breathing/?sh=fff3a7e22219.

6. This writing is based on my own learning and experience and I also consulted with my functional medicine culinary nutritionist—Karin G. Reiter, https://nutritiousndelicious.com/.

7. Alexa Gingerich, "What Is S.M.A.S.H.? Why It Should Matter to You," Philadelphia Integrative Medicine, August 9, 2020, https://philly-im.com/blog/2020/7/24/what-is-smash-why-it-should-matter-to-you.

8. Kris Gunnars, "What Is Intermittent Fasting? Explained in Human Terms," *Healthline Media*, June 4, 2017, https://www.healthline.com/nutrition/what-is-intermittent-fasting#TOC_TITLE_HDR_2.

9. Rachael Link, "16/8 Intermittent Fasting: A Beginner's Guide," *Healthline Media*, September 4, 2018, https://www.healthline.com/nutrition/16-8-intermittent-fasting.

10. Kavisha N. Abeyasekera, "Benefits of Intermittent Fasting: A Systematic Review of Randomized Clinical Trials," *Dominican Scholar*,

Dominican University of California, 2020, https://scholar.dominican.edu/physician-assistant-studies-student-articles/12/.

11. Udo Erasmus, *Fats That Heal, Fats That Kill: The Complete Guide to Fats, Oils, Cholesterol and Human Health* (Burnaby, BC, Canada: Alive, 1997).

12. Mayo Clinic Staff, "Water: How Much Should You Drink Every Day?," Mayo Foundation for Medical Education and Research, October 14, 2020, https://www.mayoclinic.org/healthy-lifestyle/nutrition-and-healthy-eating/in-depth/water/art-20044256.

13. "The Dirty Dozen & the Clean Fifteen," Nutritious & Delicious, January 4, 2019, https://nutritiousndelicious.com/2019/01/04/the-dirty-dozen-the-clean-fifteen/.

14. John Yudkin, *Pure, White, and Deadly: How Sugar Is Killing Us and What We Can Do to Stop It* (New York: Penguin, 2013).

15. Tiffany Field, *Touch* (Cambridge, MA: A Bradford Book, 2003).

16. "Harlow's Classic Studies Revealed the Importance of Maternal Contact," Association for Psychological Science, June 20, 2018, https://www.psychologicalscience.org/publications/observer/obsonline/harlows-classic-studies-revealed-the-importance-of-maternal-contact.html.

17. Field, *Touch*.

18. Sara C. Mednick and Mark Ehrman, *Take a Nap! Change Your Life: The Scientific Plan to Make You Smarter, Healthier, More Productive* (New York: Workman, 2006).

19. Jeffrey S. Durmer and David F. Dinges, "Neurocognitive Consequences of Sleep Deprivation," *Seminars in Neurology* 25, no. 1 (March 2005): 117–29, https://doi.org/10.1055/s-2005-867080.

20. Christina Neudecker, Nadine Mewes, Anne K. Reimers, and Alexander Woll, "Exercise Interventions in Children and Adolescents with ADHD: A Systematic Review," *Journal of Attention Disorders* 23, no. 4 (2019): 307–324.

21. Peter Schnohr et al., "Dose of Jogging and Long-Term Mortality: The Copenhagen City Heart Study," *Journal of the American College of Cardiology* 65, no. 5 (February 10, 2015): 411–19, https://doi.org/10.1016/j.jacc.2014.11.023.

22. John J. Ratey and Eric Hagerman, *Spark: The Revolutionary New Science of Exercise and the Brain* (New York: Little, Brown, 2013).

23. Brendon Stubbs et al., "Challenges Establishing the Efficacy of Exercise as an Antidepressant Treatment: A Systematic Review and

Meta-Analysis of Control Group Responses in Exercise Randomised Controlled Trials," *Sports Medicine* 46 (May 2015): 699–713, https://doi.org/10.1007/s40279-015-0441-5.

24. J. Eric Ahlskog et al., "Physical Exercise as a Preventive or Disease-Modifying Treatment of Dementia and Brain Aging," *Mayo Clinic Proceedings* 89, no. 9 (September 2011): 876–84, https://doi.org/10.4065/mcp.2011.0252.

25. E. G. Trapp et al., "The Effects of High-Intensity Intermittent Exercise Training on Fat Loss and Fasting Insulin Levels of Young Women," *International Journal of Obesity* 32 (2008): 684–91,https://doi.org/10.1038/sj.ijo.0803781.

4. MINDFUL RECOVERY: THE SCIENCE OF DOING NOTHING

1. Joy R. Rudland, Clinton Golding, and Tim J. Wilkinson, "The Stress Paradox: How Stress Can Be Good for Learning," *Medical Education* 54, no. 1 (November 2019): 40–45, https://doi.org/10.1111/medu.13830.

2. Alia J. Crum, Peter Salovey, and Shawn Achor, "Rethinking Stress: The Role of Mindsets in Determining the Stress Response," *Journal of Personality and Social Psychology* 104, no. 4 (2013): 716–33, https://doi.org/10.1037/a0031201.

3. Tal Ben-Shahar, *Happier: Can You Learn to Be Happy?* (New York: McGraw-Hill, 2008).

4. Jim Loehr and Tony Schwartz, *The Power of Full Engagement: Managing Energy, Not Time, Is the Key to High Performance and Personal Renewal* (New York: Free, 2003).

5. Daniel Goleman and Richard J. Davidson, *Altered Traits: Science Reveals How Meditation Changes Your Mind, Brain, and Body* (New York: Avery/Penguin Random House, 2017).

6. Ben-Shahar, *Happier.*

7. Ellen J. Langer, *Mindfulness: 25th Anniversary Edition* (Cambridge, MA: Da Capo Lifelong, 2014).

8. Manfred F.R. Kets de Vries, "Doing Nothing and Nothing to Do: The Hidden Value of Empty Time and Boredom," *SSRN Electronic Journal* INSEAD Working Paper, no. 2014/37/EFE (May 7, 2014), https://doi.org/10.2139/ssrn.2432964.

9. Will Knight, "'Info-Mania' Dents IQ More Than Marijuana," *New Scientist*, April 22, 2005, https://www.newscientist.com/article/dn7298-info-mania-dents-iq-more-than-marijuana/.

10. Julian Birkinshaw, Jordan Cohen, and Alexandra Samuel, "Conquering Digital Distraction," *Harvard Business Review*, June, 2015, https://hbr.org/2015/06/conquering-digital-distraction.

5. OVERCOMING FEAR AND OUR LIMITING BELIEFS

1. Nilima Bhat and Raj Sisodia, *Shakti Leadership: Embracing Feminine and Masculine Power in Business* (Oakland, CA: Berrett-Koehler, 2016).

2. Nilima Bhat and Raj Sisodia, *Shakti Leadership: Embracing Feminine and Masculine Power* (Oakland, CA: Berrett-Koehler, 2016).

3. Tanza Loudenback, "Spanx Founder Sara Blakely Learned an Important Lesson about Failure from Her Dad—Now She's Passing It on to Her 4 Kids," *Business Insider*, June 17, 2018, https://www.businessinsider.com/spanx-founder-sara-blakely-redefine-failure-2016-10.

4. Carol S. Dweck, *Mindset: The New Psychology of Success* (New York: Random House, 2006).

5. Arlin Cuncic, "What Is Imposter Syndrome," Verywell Mind, February 26, 2021, https://www.verywellmind.com/imposter-syndrome-and-social-anxiety-disorder-4156469.

6. Albert Ellis, "Rational Emotive Behavior Therapy," in *Current Psychotherapies*, ed. Raymond J. Corsini and Danny Wedding (Belmont, CA: Thomson/Brooks/Cole, 2005), 166–201.

7. Marianne Williamson, *A Return to Love: Reflections on the Principles of A Course in Miracles* (New York: HarperOne, 2009).

6. LEARNING TO DANCE WITH ADVERSITY

1. Jim Harter, "Dismal Employee Engagement Is a Sign of Global Mismanagement," 2017, www.gallup.com/workplace/231668/dismal-employee-engagement-sign-globalmismanagement.

2. Arpana Rai and Upasna A. Agarwal, "Workplace Bullying Among Indian Managers: Prevalence, Sources and Bystanders' Reactions," *International Journal of Indian Culture and Business Management* 15, no. 1 (2017): 58–81, https://doi.org/10.1504/ijicbm.2017.10006293.

3. Arpana Rai and Upasna A. Agarwal, "A Review of Literature on Mediators and Moderators of Workplace Bullying: Agenda for Future Research,"*Management Research Review* 41, no. 7 (October 2018): 822–59, https://doi.org/10.1108/mrr-05-2016-0111.

4. Robert I. Sutton, *The No Asshole Rule: Building a Civilized Workplace and Surviving One That Isn't* (New York: Business Plus, 2010).

5. Nilima Bhat and Raj Sisodia, *Shakti Leadership: Embracing Feminine and Masculine Power in Business* (Oakland, CA: Berrett-Koehler, 2016).

7. "SELF-FULLNESS": YOUR RELATIONSHIP WITH YOUR SELF

1. https://www.biography.com/writer/khalil-gibran; also "Kahlil Gibran," Poetry Foundation, https://www.poetryfoundation.org/poets/kahlil-gibran.

2. Jerry Kennard, "Understanding Suicide Among Men," Verywell Mind, December 10, 2020, https://www.verywellmind.com/men-and-suicide-2328492.

3. Sophie Lewis, "Simone Biles Opens Up about Withdrawal from Olympic Competitions: 'I Don't Think You Realize How Dangerous This Is,'" CBS News, July 30, 2021, https://www.cbsnews.com/news/simone-biles-olympics-gymnastics-withdrawal-twisties/.

4. Karen Attiah, "Opinion: What Men Need to Learn from Simone Biles," *Washington Post*, July 30, 2021, https://www.washingtonpost.com/opinions/2021/07/29/biles-is-helping-show-way-mental-health-lets-hope-follow-male-athletes-follow-her-lead/.

5. Adam M. Grant, *Give and Take: A Revolutionary Approach to Success* (New York: Penguin, 2013).

8. MAKING YOUR PARTNER A REAL PARTNER

1. David Schnarch, *Passionate Marriage: Love, Sex, and Intimacy in Emotionally Committed Relationships* (New York: W.W. Norton, 1997).
2. Tony Robbins, "Ultimate Relationship Guide," TonyRobbins.com, accessed July 24, 2021, http://core.tonyrobbins.com/Global/FileLib/PDF/RelGuide_Digital-opt.pdf.
3. Marc Eglon, "HBR Research: Women Score Higher Than Men in Leadership Skills," Taylor Hopkinson, July 8, 2019, https://www.taylorhopkinson.com/women-score-higher-than-men-in-leadership-skills/#:~:text=Skills%20%2D%20Taylor%20Hopkinson-,HBR%20Research%3A%20Women%20Score%20Higher%20Than%20Men%20in%20Leadership%20Skills,of%20the%2019%20competencies%20measured.

9. WORK-LIFE BALANCE AS A PARENT

1. Stephen R. Covey, *The 7 Habits of Highly Effective People: Powerful Lessons in Personal Change* (New York: Simon & Schuster, 2013).
2. Shira Offer and Barbara Schneider, "Revisiting the Gender Gap in Time-Use Patterns: Multitasking and Well-Being among Mothers and Fathers in Dual-Earner Families," *American Sociological Review* 76, no. 6 (2011): 809–833.

10. BECOMING AN INSPIRATIONAL PEOPLE LEADER

1. Gobs of Facts & Statistics on Employee Engagement, Leadership, & Strengths-Based Cultures," Lead Through Strengths, accessed October 22, 2020, https://leadthroughstrengths.com/stats/.
2. Marcus Buckingham and Curt Coffman, *First, Break All the Rules: What the World's Greatest Managers Do Differently* (London: Simon & Schuster, 1998).
3. "Re-Engineering Performance Management," Gallup Workplace, accessed June 25, 2021, https://www.gallup.com/workplace/238064/re-engineering-performance-management.aspx.

4. Jack Zenger and Joseph Folkman, "The Ideal Praise-to-Criticism Ratio," *Harvard Business Review*, March 15, 2013, https://hbr.org/2013/03/the-ideal-praise-to-criticism.

5. Peter F. Drucker, *The Effective Executive* (New York: Harper Business, 2018).

6. Marcus Buckingham and Donald O. Clifton, *Now, Discover Your Strengths* (New York: Simon & Schuster, 2001).

7. William A. Kahn, "Psychological Conditions of Personal Engagement and Disengagement at Work," *Academy of Management Journal* 33, no. 4 (1990): 692–724, https://doi.org/10.5465/256287.

8. Amy Edmondson, "Psychological Safety and Learning Behavior in Work Teams," *Administrative Science Quarterly* 44, no. 2 (1999): 350–83, https://doi.org/10.2307/2666999.

9. Charles Duhigg, "What Google Learned From Its Quest to Build the Perfect Team," *New York Times Magazine*, February 28, 2016, 20.

10. Amy Edmondson, "Unlock the Full Potential of Your Team, Check Your Psychological Safety for Free," Fearless Organization (homepage), accessed July 25, 2021, https://fearlessorganization.com/.

11. Alexander Newman, Ross Donohue, and Nathan Eva, "Psychological Safety: A Systematic Review of the Literature," *Human Resource Management Review* 27, no. 3 (2017): 521–35, https://doi.org/10.1016/j.hrmr.2017.01.001.

12. Amy C. Edmondson, *The Fearless Organization: Creating Psychological Safety in the Workplace for Learning, Innovation, and Growth* (Hoboken, NJ: John Wiley & Sons, 2018).

13. "The VIA Character Strengths Survey: Get to Know Your Greatest Strengths," VIA Institute on Character, 2021.

11. WOMEN HOLD UP HALF THE SKY

1. Camille Rainville, "Be a Lady They Said," narrated by Cynthia Nixon, Girls.Girls.Girls.Magazine, September 28, 2020, https://www.youtube.com/watch?v=c22tr74XuLU&ab_channel=BlancaP%C3%A9rez

2. V. Hunt, D. Layton, and S. Prince, "Diversity Matters," McKinsey & Company (February 2, 2015): 15–29, https://www.mckinsey.com/~/media/mckinsey/business%20functions/organization/our%20insights/why%20diversity%20matters/diversity%20matters.ashx.

3. Alexander Newman, Ross Donohue, and Nathan Eva, "Psychological Safety: A Systematic Review of the Literature," *Human Resource Management Review 27,* no. 3 (2017): 521–35, https://doi.org/10.1016/j.hrmr.2017.01.001.

4. Avivah Wittenberg-Cox, "What Do Countries with the Best Coronavirus Responses Have in Common? Women Leaders," *Forbes,* April 13, 2020, https://www.forbes.com/sites/avivahwittenbergcox/2020/04/13/what-do-countries-with-the-best-coronavirus-reponses-have-in-common-women-leaders/#68f315363dec.

5. Sheryl Sandberg, *Lean In: Women, Work, and the Will to Lead* (New York: Knopf, 2013).

6. Samyukta Mullangi and Reshma Jagsi, "Imposter Syndrome," *JAMA* 322, no. 5 (2019): 403, https://doi.org/10.1001/jama.2019.9788.

7. "Project Implicit," Project Implicit (Harvard University), accessed November 15, 2021, https://implicit.harvard.edu/implicit/.

8. Chimamanda Ngozi Adichie, *We Should All Be Feminists* (New York: Vintage, 2014).

12. POSITIVE POWER: BECOME POLITICALLY SAVVY

1. Rodd Wagner and James K. Harter, *12: The Elements of Great Managing* (New York: Gallup, 2006).

2. J. Horan, *I Wish I'd Known That Earlier in My Career: The Power of Positive Workplace Politics* (New York: John Wiley & Sons, 2011).

3. Jillian D'Onfro, "Facebook's Sheryl Sandberg Spearheaded Something Called the 'Glass Lion' to Help Shatter Gender Stereotypes," *Business Insider,* June 21, 2015, https://www.businessinsider.com/sheryl-sandberg-and-lean-in-organized-cannes-glass-lion-2015-6.

4. Stephen R. Covey, *The 7 Habits of Highly Effective People: Powerful Lessons in Personal Change* (New York: Simon & Schuster, 2013).

5. Rick Brandon and Marty Seldman, *Survival of the Savvy: High-Integrity Political Tactics for Career and Company Success* (New York: Free, 2004).

6. Simon Baddeley and Kim James, "Owl, Fox, Donkey or Sheep: Political Skills for Managers," *Management Education and Development* 18, no. 1 (1987): 3–19, https://doi.org/10.1177/135050768701800101.

7. Covey, *The 7 Habits.*

13. EMOTIONAL BRAVERY: PERMISSION TO BE HUMAN

1. Avivah Wittenberg-Cox, "What Do Countries with the Best Coronavirus Responses Have in Common? Women Leaders," *Forbes*, April 22, 2020, https://www.forbes.com/sites/avivahwittenbergcox/2020/04/13/what-do-countries-with-the-best-coronavirus-reponses-have-in-common-women-leaders/#68f315363dec.

2. Cary Cherniss and Daniel Goleman, *The Emotionally Intelligent Workplace: How to Select For, Measure, and Improve Emotional Intelligence in Individuals, Groups, and Organizations* (San Francisco: Jossey-Bass, 2001), XX.

3. Kelly McGonigal, "How to Make Stress Your Friend," TEDGlobal 2013, https://www.ted.com/talks/kelly_mcgonigal_how_to_make_stress_your_friend?language=en.

4. Joe Tomaka et al., "Cognitive and Physiological Antecedents of Threat and Challenge Appraisal," *Journal of Personality and Social Psychology* 73, no. 1 (1997): 63–72, https://doi.org/10.1037/0022-3514.73.1.63.

5. Martin E. P. Seligman, "Building Resilience," *Harvard Business Review* 89, no. 4 (April 2011): 100–106.

6. Daniel Goleman, *Emotional Intelligence: Why It Can Matter More than IQ* (New York: Bantam, 2012).

7. Victoria L. Brescoll, "Leading with Their Hearts? How Gender Stereotypes of Emotion Lead to Biased Evaluations of Female Leaders," *Leadership Quarterly* 27 (2016): 415–28.

8. Jessica Bennett, "Leaders Are Crying on the Job. Maybe That's a Good Thing," *New York Times*, May 3, 2020, https://www.nytimes.com/2020/05/03/us/politics/crying-politicians-leadership.html.

9. Tom Lutz, *Crying: The Natural and Cultural History of Tears* (New York: W. W. Norton, 2001).

10. Victoria L. Brescoll and Eric Luis Uhlmann, "Can an Angry Woman Get Ahead? Status Conferral, Gender, and Expression of Emotion in the Workplace," *Psychological Science* 19, no. 3 (2008): 268–75.

11. Laurie A. Rudman, Corinne A. Moss-Racusin, Julie E. Phelan, and Sanne Nauts, "Status Incongruity and Backlash Effects: Defending the Gender Hierarchy Motivates Prejudice Against Female Leaders." *Journal of Experimental Social Psychology* 48, no. 1 (2012): 165–79.

12. Ursula Hess, Sylvie Blairy, and Robert E. Kleck, "The Intensity of Emotional Facial Expressions and Decoding Accuracy," *Journal of Nonverbal Behavior* 21, no. 4 (1997): 241–57.

13. Jessica Bennett, "Leaders Are Crying on the Job. Maybe That's a Good Thing."

14. Sara H. Konrath, Edward H. O'Brien, and Courtney Hsing, "Changes in Dispositional Empathy in American College Students Over Time: A Meta-Analysis," *Personality and Social Psychology Review* 15, no. 2 (May 2010): 180–98, https://doi.org/10.1177/1088868310377395.

15. Brown Brené, *The Power of Vulnerability: Teachings on Authenticity, Connection, & Courage* (Louisville, CO: Sounds True, 2012).

16. David Rock, "Managing with the Brain in Mind," *Strategy+Business*, August 27, 2009, https://www.strategy-business.com/article/09306.

17. John E. Sarno, *Mind Over Back Pain: A Radically New Approach to the Diagnosis and Treatment of Back Pain* (New York: Berkley Books, 1986).

18. David Schecter et al., "Outcomes of a Mind-Body Treatment Program for Chronic Back Pain with No Distinct Structural Pathology: A Case Series of Patients Diagnosed and Treated as Tension Myositis Syndrome," *Altern Ther Health Med* 13, no. 5 (2007): 26–35,https://pubmed.ncbi.nlm.nih.gov/17900039/.

19. Adam Grant, "A Mark Of Emotional Intelligence," LinkedIn, 2020, https://www.linkedin.com/posts/adammgrant_a-mark-of-emotional-intelligence-treating-activity-6722879413844803584-AJLe/.

14. POSITIVITY AND GRATITUDE

1. Sonja Lyubomirsky, Laura King, and Ed Diener, "The Benefits of Frequent Positive Affect: Does Happiness Lead to Success?," *Psychological Bulletin* 131, no. 6 (2005): 803–855, https://doi.org/10.1037/0033-2909.131.6.803.

2. Ibid.

3. Shawn Achor, *The Happiness Advantage: The Seven Principles of Positive Psychology That Fuel Success and Performance at Work* (New York: Crown Business, 2010).

4. Barbara L. Fredrickson, "The Role of Positive Emotions in Positive Psychology: The Broaden-and-Build Theory of Positive Emotions," *American Psychologist* 56, no. 3 (March 2001): 218–26, https://doi.org/10.1037/0003-066x.56.3.218.

5. Deborah D. Danner, David A. Snowdon, and Wallace V. Friesen, "Positive Emotions in Early Life and Longevity: Findings from the Nun Study," *Journal of Personality and Social Psychology* 80, no. 5 (2001): 804–813, https://doi.org/10.1037/0022-3514.80.5.804.

6. R. A. Emmons, "Gratitude," in *Character Strengths and Virtues*, ed. M. E. P. Seligman and C. Peterson (New York: Oxford University Press/Values in Action Institute, 2004), 553–68.

7. Martin E. P. Seligman, Tracy A. Steen, Nansook Park, and Christopher Peterson, "Positive Psychology Progress: Empirical Validation of Interventions," *American Psychologist* 60, no. 5 (2005): 410.

8. Giacomo Bono, Robert A. Emmons, and Michael E. McCullough, "Gratitude in Practice and the Practice of Gratitude," in *Positive Psychology in Practice*, ed. P. Alex Linley and Stephen Joseph (Wiley, 2012), 464–81, https://doi.org/10.1002/9780470939338.ch29.

9. Kennon M. Sheldon and Sonja Lyubomirsky, "How to Increase and Sustain Positive Emotion: The Effects of Expressing Gratitude and Visualizing Best Possible Selves," *Journal of Positive Psychology* 1, no. 2 (2006): 73–82, https://doi.org/10.1080/17439760500510676.

10. Martin E. P. Seligman et al., "Positive Psychology Progress: Empirical Validation of Interventions," *American Psychologist* 60, no. 5 (2005): 410–21, https://doi.org/10.1037/0003-066x.60.5.410.

11. Maayan Boiman-Meshita and Hadassah Littman-Ovadia, "The Marital Version of Three Good Things: A Mixed-Method Study," *Journal of Positive Psychology* 16, no. 3 (January 9, 2020): 367–78, https://doi.org/10.1080/17439760.2020.1716046.

12. Jordi Quoidbach et al., "Positive Emotion Regulation and Well-Being: Comparing the Impact of Eight Savoring and Dampening Strategies," *Personality and Individual Differences* 49, no. 5 (2010): 368–73, https://doi.org/10.1016/j.paid.2010.03.048.

13. James B. Avey, Bruce J. Avolio, and Fred Luthans, "Experimentally Analyzing the Impact of Leader Positivity on Follower Positivity and Performance," *Leadership Quarterly* 22, no. 2 (2011): 282–94.

14. Teresa Amabile and Steven Kramer, *The Progress Principle: Using Small Wins to Ignite Joy, Engagement, and Creativity at Work* (Boston: Harvard Business Review, 2011).

15. Sebastian Skalski and Grzegorz Pochwatko, "Gratitude Is Female: Biological Sex, Socio-Cultural Gender versus Gratitude and Positive Orientation," *Current Issues in Personality Psychology* 8, no. 1 (2020): 1–9.

16. Todd B. Kashdan, Anjali Mishra, William E. Breen, and Jeffrey J. Froh, "Gender Differences in Gratitude: Examining Appraisals, Narratives, the Willingness to Express Emotions, and Changes in Psychological Needs," *Journal of Personality* 77, no. 3 (2009): 691–730.

17. Ronald F. Levant and Gini Kopecky, *Masculinity Reconstructed: Changing the Rules of Manhood—At Work, in Relationships and in Family Life* (Plume, 1996).

18. Irvin D. Yalom, *Becoming Myself: A Psychiatrist's Memoir* (New York: Basic, 2019).

19. Jon Kabat-Zinn, *Wherever You Go, There You Are: Mindfulness Meditation in Everyday Life* (New York: Hachette, 2005).

20. Helen Keller, *Three Days to See* (Nanjing: Yilin, 2012).

21. Michael A. Singer, *The Surrender Experiment: My Journey into Life's Perfection* (New York: Harmony, 2015).

22. Martin E. P. Seligman, *Learned Optimism: How to Change Your Mind and Your Life* (New York: Vintage, 2006).

15. BRINGING IT ALL TOGETHER: POSTTRAUMATIC GROWTH

1. Carter Center, "Mental Illness Will Cost the World $16 USD Trillion by 2030," *Psychiatric Times* 35, no. 11 (November 16, 2020), https://www.psychiatrictimes.com/view/mental-illness-will-cost-world-16-usd-trillion-2030.

2. Stefanie K. Johnson, "2021 Is a Tipping Point for Female Leaders," *Bloomberg Business*, January 31, 2021, https://www.bloomberg.com/opinion/articles/2021-01-31/women-leaders-are-doing-better-during-the-pandemic.

3. Ibid.

4. Lawrence G. Calhoun and Richard G. Tedeschi, eds., *Handbook of Posttraumatic Growth: Research and Practice* (Routledge, 2014).

5. "The Science Behind the Wim Hof Method," Wim Hof Method, accessed November 15, 2021, https://www.wimhofmethod.com/science.

6. Ryan Smith, "How CEOs Can Support Employee Mental Health in a Crisis," *Harvard Business Review*, May 1, 2020, https://hbr.org/2020/05/how-ceos-can-support-employee-mental-health-in-a-crisis.

BIBLIOGRAPHY

Abeyasekera, Kavisha N. "Benefits of Intermittent Fasting: A Systematic Review of Randomized Clinical Trials." *Dominican Scholar*. Dominican University of California, 2020. https://scholar.dominican.edu/physician-assistant-studies-student-articles/12/.

Achor, Shawn. *The Happiness Advantage: The Seven Principles of Positive Psychology That Fuel Success and Performance at Work.* New York: Crown Business, 2010.

Adichie, Chimamanda Ngozi. *We Should All Be Feminists.* New York: Vintage, 2014.

Ahlskog, J. Eric, Yonas E. Geda, Neill R. Graff-Radford, and Ronald C. Petersen. "Physical Exercise as a Preventive or Disease-Modifying Treatment of Dementia and Brain Aging." *Mayo Clinic Proceedings* 89, no. 9 (September 2011): 876–84. https://doi.org/10.4065/mcp.2011.0252.

Amabile, Teresa, and Steven Kramer. *The Progress Principle: Using Small Wins to Ignite Joy, Engagement, and Creativity at Work.* Boston: Harvard Business Review, 2011.

Attiah, Karen. "Opinion: What Men Need to Learn from Simone Biles." *Washington Post*, July 30, 2021. https://www.washingtonpost.com/opinions/2021/07/29/biles-is-helping-show-way-mental-health-lets-hope-follow-male-athletes-follow-her-lead/.

Avey, James B., Bruce J. Avolio, and Fred Luthans. "Experimentally Analyzing the Impact of Leader Positivity on Follower Positivity and Performance." *Leadership Quarterly* 22, no. 2 (2011): 282–94.

Baddeley, Simon, and Kim James. "Owl, Fox, Donkey or Sheep: Political Skills for Managers." *Management Education and Development* 18, no. 1 (1987): 3–19. https://doi.org/10.1177/135050768701800101.

Bennett, Jessica. "Leaders Are Crying on the Job. Maybe That's a Good Thing." *New York Times*, May 3, 2020. https://www.nytimes.com/2020/05/03/us/politics/crying-politicians-leadership.html.

Ben-Shahar, Tal. *Happier: Can You Learn to Be Happy?* (New York: McGraw-Hill, 2008).

———. Happiness Studies Academy. "The Science of Happiness." Accessed July 15, 2021. https://www.happinessstudies.academy/.

Bhat, Nilima, and Raj Sisodia. *Shakti Leadership: Embracing Feminine and Masculine Power in Business*. Oakland, CA: Berrett-Koehler, 2016.

Boiman-Meshita, Maayan, and Hadassah Littman-Ovadia. "The Marital Version of Three Good Things: A Mixed-Method Study." *Journal of Positive Psychology* 16, no. 3 (January 9, 2020): 367–78. https://doi.org/10.1080/17439760.2020.1716046.

Bono, Giacomo, Robert A. Emmons, and Michael E. McCullough. "Gratitude in Practice and the Practice of Gratitude." In *Positive Psychology in Practice*, edited by P. Alex Linley and Stephen Joseph, 464–81. Wiley, 2012. https://doi.org/10.1002/9780470939338.ch29.

Brandon, Rick, and Marty Seldman. *Survival of the Savvy: High-Integrity Political Tactics for Career and Company Success*. New York: Free, 2004.

Brescoll, Victoria L. "Leading with Their Hearts? How Gender Stereotypes of Emotion Lead to Biased Evaluations of Female Leaders." *Leadership Quarterly* 27 (2016): 415–28.

Brescoll, Victoria L., and Eric Luis Uhlmann. "Can an Angry Woman Get Ahead? Status Conferral, Gender, and Expression of Emotion in the Workplace." *Psychological Science* 19, no. 3 (2008): 268–75.

Brown, Brené. *The Power of Vulnerability: Teachings on Authenticity, Connection, & Courage*. Louisville, CO: Sounds True, 2012.

Buckingham, Marcus, and Donald O. Clifton. *Now, Discover Your Strengths*. New York: Simon & Schuster, 2001.

Buckingham, Marcus, and Curt Coffman. *First, Break All the Rules: What the World's Greatest Managers Do Differently*. London: Simon & Schuster, 1998.

Buettner, Dan. "How to Live to Be 100+." TEDxTC, 2009. https://www.ted.com/talks/dan_buettner_how_to_live_to_be_100?language=en.

Calhoun, Lawrence G., and Richard G. Tedeschi, eds. *Handbook of Posttraumatic Growth: Research and Practice*. Routledge, 2014.

Carter Center. "Mental Illness Will Cost the World $16 USD Trillion by 2030." *Psychiatric Times* 35, no. 11 (November 16, 2020). https://www.psychiatrictimes.com/view/mental-illness-will-cost-world-16-usd-trillion-2030.

Castrillon, Caroline. "Why Purpose Is the New Competitive Advantage." *Forbes*, April 28, 2019. https://www.forbes.com/sites/carolinecastrillon/2019/04/28/why-purpose-is-the-new-competitive-advantage/?sh=205fb56a711f.

Cherniss, Cary, and Daniel Goleman. *The Emotionally Intelligent Workplace: How to Select For, Measure, and Improve Emotional Intelligence in Individuals, Groups, and Organizations*. San Francisco: Jossey-Bass, 2001.

Collins, James C., and Jerry I. Porras. *Built to Last: Successful Habits of Visionary Companies*. New York: HarperCollins, 1994.

Covey, Stephen R. *The 7 Habits of Highly Effective People: Powerful Lessons in Personal Change*. New York: Simon & Schuster, 2013.

Crum, Alia J., Peter Salovey, and Shawn Achor. "Rethinking Stress: The Role of Mindsets in Determining the Stress Response." *Journal of Personality and Social Psychology* 104, no. 4 (2013): 716–33. https://doi.org/10.1037/a0031201.

Csikszentmihalyi, Mihaly. "Mihaly Csikszentmihalyi & Flow." Pursuit of Happiness. Accessed July 15, 2021. https://www.pursuit-of-happiness.org/history-of-happiness/mihaly-csikszentmihalyi/.

Cuncic, Arlin. "What Is Imposter Syndrome?" Verywell Mind, February 26, 2021. https://www.verywellmind.com/imposter-syndrome-and-social-anxiety-disorder-4156469.

Danner, Deborah D., David A. Snowdon, and Wallace V. Friesen. "Positive Emotions in Early Life and Longevity: Findings from the Nun Study." *Journal of Personality and Social Psychology* 80, no. 5 (2001): 804–13. https://doi.org/10.1037/0022-3514.80.5.804.

"The Dirty Dozen & the Clean Fifteen." Nutritious & Delicious, January 4, 2019. https://nutritiousndelicious.com/2019/01/04/the-dirty-dozen-the-clean-fifteen/.

DiSalvo, David. "How Breathing Calms Your Brain, and Other Science-Based Benefits of Controlled Breathing." *Forbes*, November 29, 2017. https://www.forbes.com/sites/daviddisalvo/2017/11/29/how-breathing-calms-your-brain-and-other-science-based-benefits-of-controlled-breathing/?sh=fff3a7e22219.

D'Onfro, Jillian. "Facebook's Sheryl Sandberg Spearheaded Something Called the 'Glass Lion' to Help Shatter Gender Stereotypes." *Business Insider*, June 21, 2015. https://www.businessinsider.com/sheryl-sandberg-and-lean-in-organized-cannes-glass-lion-2015-6.

Doran, G. T. "There's a S.M.A.R.T. Way to Write Management's Goals and Objectives." *Management Review* 70, no. 11 (November 1981): 35–36.

Drucker, Peter F. *The Effective Executive: The Definitive Guide to Getting the Right Things Done.* New York: Harper Business, 2018.

Duhigg, Charles. "What Google Learned From Its Quest to Build the Perfect Team." *New York Times Magazine*, February 28, 2016.

Durmer, Jeffrey S., and David F. Dinges. "Neurocognitive Consequences of Sleep Deprivation." *Seminars in Neurology* 25, no. 1 (March 2005): 117–29. https://doi.org/10.1055/s-2005-867080.

Dweck, Carol S. *Mindset: The New Psychology of Success.* New York: Random House, 2006.

Edmondson, Amy C. *The Fearless Organization: Creating Psychological Safety in the Workplace for Learning, Innovation, and Growth.* Hoboken, NJ: John Wiley & Sons, 2018.

———. "Psychological Safety and Learning Behavior in Work Teams." *Administrative Science Quarterly* 44, no. 2 (1999): 350–83. https://doi.org/10.2307/2666999.

———. "Unlock the Full Potential of Your Team: Check Your Psychological Safety for Free." Fearless Organization (homepage). Accessed July 25, 2021. https://fearlessorganization.com/.

Eglon, Marc. "HBR Research: Women Score Higher Than Men in Leadership Skills." Taylor Hopkinson, July 8, 2019. https://www.taylorhopkinson.com/women-score-higher-than-men-in-leadership-skills/#:~:text=Skills%20%2D%20Taylor%20Hopkinson-,HBR%20Research%3A%20Women%20Score%20Higher%20Than%20-Men%20in%20Leadership%20Skills,of%20the%20%2019%20competencies%20measured.

Ellis, Albert. "Rational Emotive Behavior Therapy." In *Current Psychotherapies*, edited by Raymond J. Corsini and Danny Wedding, 166–201. Belmont, CA: Thomson/Brooks/Cole, 2005.

Emmons, R. A. "Gratitude." In *Character Strengths and Virtues*, ed. M. E. P. Seligman and C. Peterson (New York: Oxford University Press/Values in Action Institute, 2004), 553–68.

"Empowering You to Your Best Negotiation Abilities!" MeD8. Accessed July 15, 2021. https://eresources.nlb.gov.sg/webarchives/details/www.med8.com.sg.html

Erasmus, Udo. *Fats That Heal, Fats That Kill: The Complete Guide to Fats, Oils, Cholesterol and Human Health.* Burnaby, BC, Canada: Alive, 1997.

Feldheim, Dalia. Dalia Feldheim. Accessed July 15, 2021. https://daliafeldheim.com/.

———. "Lead Like a Girl." TEDxJaffaWomen. YouTube. June 3, 2020. https://www.youtube.com/watch?v=nAUIJlAhW5c&t=9s&ab_channel=TEDxTalks.

Field, Tiffany. *Touch.* Cambridge, MA: A Bradford Book, 2003.

Fiorenzi, Ryan. "Sitting Is the New Smoking." Start Standing, January 31, 2021. https://www.startstanding.org/sitting-new-smoking/#extended.

Frankl, Viktor E. *Man's Search for Meaning: An Introduction to Logotherapy.* Boston: Beacon, 2006.

Fredrickson, Barbara L. "The Role of Positive Emotions in Positive Psychology: The Broaden-and-Build Theory of Positive Emotions." *American Psychologist* 56, no. 3 (March 2001): 218–26. https://doi.org/10.1037/0003-066x.56.3.218.

García, Héctor, and Francesc Miralles. *Ikigai: The Japanese Secret to a Long and Happy Life.* New York: Penguin, 2018.

Gingerich, Alexa. "What Is S.M.A.S.H.? Why It Should Matter to You." Philadelphia Integrative Medicine, August 9, 2020. https://philly-im.com/blog/2020/7/24/what-is-smash-why-it-should-matter-to-you.

"Gobs of Facts & Statistics on Employee Engagement, Leadership, & Strengths-Based Cultures." Lead Through Strengths. https://leadthroughstrengths.com/stats/.

Goleman, Daniel. *Emotional Intelligence: Why It Can Matter More than IQ.* New York: Bantam, 2012.

Goleman, Daniel, and Richard J. Davidson. *Altered Traits: Science Reveals How Meditation Changes Your Mind, Brain, and Body.* New York: Avery/Penguin Random House, 2017.

Grant, Adam M. *Give and Take: A Revolutionary Approach to Success.* New York: Penguin, 2013.

———. "A Mark Of Emotional Intelligence." LinkedIn, 2020. https://www.linked in.com/posts/adammgrant_a-mark-of-emotional-intelligence-treating-activity-6722879413844803584-AJLe/.

Groth, Aimee. "Sheryl Sandberg: 'The Most Important Career Choice You'll Make Is Who You Marry.'" *Business Insider*, December 1, 2011. https://www.businessinsider.com/sheryl-sandberg-career-advice-to-women-2011-12.

Gunnars, Kris. "What Is Intermittent Fasting? Explained in Human Terms." *Healthline Media*, June 4, 2017. https://www.healthline.com/nutrition/what-is-intermittent-fasting#TOC_TITLE_HDR_2.

"Harlow's Classic Studies Revealed the Importance of Maternal Contact." Association for Psychological Science, June 20, 2018. https://www.psychologicalscience.org/publications/observer/obsonline/harlows-classic-studies-revealed-the-importance-of-maternal-contact.html.

Harter, Jim. "Dismal Employee Engagement Is a Sign of Global Mismanagement." Gallup Workplace (blog), 2017. https://www.gallup.com/workplace/231668/dismal-employee-engagement-sign-global-mismanagement.aspx.

Hess, Ursula, Sylvie Blairy, and Robert E. Kleck. "The Intensity of Emotional Facial Expressions and Decoding Accuracy." *Journal of Nonverbal Behavior* 21, no. 4 (1997): 241–57.

Hill, Patrick L., and Nicholas A. Turiano. "Purpose in Life as a Predictor of Mortality Across Adulthood." *Psychological Science* 25, no. 7 (2014): 1482–86.

Horan, Jane. *I Wish I'd Known That Earlier in My Career: The Power of Positive Workplace Politics.* Singapore: John Wiley & Sons (Asia), 2012.

Hunt, Vivian, Dennis Layton, and Sara Prince. "Diversity Matters." McKinsey & Company (February 2, 2015): 15–29. https://doi.org/https://www.mckinsey.com/~/media/mckinsey/business%20functions/organization/our%20insights/why%20diversity%20matters/diversity%20matters.ashx.

Hyman, Mark. "ULTRAMIND®: The 6-Week Plan to Heal Your Brain." Video. Dr. Mark Hyman, November 25, 2019. https://drhyman.com/blog/2010/08/30/the-ultra-mind-solution-the-6-week-plan-to-heal-your-brain-2/.

———. *The UltraMind Solution: Fix Your Broken Brain by Healing Your Body First.* Scribner, 2008.

Johnson, Stefanie K. "2021 Is a Tipping Point for Female Leaders." Bloomberg Business, January 31, 2021. https://www.bloomberg.com/opinion/articles/2021-01-31/women-leaders-are-doing-better-during-the-pandemic.

Kabat-Zinn, Jon. *Wherever You Go, There You Are: Mindfulness Meditation in Everyday Life*. New York: Hachette, 2005.

Kahn, William A. "Psychological Conditions of Personal Engagement and Disengagement at Work." *Academy of Management Journal* 33, no. 4 (1990): 692–724. https://doi.org/10.5465/256287.

Kashdan, Todd B., Anjali Mishra, William E. Breen, and Jeffrey J. Froh. "Gender Differences in Gratitude: Examining Appraisals, Narratives, the Willingness to Express Emotions, and Changes in Psychological Needs." *Journal of Personality* 77, no. 3 (2009): 691–730.

Keller, Helen. *Three Days to See*. Nanjing: Yilin, 2012.

Kennard, Jerry. "Understanding Suicide Among Men." Verywell Mind, December 10, 2020. https://www.verywellmind.com/men-and-suicide-2328492.

Kets de Vries, Manfred F. R. "Doing Nothing and Nothing to Do: The Hidden Value of Empty Time and Boredom." *SSRN Electronic Journal* INSEAD Working Paper, no. 2014/37/EFE (May 7, 2014). https://doi.org/10.2139/ssrn.2432964.

Knight, Will. "'Info-Mania' Dents IQ More Than Marijuana." *New Scientist*, April 22, 2005. https://www.newscientist.com/article/dn7298-info-mania-dents-iq-more-than-marijuana/.

Konrath, Sara H., Edward H. O'Brien, and Courtney Hsing. "Changes in Dispositional Empathy in American College Students Over Time: A Meta-Analysis." *Personality and Social Psychology Review* 15, no. 2 (2010): 180–98. https://doi.org/10.1177/1088868310377395.

Langer, Ellen J. *Mindfulness: 25th Anniversary Edition*. Cambridge, MA: Da Capo Lifelong, 2014.

Levant, Ronald F., and Gini Kopecky. *Masculinity Reconstructed: Changing the Rules of Manhood—At Work, in Relationships and in Family Life*. Plume, 1996.

Lewis, Sophie. "Simone Biles Opens Up about Withdrawal from Olympic Competitions: 'I Don't Think You Realize How Dangerous This Is.'" CBS News, July 30, 2021. https://www.cbsnews.com/news/simone-biles-olympics-gymnastics-withdrawal-twisties/.

#LikeAGirl. "Super Bowl 2015: Always Ad." Procter & Gamble. WSJ Live. YouTube. Accessed July 19, 2021. https://www.youtube.com/watch?v=F_EpOO5fWN4&ab_channel=WallStreetJournal.

Link, Rachael. "16/8 Intermittent Fasting: A Beginner's Guide." *Healthline Media*, September 4, 2018. https://www.healthline.com/nutrition/16-8-intermittent-fasting.

"Live Dirty, Eat Clean: Robynne Chutkan, MD On Everything Microbiome." Robynne Chutkan, MD. Accessed July 15, 2021. https://www.richroll.com/podcast/robynne-chutkan-microbiome/.

Loehr, Jim, and Tony Schwartz. *The Power of Full Engagement: Managing Energy, Not Time, Is the Key to High Performance and Personal Renewal*. New York: Free, 2003.

Loudenback, Tanza. "Spanx Founder Sara Blakely Learned an Important Lesson about Failure from Her Dad—Now She's Passing It on to Her 4 Kids." *Business Insider*, June 17, 2018. https://www.businessinsider.com/spanx-founder-sara-blakely-redefine-failure-2016-10.

Lutz, Tom. *Crying: The Natural and Cultural History of Tears*. New York: W. W. Norton, 2001.

Lyubomirsky, Sonja, Laura King, and Ed Diener. "The Benefits of Frequent Positive Affect: Does Happiness Lead to Success?" *Psychological Bulletin* 131, no. 6 (2005): 803–855. https://doi.org/10.1037/0033-2909.131.6.803.

Mackey, John, and Rajendra S. Sisodia. *Conscious Capitalism: Liberating the Heroic Spirit of Business*. Boston: Harvard Business Review, 2014.

Mann, Annamarie, and Jim Harter. "The Worldwide Employee Engagement Crisis." Gallup Workplace, January 7, 2016. https://www.gallup.com/workplace/236495/worldwide-employee-engagement-crisis.aspx.

Mayo Clinic Staff. "Water: How Much Should You Drink Every Day?" Mayo Foundation for Medical Education and Research, October 14, 2020. https://www.mayoclinic.org/healthy-lifestyle/nutrition-and-healthy-eating/in-depth/water/art-20044256.

McGonigal, Kelly. "How to Make Stress Your Friend." TEDGlobal 2013. https://www.ted.com/talks/kelly_mcgonigal_how_to_make_stress_your_friend?language=en.

Mednick, Sara C., and Mark Ehrman. *Take a Nap! Change Your Life: The Scientific Plan to Make You Smarter, Healthier, More Productive*. New York: Workman, 2006.

Mei, Gina. "This Ad Just Won Sheryl Sandberg's Award for Shattering Gender Stereotypes." HelloGiggles, June 23, 2015. https://hellogiggles.com/news/sheryl-sandberg-glass-lion/.

Mullangi, Samyukta, and Reshma Jagsi. "Imposter Syndrome: Treat the Cause, Not the Symptom." *JAMA* 322, no. 5 (2019): 403. https://doi.org/10.1001/jama.2019.9788.

Neudecker, Christina, Nadine Mewes, Anne K. Reimers, and Alexander Woll. "Exercise Interventions in Children and Adolescents with ADHD: A Systematic Review." *Journal of Attention Disorders* 23, no. 4 (2019): 307–324.

Newman, Alexander, Ross Donohue, and Nathan Eva. "Psychological Safety: A Systematic Review of the Literature." *Human Resource Management Review* 27, no. 3 (2017): 521–35. https://doi.org/10.1016/j.hrmr.2017.01.001.

Offer, Shira, and Barbara Schneider. "Revisiting the Gender Gap in Time-Use Patterns: Multitasking and Well-Being among Mothers and Fathers in Dual-Earner Families." *American Sociological Review* 76, no. 6 (2011): 809–833.

"Project Implicit." Project Implicit (Harvard University). Accessed November 15, 2021. https://implicit.harvard.edu/implicit/.

Quoidbach, Jordi, Elizabeth V. Berry, Michel Hansenne, and Moïra Mikolajczak. "Positive Emotion Regulation and Well-Being: Comparing the Impact of Eight Savoring and Dampening Strategies." *Personality and Individual Differences* 49, no. 5 (2010): 368–73. https://doi.org/10.1016/j.paid.2010.03.048.

Rai, Arpana, and Upasna A. Agarwal. "A Review of Literature on Mediators and Moderators of Workplace Bullying: Agenda for Future Research." *Management Research Review* 41, no. 7 (October 2018): 822–59. https://doi.org/10.1108/mrr-05-2016-0111.

———. "Workplace Bullying Among Indian Managers: Prevalence, Sources and Bystanders' Reactions." *International Journal of Indian Culture and Business Management* 15, no. 1 (2017): 58–81. https://doi.org/10.1504/ijicbm.2017.10006293.

Rainville, Camille. "Be a Lady They Said." Narrated by Cynthia Nixon. Girls. Girls.Girls.Magazine. Accessed September 28, 2020. https://www.youtube.com/watch?v=c22tr74XuLU&ab_channel=BlancaP%C3%A9rez.

Ratey, John J., and Eric Hagerman. *Spark: The Revolutionary New Science of Exercise and the Brain*. New York: Little, Brown, 2013.

Reavis, G. H. "The Animal School." *Agricultural Education Magazine* 80, no. 2 (2007): 21.

"Re-Engineering Performance Management." Gallup Workplace. Accessed June 25, 2021. https://www.gallup.com/workplace/238064/re-engineering-performance-management.aspx.

Reiter, Karin G. "Healthy Eating Plate." Nutritious & Delicious. Accessed July 19, 2021. https://nutritiousndelicious.com/.

Ritvo, Eva. "The Neuroscience of Giving: Proof that Helping Others Helps You." *Psychology Today*, April 24, 2014. https://www.psychologytoday.com/us/blog/vitality/201404/the-neuroscience-giving.

Robbins, Tony. "Tony Robbins: Rapid Planning Method." Robbins Research International, 2016. https://cdnwp.tonyrobbins.com/wp-content/uploads/2016/11/RPM-Sample-Book2.pdf.

———. "Ultimate Relationship Guide." TonyRobbins.com. Accessed July 24, 2021. http://core.tonyrobbins.com/Global/FileLib/PDF/RelGuide_Digital-opt.pdf.

Rock, David. "Managing with the Brain in Mind." *Strategy+Business*, August 27, 2009. https://www.strategy-business.com/article/09306.

Rosen, Larry, and Alexandra Samuel. "Conquering Digital Distraction." *Harvard Business Review*, June 2015. https://hbr.org/2015/06/conquering-digital-distraction.

Rudland, Joy R., Clinton Golding, and Tim J. Wilkinson. "The Stress Paradox: How Stress Can Be Good for Learning." *Medical Education* 54, no. 1 (2019): 40–45. https://doi.org/10.1111/medu.13830.

Rudman, Laurie A., Corinne A. Moss-Racusin, Julie E. Phelan, and Sanne Nauts. "Status Incongruity and Backlash Effects: Defending the Gender Hierarchy Motivates Prejudice Against Female Leaders." *Journal of Experimental Social Psychology* 48, no. 1 (2012): 165–79.

Sandberg, Sheryl. *Lean In: Women, Work, and the Will to Lead*. New York: Knopf, 2013.

———. "Why We Have Too Few Women Leaders." TED Talk. YouTube. December 21, 2010. https://www.youtube.com/watch?v=18uDutylDa4&t=731s&ab_channel=TED.

Sarno, John E. *Mind Over Back Pain: A Radically New Approach to the Diagnosis and Treatment of Back Pain*. New York: Berkley, 1986.

Schecter, David, Arthur Preston Smith, Jennifer Beck, Janine Roach, Roksana Karim, and Stanley Azen. "Outcomes of a Mind-Body Treatment Program for Chronic Back Pain with No Distinct Structural Pathology: A Case Series of Patients Diagnosed and Treated as Tension Myositis Syndrome." *Altern Ther Health Med* 13, no. 5 (2007): 26–35. https://pubmed.ncbi.nlm.nih.gov/17900039/.

Schnarch, David. *Passionate Marriage: Love, Sex, and Intimacy in Emotionally Committed Relationships*. New York: W. W. Norton, 1997.

Schnohr, Peter, James H. O'Keefe, Jacob L. Marott, Peter Lange, and Gorm B. Jensen. "Dose of Jogging and Long-Term Mortality: The Copenhagen City Heart Study." *Journal of the American College of Cardiology* 65, no. 5 (February 10, 2015): 411–19. https://doi.org/10.1016/j.jacc.2014.11.023.

"The Science Behind the Wim Hof Method." Wim Hof Method. Accessed November 15, 2021. https://www.wimhofmethod.com/science.

Seligman, Martin E. P. "Building Resilience." *Harvard Business Review* 89, no. 4 (April 2011): 100–106.

———. *Learned Optimism: How to Change Your Mind and Your Life*. New York: Vintage, 2006.

Seligman, Martin E. P., Tracy A. Steen, Nansook Park, and Christopher Peterson. "Positive Psychology Progress: Empirical Validation of Interventions." *American Psychologist* 60, no. 5 (2005): 410–21. https://doi.org/10.1037/0003-066x.60.5.410.

Sheldon, Kennon M., and Sonja Lyubomirsky. "How to Increase and Sustain Positive Emotion: The Effects of Expressing Gratitude and Visualizing Best Possible Selves." *Journal of Positive Psychology* 1, no. 2 (2006): 73–82. https://doi.org/10.1080/17439760500510676.

Sinek, Simon. *Start with Why: How Great Leaders Inspire Everyone to Take Action*. New York: Penguin, 2009.

Sinek, Simon, David Mead, and Peter Docker. *Find Your Why: A Practical Guide for Discovering Purpose for You and Your Team.* New York: Portfolio, 2017.

Singer, Michael A. *The Surrender Experiment: My Journey into Life's Perfection.* New York: Harmony, 2015.

Skalski, Sebastian, and Grzegorz Pochwatko. "Gratitude is Female. Biological Sex, Socio-cultural Gender versus Gratitude and Positive Orientation." *Current Issues in Personality Psychology* 8, no. 1 (2020): 1–9.

Sloan, Rennie. "Mental Illness Will Cost the World $16 USD Trillion by 2030." The Carter Center, October 9, 2018. https://www.cartercenter.org/news/pr/mental-health-lancet-report-100918.html.

Smith, Ryan. "How CEOs Can Support Employee Mental Health in a Crisis." *Harvard Business Review*, May 1, 2020. https://hbr.org/2020/05/how-ceos-can-support-employee-mental-health-in-a-crisis.

Stubbs, Brendon, Davy Vancampfort, Simon Rosenbaum, Philip B. Ward, Justin Richards, Michael Ussher, and Felipe B. Schuch. "Challenges Establishing the Efficacy of Exercise as an Antidepressant Treatment: A Systematic Review and Meta-Analysis of Control Group Responses in Exercise Randomised Controlled Trials." *Sports Medicine* 46 (May 2015): 699–713, https://doi.org/10.1007/s40279-015-0441-5.

Sutton, Robert I. *The No Asshole Rule: Building a Civilized Workplace and Surviving One That Isn't.* New York: Business Plus, 2010.

Swant, Marty. "20 Memorable Ads From the Past Decade (for Better and for Worse)." *Forbes*, December 29, 2019. https://www.forbes.com/sites/martyswant/2020/12/29/20-memorable-ads-from-the-past-decade-for-better-and-for-worse/#1e9d76631cdd.

Tomaka, Joe, Jim Blascovich, Jeffrey Kibler, and John M. Ernst. "Cognitive and Physiological Antecedents of Threat and Challenge Appraisal." *Journal of Personality and Social Psychology* 73, no. 1 (1997): 63–72. https://doi.org/10.1037/0022-3514.73.1.63.

#TouchThePickle. "Cannes Lions Case Study: P&G Whisper Gets 3M Indian Women to 'Touch the Pickle'." Digital Training Academy. Accessed July 19, 2021. http://www.digitaltrainingacademy.com/casestudies/2015/07/cannes_lions_case_study_pg_whisper_gets_3m_indian_women_to_touch_the_pickle.php.

Trapp, E. G., D. J. Chisholm, J. Freund, and S. H. Boutcher. "The Effects of High-Intensity Intermittent Exercise Training on Fat Loss and Fasting Insulin Levels of Young Women." *International Journal of Obesity* 32 (2008): 684–91. https://doi.org/10.1038/sj.ijo.0803781.

"2 FINAL Mind Body Connection Recording." Dalia Feldheim. YouTube. May 25, 2020. https://www.youtube.com/watch?v=Tdb5okIuWEI&t=640s&ab_channel=daliafeldheim.

"The VIA Character Strengths Survey: Get to Know Your Greatest Strengths." VIA Institute on Character, 2021. https://www.viacharacter.org/survey/account/register.

Wagner, Rodd, and James K. Harter. *12: The Elements of Great Managing.* New York: Gallup, 2006.

Williamson, Marianne. *A Return to Love: Reflections on the Principles of* A Course in Miracles. New York: HarperOne, 2009.

Wittenberg-Cox, Avivah. "What Do Countries with the Best Coronavirus Responses Have in Common? Women Leaders." *Forbes*, April 13, 2020. https://www.forbes.com/sites/avivahwittenbergcox/2020/04/13/what-do-countries-with-the-best-corona-virus-reponses-have-in-common-women-leaders/#68f315363dec.

Yalom, Irvin D. *Becoming Myself: A Psychiatrist's Memoir.* New York: Basic, 2019.

Yudkin, John. *Pure, White, and Deadly: How Sugar Is Killing Us and What We Can Do to Stop It.* New York: Penguin, 2013.

Zenger, Jack, and Joseph Folkman. "The Ideal Praise-to-Criticism Ratio." *Harvard Business Review*, March 15, 2013. https://hbr.org/2013/03/the-ideal-praise-to-criticism.
———. "Research: Women Score Higher Than Men in Most Leadership Skills." *Harvard Business Review*, June 25, 2019. https://hbr.org/2019/06/research-women-score-higher-than-men-in-most-leadership-skills.

INDEX

ABOUT THE AUTHOR

Dalia Feldheim is a passionate advocate of women and feminine leadership—encouraging women (and men) to lean into their feminine leadership traits and "lead (more) like a girl." Her standing ovation TED talk speaks to the power of this idea: https://www.youtube.com/watch?v=nAUIJlAhW5c.

Her book, *Lead Like a Girl*, with a foreword by Sheryl Sandberg, will direct 100% of book proceeds (after expense) of first publication to "Lead Like a Girl" programs for underprivileged women around the world ("Lead Like a Girl" programs in India, Africa, and United Kingdom being defined).

Dalia is founder and CEO of Flow Leadership Consultancy, and draws on her own extensive corporate leadership experience and her passion for championing for others to enable organizations to promote a more authentic, happier, and psychologically safe working culture.

Before founding Flow Leadership Consultancy, Dalia spent over two decades as a C-suite global marketing executive at Procter & Gamble, where she led some of the world's most iconic Cannes award-winning women's empowerment ad campaigns, including Tampax "Mother Nature" and Whisper India "Touch the Pickle," as well being a part of the global team leading the Always "#LikeAGirl" campaign, which was ranked by *Forbes* as the most influential campaign of the decade: https://www.youtube.com/watch?v=XjJQBjWYDTs.

Dalia holds a psychology and business degree (summa cum laude 1998), an executive master's degree in organizational psychology from INSEAD business school, and a "Happiness teacher diploma" from the Happiness Studies Academy in partnership with Miami University.

She is an adjunct professor for "The Science of Happiness and Resilience" program at the Singapore Management University and an executive coach and organizational consultant working with top tech companies (like Microsoft, Netflix, Facebook, and Google), focusing on bringing resilience and joy to the workplace. To complement her mission, she recently founded a small start-up online game, "Uppiness: Up your game at work," together with Dr. Tal Ben-Shahar and the Happiness Studies Academy, designed to solve daily challenges through the use of positive psychology interventions.

She is also an ICF (International Coaching Federation) accredited coach, a qualified psychodynamic group therapist, and a yoga, Stand Up Paddle Board (SUP) yoga, and meditation trainer.

And above all, she is a devoted mum of three (nineteen-year-old Mia, eighteen-year-old Liam, and thirteen-year-old Anna) and wife to serial entrepreneur Dror.

To keep it all in flow, she lives her life by her values of Compassion, Contribution, Continuous growth, and Crazy adventure ;-)

City, State: Singapore, Singapore.